MARKETING

Change and Exchange

MARKETING
Change and Exchange

Readings
from
FORTUNE

Edited by H. C. Barksdale
NEW YORK UNIVERSITY

Holt, Rinehart and Winston, Inc.

New York • Chicago • San Francisco
Toronto • London

Preface

While always important, change has suddenly become a predominating concept. Thus it is not surprising that change has become a subject of serious study for many groups in business, education, and government—and a topic of discussion for everyone.

Some of the more obvious areas of change have been frequently described and widely reported. For example, it is generally known that knowledge is expanding at an accelerating pace, increasing man's control over the world in which he lives. Population is growing in geometric patterns, creating new pressures on resources and living conditions. Productivity is increasing, raising personal income and levels of aspiration for many people. Political power is shifting, creating new nations and redefining political boundaries.

The forces of change are not independent; rather they are interrelated and affect one another. While these relationships and reciprocal effects cannot be measured directly, at present, there is increasing awareness that business firms operate in an environment that is continually churning and changing. Here are some illustrations: The dimensions of markets are altered as population increases and new patterns of consumption emerge. New products and new industries evolve from scientific and technological developments. The structure and functions of institutions serving business and society change, creating new competitive situations. Operating processes and policies are revised to improve customer service and increase business efficiency.

Profitable existence in a dynamic environment requires continuous adjustment of operations to capitalize on opportunities and meet the challenges of changed conditions. More specifically, to survive and prosper producers of goods must constantly adjust to changing situations in the marketplace. Since marketing is concerned with the exchange of goods, and supplies the link or bridge between the producer and consumer, it plays a key role in adapting the activities of modern business to the requirements of ever-changing markets.

No other publication has reported the changes in technology, business, and marketing as completely and as authoritatively or has attempted to project the dimensions of markets and future marketing developments as carefully and as thoroughly as *Fortune*. And the publishers of *Fortune* have allowed complete freedom in the selection of articles to illustrate the dynamics of marketing, the basic theme of this book.

The articles selected describe and define the dramatic changes that are taking place in markets and products. They also report the adjustments being made in marketing institutions and distribution processes to adapt to new conditions. Together they present a picture of marketing—change and exchange—in four dimensions: markets, products, institutions, and processes.

Markets

During the past two decades, explosive forces have reshaped almost every aspect of American society, the United States economy, and the market for all kinds of products. The articles in this part of the book examine the changes taking place in markets and project developments expected through 1970. Topics discussed include growth of production, shifts in income distribution, changes in consumer tastes, and the market implications of these developments.

Products

Planning products to meet the needs of consumers is one of the major functions of marketing. It is also one of the most challenging tasks in business. Since products are the medium through which business is conducted, products play a crucial role in the success of any firm. The articles in Part II examine technological developments that promise a rising flood of new products and describe the problems involved in developing and modifying products to meet the demands of new markets.

Institutions

Since World War II, there have been some important changes in retailing and wholesaling. These changes—whether they are called a revolution, evolution, or rebellion—have had tremendous impact on the distribution of goods. The articles in this section describe the conflict between the older, established retailers and the newer discount houses and illustrate the shifting structure of marketing institutions.

Processes

Markets are never static, products are constantly being improved, institutions are forever evolving, and the processes of marketing are continually changing. Innovation and modification of marketing processes are essential in the adjustment of business operations to the changing needs of customers. The articles in Part IV examine some recent developments in marketing processes, including the vanishing salesman, the credit pump, computer systems of distribution, and the dark continent of marketing.

Finally, I wish to acknowledge the cooperation of the publishers of *Fortune* and express my appreciation to them for making this book of readings possible.

H. C. Barksdale

Fall 1964

Contents

MARKETING

Change and Exchange

part I

MARKETS

Rapid economic growth during the 1960s is expected to push total production of goods and services up to $750 billion—an increase of 50 percent—the largest gain of any decade in United States' history. Defense and investment spending will probably make heavy demands on production, yet consumers' buying power also promises to increase at a higher rate than ever before. While it is difficult to grasp the meaning of such rapid economic growth, it will certainly change consumption patterns and influence the market for all kinds of products.

The Good Uses of $750 Billion*

Those who are anxious lest the Soviet Union soon "catch up" with the U.S. can take some comfort in the fact that the prospective *increase* in American production in the 1960's is almost as much as the total current national production of the Soviet Union and West Germany combined. Recovery from recession will carry total U.S. production of goods and services from $475 billion this year to about $500 billion in 1960. But the "half-trillion economy," once considered such a breath-taking (or unlikely) achievement, will enjoy only a momentary glory. For so rapid is the economic expansion in prospect for the 1960's that by 1970 U.S. production will probably come to about $750 billion (in today's prices), up no less than $250 billion or 50 per cent—the largest percentage growth in any decade of our history. A major reason for anticipating

by Gilbert Burck
and
Todd May

* Vol. 59, April 1959, pp. 104–107, 226–238.

such a rise is that national productivity, measured in output per man-hour, can be expected to continue to increase at its record postwar average rate of 3 per cent or more a year. Meantime the U.S. labor force, which grew slowly in the 1950's, is now, owing to the high birth rate that began during World War II, beginning to expand rapidly. With more workers turning out more per hour, the economy as a whole probably will grow at the unprecedented rate of 4.2 per cent a year. Since the population will be rising steeply, G.N.P.—total national production of goods and services—*per person* will not rise as much. But it will increase at the rate of 2.9 per cent a year or 33 per cent for the decade—or, to put it in dollars at today's prices, from $2,700 to $3,600 per person.

To grasp the dimensions and promises of so stupendous an advance, glance at it in historical perspective. During the *two* decades 1910–30, G.N.P. per person increased from $1,250 to about $1,600, or by only 30 per cent. Yet in those two decades mass production and mass consumption transformed the nation's way of life. By the end of the so-called Golden Twenties, food became plentiful and cheap and the automobile was counted a necessity by millions.

During the three following decades, 1930–60, G.N.P. per person increased from about $1,600 to $2,700 or by 70 per cent. (Owing to mounting defense needs, civilian output increased by only 55 per cent.) Yet this growth enabled the country to catch up on the civilian production it lost during World War II, to take the Korean war in stride, to multiply its outlays for research and development, to inaugurate the electronic age, and to overcome more than half of its shortages (as estimated by the Twentieth Century Fund) in health, education, and public works.

During the past fifty years, in other words, U.S. production rose by 1.5 per cent a year or $1,450 per person; just in the next ten years, it will probably increase by 2.9 per cent a year or $900 per person. What this remarkable expansion holds in store for America will be the subject of the articles in this section. The present article is devoted mainly to projecting the probable needs of investment and defense in the 1960's, and to constructing a preliminary fix on consumption; future articles will refine that fix in terms of specific consumer markets.

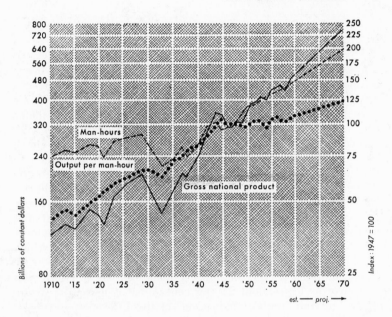

FIGURE 1. The Rising Tempo of American Economic Growth.
Total output of United States goods and services, which has been
growing at an average rate of almost 4 percent a year since World
War II, will probably grow by more than 4 percent a year in the
1960s and amount to $750 billion by 1970. The basic force in this
growth is accelerating productivity, measured in output per man-
hour. United States' productivity, which increased at the rate of
1 percent a year between 1850 and 1889, 2 percent between 1889
and 1919, and 2.5 percent between the wars, has been increasing
about 3 percent since World War II. In the 1960s it will probably
equal, if not surpass, its average postwar rate of increase. What
will make total production boom is that man-hours worked will be
expanding more than in many decades, for the labor force will
grow faster than it has in a generation and the work-week will
probably decline only moderately. With man-hours growing at a
near-record rate and productivity continuing to grow at a record
rate, total production is plainly bound to grow at a record rate.

Magnificently Easy to Bear

Obviously the expansion of the Sixties is going to affect every business and person. Of course, it does not mean a 33 per cent increase for every company and person, across the board. Nor does it mean exactly proportionate increases in each of the major uses of production—defense, investment, and consumption. On the contrary, defense should expand greatly. And the country must pay a certain "price" for its swift growth—a disproportionate rise, for a while, in industrial investment and what might be called social investment, and hence a less than proportionate rise in the output of purely consumer goods and services. For about five years of the decade, or till about 1965, the needs of investment and probably defense may well rise enough to hold the rate of increase in consumption down to about 3.5 per cent a year, which is still a little higher than the rate of the past ten years. Increase in consumption per person, since population will be rising, will of course be less—about 2.2 per cent. What is more, the steady upgrading and "professionalization" of the U.S. labor force will mean that a considerable part of the increase in consumption will fall to the people whose skills have been improved. The disposable income of many other people may rise by no more than 1.5 per cent a year—though even this, compounded over five years, works out to an 8 per cent increase.

But for the U.S. as a whole, the price of growth will be magnificently easy to bear; the economic pie will expand so enormously that almost everybody can get a substantially bigger cut. Although consumption's *share* of the country's production will probably decline in 1960–65, consumption will still increase by $55 billion—an amount greater than the present national production of Italy.

And a still bigger increase in consumption will lie just ahead. By about 1965, as will be shown later, heavy demands of investment and defense on the economy should be leveling off. Between 1965 and 1970, therefore, output going to consumption should increase by some 25 per cent, or by $90 billion—unless even more of the productivity increase than assumed here is taken in the form of a shorter work week. From 1965 on, in other words, the U.S. should enter a new age of abundance that will make even the great days of the 1950's look a little austere.

Not Quite Guaranteed

It is not guaranteed, of course. If the Russians should somehow succeed in breaking our alliances or taking over more of the previously "uncommitted" regions, the U.S. could be forced to accelerate its defense expenditures to the point where they would squeeze everything else unmercifully. The race to space may yet pile egregious burdens on people who would rather be happy on earth than miserable on Mars. Or, at the other extreme, if the cold war were somehow ended, and U.S. defense outlays could be cut back sharply, the U.S. economy might experience a hard jolt before ascending to even higher levels of civilian abundance than those projected here.

Aside from such earth-shaking and unpredictable possibilities, there is the more mundane possibility that the U.S. itself, in the pursuit of higher consumption, may not levy sufficient taxes, or save enough, to put its defense and investment needs on a sound financial basis. Financing them will be doubly onerous because the prices of both defense and investment goods are rising faster than the prices of consumption goods and services. Between 1948 and 1957, for example, their share of the country's physical output rose from 37 to 39 per cent, while their share of the nation's money outlays rose from 34 to 39 per cent. To put it another way, more than $20 billion had to be diverted from consumer spending to investment and defense.

By the mid-Sixties defense and investment will probably have risen from 39 to 42 per cent of G.N.P. This is only a three-point increment, to be sure, but it means that $20 billion more must be diverted from consumer spending—in the form of taxes, personal savings, and corporate depreciation and profits. If these savings are not forthcoming, if the government does not pay for its needs as it goes, and if corporations cannot accumulate their investment needs, the needs will be realized only through inflation—if at all.

Who Takes What

To demonstrate the basic trends in the growth of U.S. markets *Fortune* has divided the country's total expenditures into three functional groups:

1. Defense outlays, which in 1957 accounted for about 10 per cent of G.N.P.; and international payments (or the excess of exports over imports), which in 1957 accounted for 1.2 per cent of G.N.P.

2. Investment goods and services, which in 1957 took nearly 28 per cent of G.N.P. These include such familiar items as capital investment (10.3 per cent of G.N.P.) and inventory accumulation (0.2 per cent) by business; house construction (4 per cent), and construction of public works like highways, hospitals, and schools, either public or private (3 per cent). *Fortune* is also including under "investment" several items that are general investments in the nation's well-being or proficiency and hence in its future productivity: expenditures for education, both public and private (3 per cent); expenditures for medical care and hospital services, etc., largely private (nearly 5 per cent). Finally there are government expenses not included elsewhere—i.e., on general administration, police and fire departments, etc. (2.3 per cent).

3. Consumption goods and services encompass everything else. They are all bought out of individuals' income after taxes, and in 1957 accounted for nearly 61 per cent of G.N.P. The chief categories are food, alcohol, and tobacco (18.5 per cent of G.N.P.); rent (8 per cent); clothing (7.7 per cent); auto purchases (3.3 per cent); current transportation, including auto upkeep and fares (5.5 per cent); household and recreation goods (7.1 per cent); and personal and household services and utilities (10.7 per cent).

The Dynamics of Price

To project the country's future expenditures on these groups of goods and services we must first estimate, at today's prices, the physical quantities the country will demand. Since prices change, however, the actual amount the country will spend on these various groups almost certainly will not be the same as the estimates of physical demand. For one thing, there is the general upward price movement known as inflation (or what has been practically nonexistent since the 1930's, the general downward movement known as deflation). Since there is no way of telling what general inflation will do to prices, we must disregard it. What we cannot disregard, however, is the *relative* movement of prices. As everyone has observed, prices of all goods and services do not move in the same way. The prices of goods like appliances, whose finished costs benefit from the economies of mass production, can and sometimes do decline even when the cost of everything going into them is rising. On the other hand, the costs and selling prices of goods like machines for factories may rise relatively fast. They rise fast because the machines are virtually handmade and the labor that goes into them is increasingly expensive, inflation or no. Labor in capital-goods industries, even if its productivity does not rise, benefits from the general rise in productivity.

And how does the relative movement of prices affect future sales? If real, i.e., relative, costs and prices of certain goods and services are rising, say, at an average of 2 per cent a year, the country must pay better than 20 per cent more for the same quantity of goods and services ten years from now. And if the country is buying 50 per cent more of these goods and services ten years from now, measured in physical quantity, then it will be spending 80 per cent more on them than it is today.

Of course, goods and services whose prices are rising inordinately fast tend to run into sales resistance, just as goods and services whose prices are falling tend to sell easily. Let anything claim too much of the resources of a market economy, and the country will try to choose something cheaper. Over the short run, however, the country has relatively little option in some purchases, such as defense and certain capital goods. If a particular company is going to need a special machine and the price of that machine rises 25 per cent, it will usually go ahead and spend 25 per cent more for it. If the nation needs new missiles in 1965, it will presumably lay out the money for them even if the price of those missiles doubles.

Where Choice Matters

But consumers do have relatively free choice in buying such things as cars and appliances. If the goods become too costly, people will tend to buy less of them. But will this tendency be strong enough to reduce actual dollar sales—or, since population is increasing, per capita dollar sales? If their relative costs and prices are falling, people will tend to buy more of them. But will this tendency be strong enough to offset declining prices and actually raise dollar sales—or again, since population is increasing, per capita dollar sales? To project future markets with any accuracy, questions like these must be considered. Past price movements must be appraised. So must the inherent demand for the goods and services themselves.

Defense Needs Are Rising

The future physical volume of defense needs, depending as they do on domestic as well as international politics, is hardly to be divined by economic insight or statistical method. But to project the economy as a whole, one must make assumptions about defense spending. *Fortune*'s assumption is that defense expenditures will rise a little faster than G.N.P., at least until the middle of the decade. Last year the country spent $45 billion on defense—mainly Defense Department outlays, but also including the AEC, foreign military aid, and stockpiling. The pressure is rising to ensure our capacity to deter the enemy by spending a good deal more, and not only on nuclear retaliatory power.

The question is how much. There is a large and vocal school of thought that would mount a greatly increased defense program embodying the main points of the so-called Gaither and Rockefeller committees, including stepped-up ICBM production, heavy reinforcement of the Strategic Air Command, and a large improvement of "limited-war" capability. Such a program would call for increasing spending by more than $3 billion a year to $65 billion by 1965 and then tapering off to perhaps $70 billion in 1970. The pace of Administration programs, on the other hand, suggests nothing like this. The Administration has been increasing outlays for retaliatory power by perhaps $1.5 billion a year. But it has been meeting some of these costs by trimming limited-war capabilities, such as troop strength. But these savings obviously cannot go on indefinitely, and a $1.5-billion increase a year would work out to $54 billion in 1965 and $61 billion in 1970.

Fortune is striking a balance between the "big" defense program and the "Administration" rate of increase in defense spending, and is assuming a physical volume of defense needs at $60 billion in 1965 and $65 billion in 1970. Now, the relative prices of defense goods held fairly steady between 1948 and 1953, rose between 1953 and 1957, then steadied again, but will probably rise somewhat during the Sixties. Thus actual defense outlays would come to about $61 billion in 1965, or 9.9 per cent of G.N.P., and $68 billion in 1970, or 9 per cent of G.N.P. In other words, they would squeeze the rest of the economy a little until the middle of the Sixties and then grow somewhat more slowly than G.N.P.

But as things look now, it is investment, and particularly business' outlays for capital goods, that will provide the major squeeze on the consumption sector of the economy in the early Sixties. In 1957 capital-goods outlays came to $46.6 billion or 10.3 per cent of G.N.P. But demand for capital goods, measured in physical volume, should soon rise and reach 11.2 per cent of G.N.P., or $69 billion, by 1965. Then, as the rate of increase tapers off somewhat, physical volume should amount to 10.8 per cent of 1970's G.N.P., or $81 billion.

The average price of capital goods has risen 14 per cent, relative to other goods, between 1948 and 1957. Fortunately, the price increases have begun to slow down, and between now and 1970 the increase will probably be not more than 5 per cent relative to other goods. Thus actual dollar outlays for capital goods would come to $71 billion in 1965 and to $85 billion in 1970.

The Price of Growth

Why are capital-goods outlays likely to rise so steeply during the first half of the decade? Replacement requirements, based on *Fortune*'s calculations of the survival rate of the existing stock of capital goods, will not be responsible. These have been rising, but they will reach a peak of 5.5 per cent of G.N.P. by 1960 and then decline slightly to 5.4 per cent in 1965, and to 5.1 by 1970.

The answer lies in the rapidly increasing labor force, and the drive for still higher productivity. Both mean large *additions* to plant and equipment, as soon as existing plant and equipment are fully utilized—as they should be by the end of 1960. On the average, U.S. business has to spend about $1.65 on capital goods to increase its capacity by $1—i.e., by $1 a year for ten or twenty years or even more, depending on how long the capital goods last. Thus, business in the 1950's spent the equivalent of 6 per cent of private G.N.P. to realize an increased annual output of 3.7 per cent. In the Sixties it will have to spend the equivalent of 7 per cent of private G.N.P. on capital goods in order to get a 4.2 per cent annual growth in output.

Economists have often argued, it is true, that plant and equipment outlays should increase more slowly than production at capacity because new capital goods are usually more efficient than the ones they replace. But U.S. experience since World War II does not bear this out. Some industrial groups, such as manufacturing, have not added capital goods quite so fast as their capacity to produce has increased. But these industries have accelerated their use of energy to increase their efficiency, and this has led to an increase in the capital investment of the energy-producing industries at a rate rapid enough to offset the lag in investment of other industries. Notwithstanding the postwar experience, *Fortune*'s projections for the 1960's are conservative, and so allow a little for a possible increase in the efficiency of capital. Therefore additions to plant and equipment should easily equal or even exceed the projections here.

Research outlays, in the sense that they constitute an investment in the future that will swell capital-goods volume, should be noted here. Owing to the nature of G.N.P. statistics, only about half of present research outlays are classed as research, and this actually comes under the heading of government defense purchases. The other half is financed by business, and appears as a small fraction of the value of various goods and services. Private research outlays have risen from 0.5 per cent of G.N.P. in 1948 to nearly 1 per cent today and will doubtless rise between 1.5 and 2 per cent by 1970.

Education Comes into Its Own

Investment in the nation's education is, of course, investment in its future productivity as well as its culture. To Americans exercised about the "lag" in U.S. education it may come as a surprise that the country's accomplishments in education during the past decade have already anticipated even the most liberally conceived tasks of the next. The Twentieth Century Fund, whose

America's Needs and Resources was a pioneering effort to define some of the country's potentials and shortages, defined educational needs for 1950 as more students, more teachers, and higher pay per teacher. The fund estimated that U.S. education outlays were then meeting only 70 per cent of the needs of elementary and secondary schools and 50 per cent of the needs of colleges. Since then primary and secondary-school enrollments have risen 50 per cent. The average schooling of the labor force has risen from 10.6 years in 1948 to twelve years in 1958, a palpable investment in future productivity in a new age of research and automation. Yet more than half the educational deficit estimated by the fund has already been made good, and this article's projections assume it will all be made good by 1970.

The country's outlays for education (not including school construction, which will be discussed later) were 3.1 per cent of G.N.P. or $14 billion in 1957, against only 2.4 per cent in 1948. Half the increase has been accounted for by rising salaries—teachers' salaries have been actually going up faster than factory wages—and the other half by more teachers and facilities.

Boom in Higher Education

Expenditures for education will probably account for 3.1 per cent of G.N.P. or $15.5 billion by 1960. And how will they shape up during the Sixties? The big surge will come in advanced education, which is three times as expensive per student than primary or secondary education. A steadily increasing percentage of the young are attending college—the figure was 30 per cent in 1950, is 40 per cent today, and will probably be at least 45 per cent in the 1960's. What is more, the population of college age will increase 50 per cent by 1970. Thus college enrollment, which has risen 50 per cent since 1950 to perhaps four million next year, may amount to seven million by the end of the decade. (Some authorities say as high as ten million.)

On the other hand, the baby boom is leveling off, and the elementary and secondary-school enrollment in the 1960's will increase only 20 per cent, against 50 per cent in the 1950's. As the decade ends, the children born in the baby boom of the 1940's will begin to have children of their own, and enrollment will begin to rise again. So educational needs will probably level off to 3.1 per cent of G.N.P., or better than $19 billion in 1965, and nearly $24 billion in 1970. Since the price of education will rise relatively, actual outlays will probably be something like $20 billion in 1965 and $25.5 billion in 1970.

Health as Investment

Another great but unsung social investment in the past decade has been the improvement of the national health. The Twentieth Century Fund estimated that medical care was only two-thirds adequate in 1950. Today, even when full account is taken of the increased number of people, and particularly of the aged, more than half of this inadequacy has been made good. Expenditures for medical and hospital services (but not hospital construction) increased from 4.1 per cent of G.N.P. in 1948 to 4.8 percent or $21.6 billion in 1957. At the same time, life expectancy and other measurements of well-being show great improvement. Owing to the unmeasured but doubtless rising effectiveness of new drugs, new medical techniques, less hospitalization time, etc., the productivity of health services may have grown enormously, and therefore expenditure figures do not reflect the true progress the country has made.

It is hard to gauge accurately health standards and needs. But to take care of current demands and at the same time make good the remaining inadequacy in health as estimated by the Twentieth Century Fund, the U.S. will have to spend, as prices stand today, about $30 billion in 1965 and $38 billion in 1970. Since the relative prices of health goods and services (mostly services) will probably be rising by at least 10 per cent during the 1960's—more than prices of all other investment goods and services—actual outlays may come to $33 billion in 1965 and $43 billion in 1970. This latter figure is twice the 1957 figure.

More House per House

Although the country's housing "requirements" ought to be easy to meet in the Sixties, needs will change to some extent as standards change. In recent years the U.S. has been building more than

1,300,000 new nonfarm housing units a year for a million new households, and thus more than 300,000 units a year have been replacements. By 1970 the number of nonfarm households will be increasing by about 1,300,000 a year, so the number of housing starts will probably rise to 1,600,000 a year. But unless people spend more on the houses than they do now, the share of G.N.P. claimed by housing construction will decline from 4.3 per cent in 1960 to 3.4 per cent in 1970.

From the end of World War II to the mid-Fifties, the housing industry failed to persuade Americans to spend as much of their income on houses as they did in the 1920's. Or to put it another way, the country's disposable income rose faster than the value of its stock of houses. The trouble seemed to be the persistently high cost of new houses even when other consumer prices (relative to all prices) were declining.

Several years ago, however, the trend changed. Partly because growing families needed larger quarters, the building industry succeeded in selling more house per house—somewhat as the auto industry sold more car per car. Between 1953 and 1957 the real value of the country's houses rose 17 per cent, while real disposable income rose only 14 per cent. Obviously people are now buying more expensive houses. And as new techniques such as prefabricated modules and new low-cost materials are employed more widely, housing costs and prices may actually decline— relative, that is, to the trend of all prices. So the share of G.N.P. accounted for by house construction should rise to 4.3 per cent in 1960, and then, with a continued rise in quality, can plausibly be expected to decline to about 4 per cent in 1965 and 1970. This would mean actual outlays of $25 billion in 1965 and $30 billion in 1970.

Investment in "Public Works"

A large category of investment needs that will increase faster than G.N.P.—and thus at the expense of consumption—consists mainly of public works such as highways, and schools and hospitals both privately and publicly financed. In 1957 this group took $13.6 billion or 3 per cent of G.N.P. By 1965, *Fortune* estimates, physical volume will rise to 3.7 per cent of G.N.P., and by

1970 to 4 per cent. Since construction prices are rising, relatively, actual outlays would come to more than $23 billion in 1965 and to about $31 billion in 1970.

The biggest single factor in the increase is the $40-billion-plus interstate highway network, whose construction will lift annual outlays on highways by federal, state, and local governments from close to $7 billion now to as much as $12 billion a year by the end of the decade. School construction now takes more than $3.5 billion a year as against $2.2 billion in 1950. But despite the heavy outlays of the past decade, school construction will probably continue to advance faster than G.N.P. Another large element in public works is hospital construction, which now takes $1.1 billion a year and will take $1.6 billion in 1965 and more than $2 billion in 1970. And there is a miscellany of $5.5 billion devoted to sewerage, waterworks, etc., which will rise to almost $8 billion by 1970.

Finally, under the general heading of "Investment" there are three other items: (1) "other government"—general administration expenses and police and fire departments—which over the years has accounted for 2.5 per cent of G.N.P. and will probably continue to do so; (2) net exports, which have been averaging 1 per cent of G.N.P. and will probably continue to do so; and (3) net additions to inventory, including farmers' and CCC stocks which fluctuate widely but probably will average 1 per cent of G.N.P.

So much for investment and defense needs. Note that all their prices have been rising relative to consumption prices, and will continue to do so. If their prices were to remain level, outlays for them of course would be the same as the estimates of their physical volume, or a total of $252 billion in 1965 and of $298 billion in 1970. Instead, the country will probably be spending a total of $260 billion on investment and defense in 1965, and $315 billion in 1970.

$436 Billion Plus to Spend

The prices of consumption goods and services, compared to prices of investment goods, have been falling and will continue to fall. Although the country will probably have $355 billion available for them in 1965 and $436 billion in 1970, it will be able to buy more than these sums could buy today. The total "physical" volume of consumer goods and services in the 1960's, in other words, will rise faster than consumers' actual dollar payments for them—assuming, of course, no general inflation.

How consumers will allocate these dollars will depend on a variety of factors that can now be only tentatively appraised: although population will increase less than half as fast as personal income, the number of teen-agers and young adults (up to twenty-five) will increase by 45 per cent; income distributions may shift, and the largest income gains will not go to the unskilled workers, but rather to the skilled and the professionals.

The trend of consumer spending will also depend on relative price movements. Prices of food, clothing, and home and recreation goods have tended to show steady declines, relative to other prices; rents and car prices have been fairly stable; prices of most services have tended to rise. So here are estimates of the prospects for the major consumer markets:

1. Food, drink, and tobacco. Per capita volume in this group fluctuates from year to year with the so-called meat-production cycle, but in recent years it has tended to rise about two-thirds as much as total consumption. This seems only natural, given the limits of man's stomach, though in fact sales of many food products incorporating service features have risen briskly, and more or less static sales of tobacco and alcohol are responsible for the group's sluggishness. The demand for special food products may yet cause that group's volume to rise faster; but its volume will probably continue to rise a third less rapidly than the volume of total consumption. In the latter years of the decade, owing in part to the rapid increase in the numbers of teen-agers and young adults, food consumption will accelerate along with total consumption.

Relative prices of food, which dominate the group, have tended to decline in recent years, and should continue the tendency as farm productivity rises. Actual dollars spent on food, drink, and tobacco, therefore, may rise only 11 per cent between 1960 and 1965 or from $91 billion to $101 billion, and 16 per cent between 1965 and 1970, or from $101 billion to $117 billion.

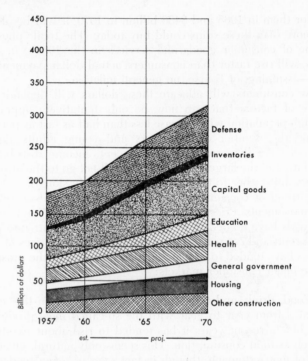

FIGURE 2. This Is the Way It Will Work Out in Dollars. Investment and defense expenditures together should rise from $177 billion in 1957 to $195 billion in 1960 to $260 billion in 1965 and $315 billion in 1970 (inflation would raise all the figures). Defense expenditures (which on the charts include several billions sent abroad) are projected to rise from $51 billion to $67 billion in 1965 and $75 billion in 1970. Capital-goods outlays are projected to rise from $47 billion to $71 billion in 1965 and $85 billion in 1970. All other investment outlays are projected to rise from $79 billion in 1957 to $96 billion in 1960, and to $122 billion in 1965 and $155 billion in 1970.

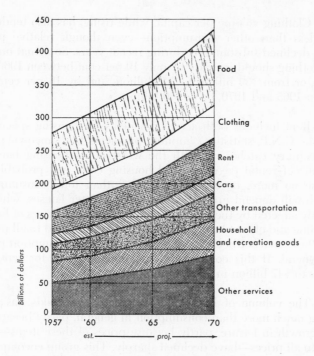

But consumption outlays, though accounting for a smaller *share* of G.N.P., will show an immense actual rise. Total consumption should increase from $275 billion in 1957 to about $355 billion in 1965 and $436 billion in 1970. The breakdown may look something like this: outlays for food, drink, and tobacco will increase from $84 billion in 1957 to $101 billion in 1965 and $117 billion in 1970; for personal services and utilities, from $48 billion in 1957 to $67 billion in 1965 and $89 billion in 1970; for autos, from $15 billion in 1957 to $21 billion in 1965 and $26 billion in 1970.

2. Clothing volume per capita, while rising, has also tended to rise less than other consumption—even though relative prices have declined substantially during recent years. So actual outlays on clothing should increase by only 10 per cent between 1960 and 1965, or from $39 billion to $43 billion, and by 16 per cent between 1965 and 1970, or to $50 billion.

3. Rent includes both actual payments for housing space and (in the G.N.P. statistics) imputed payments by homeowners. As the country catches up with the worst of its housing backlog, volume of rental payments and housing costs will probably increase no more, or even slightly less, than total consumption. Much will depend upon the demand for better houses, which is greatly affected by the prices of new construction. Prices of house-building and of rent have held stable when compared to all prices, i.e., they have not been going down as fast as consumption prices in general. If this continues, actual dollars spent for rent will come to $47 billion in 1965 and $57 billion in 1970.

4. The volume of household and recreation goods has been rising much more than consumption in general, partly because of the growth in leisure, partly because prices of these items—relative to all prices—have declined sharply. This group encompasses a great variety of products—TV, hi-fi, washers, freezers, air conditioners, cameras, records, sporting goods—and their prices have not declined, nor have their sales risen, in unison. However, the trends toward bigger volume and still lower (relative) prices may be safely projected into the 1960's, and this means that outlays for household and recreation goods would come to $42 billion in 1965, and to $53 billion by 1970.

5. Car purchases have tended to rise faster than consumption in general for nearly two generations and, despite the auto industry's recent troubles, will probably continue to do so in the 1960's. By 1960, it is true, car volume may not have completely recovered from the recent debacle. But the development of compact cars and the consequent broadening of the market should help sales over most of the decade, and so will the impending large additions to the car-driving population.

Relative prices of cars, as well as they can be measured in the face of major shifts in size, power, and appointments, have fluctuated sharply. They declined, relatively, in the mid-Fifties, and then rose in the last few years. In light of recent market troubles and the trend to cheaper compact cars, the relative price trend should be down again in the 1960's. Outlays on cars can be expected to rise 19 per cent in 1960–65 and 24 per cent in 1965–70, or to $21 billion in 1965 and $26 billion in 1970.

6. Expenditures on "transportation"—automobile operation, as distinct from car purchases, and fares for public transport—are geared closely to the number of cars on the road. Seventy-five per cent of the total goes for auto operation: gas and oil (42 per cent), tires and parts (10 per cent), and car repair, insurance, etc. (23 per cent). The number of cars has been growing faster than the population and will continue to do so if the accompanying projection of car purchases is realized. During most of the Fifties, relative prices in the transportation category tended to increase, but they have dipped a little recently. We can assume a very slight rise in the 1960's, owing mainly to the tendency of service costs (repair, insurance, etc.) to mount. So outlays should come to about $34 billion in 1965 and to $44 billion in 1970.

7. Personal services and utilities are a vast miscellany that totaled $48 billion in 1957. This included $15 billion for gas, electricity, and telephones, and $33 billion for domestic servants, spectator amusements, insurance and bank charges, brokerage commissions, and foreign travel. Growth trends and price trends have been somewhat diverse—e.g., more utilities and fewer servants, more tourists and fewer movie-goers. But there are crosscurrents: recently the number of domestic servants has risen, and utility rates have not been declining as much as they did in the 1940's. The most spectacular volume increases over recent years have been shown by foreign travel—and brokerage charges.

The volume of services, though growing, lagged behind the volume of other consumption between 1929 and the end of the war. But since then it has been making up for lost time, and has expanded far more rapidly than total consumption. More recently, however, the increase slowed down, partly because of rising prices. In the coming decade a slow uptrend in relative prices of services may limit the rise; outlays will nevertheless increase at a faster rate than outlays for other major consumption groups. So they should come to about $67 billion or 11 per cent of G.N.P. in 1965 and $89 billion or 12 per cent of G.N.P. in 1970.

Enough Is Not Too Much

Such a plenitude of consumer goods and services suggests that the American people may take a slice of their increased capacity to produce in the form of leisure. This, as a matter of fact, they have been doing for a century. A hundred years ago the average work week (nonfarm) was around sixty-five hours, and at the turn of the century it was still fifty-six hours. But by 1950 it had been shortened to less than forty-one hours. It is still about forty hours. The projections in this article assume that the work week will shrink more in the 1960's than it did in the 1950's, but less than in previous decades. There has been no basic change in the standard nonfarm work week since 1938, when the forty-hour week was adopted by many industries; the average work week has been declining by 1.5 hours a decade since then because the nation as a whole has been gradually adopting the forty-hour week, and because many women and students have been working part time. Although there is as yet no sign of a new basic work week, the thirty-five or thirty-six-hour week (five seven-hour days) is common in a good many big-city offices and is bound to spread (perhaps in the form of four nine-hour days).

Despite such trends, however, the labor force is increasing more than enough to offset them. In the 1950's it grew by about 8 per cent. In the 1960's, as the babies of the 1940's come of age, the population of working age should expand twice as fast as it did in the 1950's, or by about 16 per cent a year. It is this accelerated growth in the labor force, coming at a time when the country's productivity will also be increasing at a record rate, that will enable the U.S. of the 1960's to meet the demands of defense, public service, and capital investment, and still have such stupendous quantities of goods and services left for the consumer.

A revolution in income distribution is turning the traditional income pyramid upside down. Though it sounds fantastic, it is predicted that almost one-half of all families will be earning more than $7500 a year after taxes in 1970. But even more intriguing is the promise that by 1970, more than half of all disposable personal income will be "discretionary," that is, over and above the amount needed for necessities such as food and clothing. Potentially, there is the possibility of an entirely new kind of market—endlessly fragmented by the individualistic spending decisions of the high-income masses.

The Decade of the
"Discretionary" Dollar*

The U.S. is now entering an astonishing new phase of the great income revolution that has transformed U.S. society—and the U.S. market—in the last few decades. Indeed, some of the changes in prospect for the 1960's are so extraordinary that they sound less like economic projections than like some utopian manifesto. Real poverty will be largely abolished in the U.S. A vast number of adult Americans, perhaps 25 million, will be "making a living" without actually working; most of them, of course, will be retired, and retirement income will be substantial enough so that Americans will be largely free of the old fear of destitution in their late years. Meanwhile, the ancient image of work as something manual and

by Sanford S. Parker
and
Lawrence A. Mayer

* Vol. 59, June 1959, pp. 136–138, 260–264.

tedious will be fading rapidly: by 1970 a substantial majority of workers will be in white-collar or highly skilled blue-collar jobs —in jobs that characteristically require real training and thought. In part because of this occupational upgrading, personal income will grow furiously during the 1960's; it will, in fact, grow even more rapidly than it has grown in the booming 1950's. By the end of the decade, families *above* the middle-income level will constitute the new mass market.

These high-income masses will provide the essential difference between the markets of this decade and those of the 1960's. The markets of the 1950's were expanded and reshaped by the emergence of an appreciable new supply of "discretionary" income. While the exact dividing line has to be set somewhat arbitrarily, it is broadly true that families with after-tax incomes under $4,000 are obliged to spend just about everything on the necessities of food, clothing, shelter, transportation, and medical care. As they move over the $4,000 line, they have extra income with which they can exercise a number of options. They can buy better food and drink, or better furniture, or they can take a small flyer in the stock market; or, conceivably, all of the extra income may go for one big fling in the luxury market (e.g., the $5,000 family that saves for years to take a trip to Europe). Right now, about three-fifths of all family units[1] in the U.S. have some discretionary income.

By the time that families move over the $7,500 line, about half their income is discretionary, and the range of options is now so wide that it is no longer just a question of this purchase or that purchase, but of choosing a whole *style of life*. A skilled mechanic who earns $7,500 after taxes may choose to continue living in "working class" style, meanwhile saving sizable sums for his children's college education; or he may choose to live like a junior executive in his own $17,000 suburban house; or he may choose to live in a city apartment house otherwise occupied by business and professional men. When the American "masses" have options

---

[1] Except for those who are institutionalized, and some members of the armed forces, every American is counted as belonging to some "family unit." Besides families in the ordinary sense, the term applies to individuals living alone, three bachelor girls sharing an apartment, etc. There are 55 million family units in the U.S. today.

of this breadth, it is scarcely an exaggeration to suggest that we will have arrived at a landmark in all the history of human freedom.

Like the other predictions ventured in this *Fortune* series, these extravagant-sounding statements assume that there will be no general war in the years ahead; and they also assume that no large, presently unforeseeable events will send the economy into a recession more severe than those of 1949, 1953–54, and 1957–58. If these assumptions prove correct, it is safe to say that we are in for a gradual, but nevertheless breath-taking, change in the character of life in America.

Another kind of reservation may be expressed. If the marketing implications of a high-income mass society are exhilarating, the moral implications of a world in which sizable sums of money come to millions of Americans easily, almost "automatically," are somewhat harder to express. It is at least conceivable that the opulent masses might develop a kind of moral flabbiness over the years, and that endless preoccupation with problems of consumption might turn us into a race of people poorly equipped to cope with the realities of the thermonuclear age. In the years just ahead it is likely that we will be hearing a great deal about this problem.

The extraordinary proliferation of high-income families in the next decade is the principal subject of this article. The article will also deal with the occupational shifts in prospect for the 1960's, and will explore the marketing implications of both the new jobs and the higher incomes.

Perhaps the best way to gain an appreciation of this coming phase is to consider what has preceded it:

• In the first three decades of this century the U.S. began to develop what was then glorified as a "mass market." It was, at first, a very impoverished market by modern standards: in 1900, almost half the family units in the U.S. had less than $2,000 of income—in terms of today's money. (Past and future income figures in this article are all given in 1959 dollars and after taxes.) During the 1920's the most significant market development was the creation of a sizable "lower-middle-income" class, based on family units in the $2,000-to-$4,000 income class. It was these families and individuals who made possible the development of a mass consumer market for products like the Model T; by 1929 there were 14 million such family units—three times as many as in 1900—and they represented almost 40 per cent of all the units. But the division between the mass and the "class" markets persisted: these 14 million, together with the 12 million below $2,000, had less aggregate spending power than the 3,300,000 family units with more than $7,500 of income.

• The welfare legislation introduced under the New Deal, and the higher taxes imposed during the 1930's and the war years, comprised the second phase. These measures tended to equalize incomes somewhat—i.e., to prop up the mass market and to limit the growth of the class market—and when World War II finally ended the depression these measures contributed to the extraordinary growth of a real middle-income class—i.e., of family units with income after taxes of $4,000 to $7,500. By 1947, family units in this bracket already had 43 per cent of all the disposable income in the U.S. But about half of all family units in 1947 were still under the $4,000 line.

• In the third phase, which began after the war and is now ending, the moneyed middle-income class came to dominate the market in almost every respect. In 1953, when *Fortune* began its series on "The Changing American Market," over 40 per cent of all family units had after-tax incomes between $4,000 and $7,500, and their income was about 40 per cent of the total. These proportions have remained fairly constant during the 1950's. All together, the number of family units with $4,000 to $7,500 of income is now about 22 million (a gain of 30 per cent over 1947), and within this group there are now over seven million family units with more than $6,000. The number of family units under $4,000 has declined both absolutely and relatively: today only two-fifths of all family units are under $4,000. Meanwhile, the number of units with more than $7,500 has roughly doubled—to over 12 million—in the years since 1947.

• During the next decade, the market will come to be dominated by this mass high-income class. By 1970 there will be around 25 *million* family units with more than $7,500; they will comprise nearly two-fifths of all the family units; and they will have over three-fifths of all consumer spending money. The middle-income family units, whose spending power dominated the markets of the early 1950's, will have only 28 per cent of the disposable income by 1970—down from 43 per cent in 1947.

Or look at it another way: If all family units in the U.S. are divided into a low (under $4,000), middle ($4,000 to $7,500), and high (over $7,500) income class, then the income pyramid that has traditionally characterized all societies is now being stood on its head in the U.S. Even in 1947 about 50 per cent of family units were low income, about 40 per cent were middle income, and about 10 per cent were high income. During the 1950's, this pyramid began to assume a diamond shape. (The diamond shape is more marked if we consider only actual families and forget for the moment about "family units"; the latter include a number of relatively low-income single individuals just starting their careers and older persons who are not working, e.g., widows.) Right now there are more families in the middle than at the top or bottom. And by 1970 the pyramid will be finally inverted. Families with incomes over $7,500 will be 45 per cent of all families; the middle-income families will be another 39 per cent (and they will still be moving rapidly toward the top group); and those with less than $4,000 will be only 16 per cent.

Where It Comes From

The basis for the coming income boom has been set forth in the previous article. The heart of the matter is the very rapid growth of productivity anticipated for the 1960's; the increase is likely to average 3 per cent a year—as it has in the years since World War II. Meanwhile, the total man-hours worked should rise about 1.2 per cent a year, an increase over the growth rate that prevailed during the 1950's. The over-all increase in the output of goods and services, then, will be more than 4 per cent a year compounded, and suggests a gross national product in 1970 of $750 billion. About a third of this total will be absorbed by defense expenditures and by business and "social" investment (e.g., for schools, highways). This would leave about $500 billion of disposable income in 1970 (a rise from $320 billion today).

It is not only the sheer magnitude of this figure that compels attention. What may prove even more intriguing, and more challenging, to marketing men is the fact that so much of this money

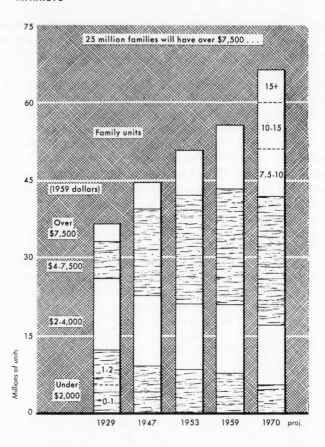

FIGURE 3. **The High-Income Masses.** The next American market will be dominated by family units with more than $7500 income (after taxes), just as the market of the early 1950s was dominated by families in the middle range ($4000 to $7500). By 1970, families over the $7500 line will actually outnumber families in the middle,

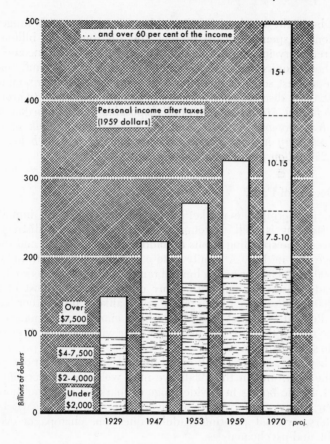

even though these too will grow a little during the 1960s. Meanwhile there will be a steep decline, both absolutely and relatively, of families under the $4000 line (who will be only a sixth of the total by 1970).

will be in the hands of families able to exercise a wide range of options in spending it. At present, there is some $135 billion of discretionary income in the U.S., i.e., of "after-$4,000 income" to the family units that have it—and 60 per cent of U.S. family units have at least some of this after-$4,000 money. Between now and 1970, these discretionary dollars will just about double, *to around $255 billion. More than half of all disposable personal income will be discretionary by 1970. And the overwhelming bulk of this discretionary income, perhaps 85 per cent of it, will belong to the 25 million families with more than $7,500.*

A Decade of Fads?

In pondering the marketing implications of these imposing statistics, it is well to retain a firm focus on the distinction between the spending habits of middle-income families and those above the middle. A family whose income goes up from, say, $4,000 to $5,000 has only a limited range of discretions, as we have already observed; and within any one community most of the $5,000 families have to live pretty much alike. On the other hand, families with incomes over $7,500 have enough discretionary income so that they are free to change their whole style of life—and to do so repeatedly.

They may, in fact, go off on all sorts of tangents from one year to the next, and in the 1960's we may well see a succession of brief, hectic booms in a wide range of markets, with the money-laden masses conferring their favors alternately on boats, helicopters, original paintings, adult education, champagne-every-night, and psychoanalysis.

Historically, the spending habits of the American masses have been heavily influenced by "spending leaders" whose income was well above the average. As the incomes of the leaders were steadily increased, and a wider range of goods became available, they tended to spend their additional income. In following the leaders, the masses have tended, over the years, to reduce the proportion of income saved by any one income class, and they have also tended to build up mass markets for a wide range of consumer products, like refrigerators, that were regarded as luxuries when the leaders first began to buy them. Out of this process there has emerged, somehow, a remarkable kind of stability in spending patterns, i.e., the proportions of income spent on food, transportation, furniture, etc., have held fairly constant. This constancy may well persist during the 1960's, even while the new spending leaders continue to upgrade the country's notions about necessities. But it is also possible that these families, which have the capacity to *save* in a big way, will lead millions of Americans to own more common stocks, say, and fewer physical goods. (Stock ownership is already becoming, for many families, an important symbol of "having arrived.")

These are speculations, of course, not predictions. We can summarize matters by saying that there is a *potentiality*, at least, for an entirely new kind of market, endlessly fragmented by the individualistic spending decisions of millions of well-heeled families; and there is also a potentiality for a cohesive but quite volatile market, dominated by families keeping up (or down) with the Joneses, and moving from one gigantic fad to another. If the spending possibilities cited above sound extreme for many families that have just crossed the $7,500 line, it should be noted that most families over that line will be well over it (see Fig. 3). More than three-fifths of the over-$7,500 families of 1970 will also be over $10,000.

Seated Employment

In estimating how Americans are likely to be spending their money in the 1960's, it is important to know something about their occupations as well as incomes—though the living styles of families with different occupational backgrounds are coming to be "homogenized" to some extent.

Perhaps the first point to make about the occupations of the 1960's is that fewer of them will be physical than they have been in the past. Perhaps half of all employed Americans already do their work *sitting down*. During the 1960's, the trend will continue; an increasing number of jobs will require special kinds of skill, judgment, training, and in turn will offer (along with good pay) challenge and stimulus.

This trend is commonly viewed as the "white-collar revolution," and there is certainly some basis for that view, even if one looks only at the changes in male jobs—the jobs that principally determine the way a family looks at itself. Only about 15 per cent of men held white-collar jobs in 1900 (they were mostly small proprietors). This proportion rose to 25 per cent in 1940 and will rise to 40 per cent by 1970.

But meanwhile, there has been a significant change in farm and blue-collar work. At the turn of the century, more than half of the male labor force in the U.S. consisted of farmers and laborers whose skills were primitive, whose work was arduous, and whose income was not much above a subsistence level. By 1940 only 40 per cent of men were farmers or laborers, and by 1957 only 25 per cent—and they were much better paid. Meanwhile, skilled and semiskilled workers grew from 20 per cent of the male labor force in 1900 to 40 per cent in 1957.

In the coming period, work will be predominantly brain work. By 1970, about two working men out of five will be white collars; there will be about 20 million of them, and two-thirds will be congregated in the very best white-collar jobs, i.e., they will be working, in Census Bureau terms, as "managers, officials, and proprietors," or as "professional, technical, and kindred workers."

Within the blue-collar and farm groups there will also be significant kinds of "upgrading" during the 1960's. In each of these categories, work will not only be less physical, but it will also have a new dignity attached to it. The characteristic blue-collar of 1940 was a man on an assembly line whose work was intensely monotonous. But a high proportion of blue-collar workers are now skilled, and by 1970 over ten million of the blue-collars will be "craftsmen, foremen, and kindred workers," exercising a great deal of judgment and entrusted with the care and operation of some very sophisticated kinds of capital equipment. One modern oil refinery, for example, now requires a high-school education for production workers, and hires only foremen with engineering degrees.

The prototypical farmer of 1970 will also be exercising new kinds of judgment. Indeed, it is already somewhat unrealistic to think of the farmer as a manual worker; a great many of them are beginning to look (and to earn) more like highly trained technicians and entrepreneurs, exercising skills that depend on detailed knowledge of soil chemistry, and even making use of electronic computers, e.g., to determine the best genetic combinations in breeding chickens. The continuing decline in the farm labor force—which had about 8,500,000 men in 1940 and will have about half that many in 1970—has been chiefly at the expense of the least-skilled farmers and laborers, e.g., sharecroppers and field hands.

The Helpmates

Their flexibility will also be enhanced by the continuing expansion of opportunities for their wives to work, especially in white-collar fields. In "The Changing American Market" series of 1953–54, *Fortune* observed that the rapid increase in middle-income families during the 1950's was based in large measure on the growth of supplementary earners; and that about two-fifths of all these families would be *below* the middle if they did not have more than one member at work. A similar point may now be made about the growth of over-$7,500 families, recent and prospective. During the 1960's there will be more working wives; the wives are already about half of all the supplementary earners.

Jobs that require skills and judgment have, almost inherently, a greater dignity than jobs that are simply manual or repetitive; and the faster growth of "judgment jobs," combined with sharply rising levels of pay, suggests that during the 1960's millions of workers will begin to enjoy something like the status that once was conferred exclusively on certain kinds of professionals and proprietors—traditionally the "individualists" par excellence.

Who Are the Poor?

One corollary of the prospective upgrading of the labor force is that, in the aggregate, the lowest-paid jobs—for service workers, farm and nonfarm laborers—will show no significant growth. Indeed, the attrition in these jobs since 1940, and the rising pay scales attached to them, have already created a situation in which very few Americans can be considered "permanently poor" because they hold bad jobs. In 1957 there were some 3,600,000 families with incomes under $2,000. But more than half of them were either unemployed or retired, i.e., the low income was temporary or it was being bolstered by savings or help from relatives. Only about a million domestic servants, marginal farm operators, and farm laborers still look truly poor.

Discretionary Anxiety

By the end of the 1960's, it is manifest, Americans will be free to order their lives in a dramatically new and different fashion. They will have incomes and jobs that offer the prospect of a new kind of human dignity. But the freedoms of the 1960's imply some new kinds of problems too. Masses with high incomes and diverse job opportunities may not only baffle the marketing man, they may baffle themselves. The expanded range of options will call for new and sometimes difficult decisions—how to spend, how much to spend or save, how much, indeed, to work. A man whose career is determined, and whose spending habits are largely determined, by necessity may simply take his position in life as "fixed"—and not worry about it. People with new options about their style of living and position in life may find themselves exposed to new anxieties. Most of them, presumably, will be willing to put up with this.

THE NEW "RENTIER" CLASS

Not working is the fastest growing of all major "occupations" in the U.S. today. The number of nonworkers has roughly doubled in the past decade, and might well double again by 1970. In the process, the U.S. is forming a new kind of rentier class, which poses some intriguing challenges for marketing men.

In 1949 there were 2,700,000 able-bodied Americans over fourteen who were not working or looking for work, not going to school, and not keeping house. Today there are about 5,500,000 persons over fourteen who are doing none of these things, and a sizable number of them appear to have resources that enable them to "not work" fairly early in life: about 1,500,000 of them are under sixty-five. The remaining four million are predominantly retired men. In all, there are seven million men in the U.S. over sixty-five, of whom 2,200,000 are still working (and half a million are considered disabled rather than retired). Of the eight million women over sixty-five, 6,500,000 are listed as "keeping house"—and more than a million are employed.

By 1970 about eight million men and eleven million women will be over sixty-five, and they will comprise about 9 per cent of the U.S. population. The significant marketing fact about these men and women is that, for the first time, they are coming to represent a big sales potential for a very wide variety of consumer products—for more and more leisure products like cameras and fishing gear, but also for furniture, household appliances, etc., since the retired are frequently setting up new homes. They can devote a lot more time to consumption than workers can; and given the swelling income that is becoming available to them, one might conceive of these elder Americans becoming an important new influence on taste and consumption habits generally.

In 1950 the median income of all men over sixty-five was about $1,000 (in 1959 dollars). Over 40 per cent of all these men were then in the labor force—i.e., they were either employed or looking for work. Today the median income of men over sixty-five is about $1,450—but only a third of them are in the labor force. In 1950 about 15 per cent of men over sixty-five had incomes over $3,500; today the proportion is 20 per cent. These figures, moreover, include only the sums going directly to men over sixty-five, but many of their wives also have pensions and other income. Of the seven million men over sixty-five, about 4,500,000 are living with their wives (and another 400,000 are the heads of families that do not include their wives). About 40 per cent of these families have incomes over $3,500.

Retirement and retirement income will grow rapidly during the 1960's, principally because Americans have been deferring sizable quantities of current income in order to build nest eggs for the future. The eggs will be hatched, in the 1960's, out of income that had been deferred in several different ways: by paying taxes (e.g., social-security taxes, payroll taxes to finance unemployment insurance) that are ultimately transferred to people who are not working; by limiting payrolls in order to build up pension funds for employees; by saving in order to build up annuities or capital that can later be used to produce income. Here are some figures on the recent and prospective payout to the new rentier class:

Social security. In 1940 about a million Americans received old-age and survivors' payments; the annual payout was $24 million. Today about 13 million Americans receive social security (which has included disability payments since 1957); the annual total is about $10 billion—more than double the payroll of the U.S. automobile industry. By 1970, the Social Security Administration has estimated, about 19 million will be receiving payments; and the annual payout will be about $18 billion. In 1970, even with no further changes in coverage, about 80 per cent of all people over sixty-five will be receiving social-security benefits.

Other federal programs. A miscellany of other benefits for civil servants, railroad workers, regular military personnel, and veterans provide regular payments to some 5,200,000 individuals or families. The total annual payout is about $4.7 billion. There has been a fivefold increase in the number of beneficiaries since 1940 and a sevenfold increase in the payout. It is hard to project these totals ahead to 1970—but they will surely continue to rise.

State and local programs. These afford benefits under a diverse and bewildering assortment of laws—which provide for teachers' and policemen's pensions, unemployment insurance, workmen's compensation, public assistance (i.e., "relief") etc. Not all the payments are made regularly (e.g., unemployment-insurance payments), and the total number of beneficiaries is not known; but the total payout from all these sources has increased from $1.4 billion in 1940 to around $4.5 billion this year. Again, future payouts are certain to increase.

Private pensions. In 1940 about 160,000 families or individuals received regular payments under privately financed group pension plans; the figure is up to about 1,300,000 today. Total payments are up from $140 million in 1940 to about $1.2 billion. Right now about 18 million workers are covered by these plans; if we assume that these workers have the same age composition as the labor force as a whole, then it would appear that there will be about three million regular beneficiaries by 1970. The monthly payments will vary considerably, of course, but to cite a possibility under one of the more generous plans, a welder who began at Grumman Aircraft in 1935 and now earns $130 a week might be eligible to retire in 1970 with $300 a month—$425 counting his social security.

Life-insurance payments, not counting payments under group pension plans, rose from $2.6 billion in 1940 to about $7.4 billion this year. It is reasonable to expect a further rise to $13 billion by 1970.

Dividends, interest, and rent—the traditional sources of rentier income—have increased from an aggregate of $9.2 billion in 1940 to $29 billion of cash payments this year. Forecasting the future of these payouts is a parlous business, but it is quite possible that by 1970 the total will be more than $40 billion. However, the figures on dividends, interest, and rent include some payments that are not really to individuals—e.g., payments made to pension funds—and so the totals should be reduced somewhat, perhaps by 15 per cent, to avoid an overlap with some of the newer kinds of rentier income.

The significant fact about these newer kinds of income is that they are growing much more rapidly than personal income as a whole, while dividends, interest, and rent have been declining as a share of all personal income—from 12 per cent in 1940 to 8 per cent today. The newer kinds of rentier income are already close to 8 per cent—i.e., they add up to about $28 billion of the total $375 billion in personal income. Something like 15 per cent of all personal income, then, is already paid out for nonwork—which is getting to be an extremely attractive occupation.

American taste is changing and will continue to do so. The changes taking place are pervasive, encompassing nearly all social classes and income groups, and are reflected not only in the things people buy but in the ways they use their leisure. This article explores the forces working to elevate American taste and concludes that business can look forward to increasing demand for "better" products—both functionally and esthetically.

*How American Taste Is Changing**

Not so long ago American taste was the concern chiefly of the country's architects, artists, writers, and intellectual leaders. Now it is also the concern of its business leaders—of anyone, that is, who sells consumer goods and services. Price is important and always will be, but in

by Gilbert Burck

a society looking forward to an average family income approaching $7,500 a year after taxes, price becomes relatively less important. Just as a woman who can afford to spend $50 for a frock will pay $65 for one that delights her, but begrudges $35 for one that does not, so American consumers as a group today tend more and more to let their senses make up their minds.

As with price, so with utility and efficiency of products. In these days when consumer testing services are hard pressed to find important technical differences between brands of similar products, what counts more and more is the aesthetic quality of

* Vol. 60, July 1959, pp. 114–116, 186–196.

the products. It is not for nothing that industrial designers are getting into almost everything.

Business' growing concern with American taste is intensifying the intellectuals' concern about it. Taste is perhaps best defined as the capacity to discern fitness, beauty, order, congruity, or whatever constitutes excellence. When patterns of taste are dictated by purely commercial considerations, one argument goes, this capacity is stunted, and nearly all taste must conform to the average. Creative talent is diverted from writing novels or composing sonatas into such tasks as confecting advertising slogans; and intellects that are capable of unlocking the secrets of the universe are diverted into such pursuits as designing better cigarette-making machinery.

What *is* the state of American taste? In this essay *Fortune* puts aside statistics to argue a speculative and controversial thesis: it is that American taste, at least by prevailing standards, is changing for the better, and will continue to do so. The change will be pervasive, encompassing nearly all social and income groups, and will be evident not only in the things people buy, but in the ways people use their leisure. And despite the apprehensions of the intellectuals, the part that business plays in forming tastes will tend not to corrupt but to improve them.

About Taste There Is Much Dispute

But is it possible to talk about absolute standards of taste? A lot of cagey thinkers, from the dawn of civilization, have maintained that anybody laying down such standards is simply describing his personal inclinations. It is certainly true that taste cannot be analyzed and graded to close standards, like aluminum alloys, or internal-combustion engines. Moreover, taste is often the cloak of the intellectual snob who automatically defines as bad anything that is popular. Yet there appear to be some fundamentals of fitness, proportion, and beauty. Give a group of people a series of pictures of objects and tell them to pick the best and the worst, and they agree remarkably on the extremes of both good and bad. What is more, a nation's taste is the measure of its culture, and to deny the reality of qualitative differences in taste is to slam the door on all inherited cultural values. If those values

mean anything at all, there is an important difference between
J. D. Salinger and Mickey Spillane, between the *Eroica* and
Pink Shoe Laces, between O'Neill and soap opera, between the
Parthenon and a hot-dog stand.

Perhaps the most practical approach to taste values is simply
to observe that "good" taste is usually the taste of the "upper"
classes, the artistically proficient, or the learned. But the arbiters
or makers of taste are not only educators, the *avant-garde,* the
intellectuals, the writers, the designers, they are also, as we shall
see, often manufacturers and merchandisers. These arbiters, of
course, don't always agree among themselves, but whether they
agree or not, they do set standards. So let us say that "good"
taste in the U.S. is represented by the preferences of its tastemakers.

Four major forces are working to elevate American taste:
(1) rising real income; (2) more education, both formal and informal; (3) the efforts of the tastemakers to spread their own
gospel; and (4) the old American striving for self-betterment.

The effect of rising real income on U.S. taste is not merely that
it enables people to buy more. It usually enables business to provide consumers with a steadily wider range of choices, thus making mass production the agent not of uniformity but of constantly
widening variety. And along with more money, Americans are
getting more leisure in which to develop their taste.

But income and leisure without education are like force without
direction. As the excesses of America's own newly rich suggest,
more leisure and more money for masses of Americans without
more and better education could produce a temporary decline in
public taste. Immediately after World War II, for example, war-
plant workers splurged on the elaborate, overstuffed "Borax"
furniture they had set their hearts on years before.

Not that formal education necessarily improves anyone's taste.
But it does help; in fact it is probably the most powerful single
factor in the improvement process. And never in American history
has education expanded so fast as it is now expanding. The number of adult Americans who have completed high school rose from
27 million, or 33 per cent of the adult population, in 1947 to 39
million, or 40 per cent of the adult population, in 1957; during
the next decade it will surely rise to about 55 million, or 50 per

cent of the adult population. During the past decade the number of youths attending college has risen from 2,200,000 to 3,200,000, and during the next decade it will rise to at least six million, more than 40 per cent of the number of youths of college age. According to the U.S. Office of Education, 35 million to 40 million adults are "interested" in after-hours study programs, and some nine million are actually enrolled in organized courses.

Surely not far behind the formal educators as molders of taste are the informal educators or tastemakers. They have always existed, but never in such quantity. In the past they consisted of a tiny aristocracy, who so to speak administered a nation's culture; today America probably supports the largest taste-conscious *haute bourgeoisie* in history, expressing itself through an extraordinary variety of communications. People who think they possess good taste, like people who believe they possess the one true religion, often harbor a missionary's urge to convert others; and the American people, for the good of their taste, are being subjected to a constant drumfire of instruction, persuasion, and information. The so-called shelter or home-service magazines, for example, play an enormous role in creating the demand for houses and furnishings gratifying to behold. The mass magazines have made such subjects as America's Arts and Skills and Adventures of the Mind interesting to millions of people without talking down or unduly oversimplifying.

What People Don't Know Helps Them

And then there are the corporate managers and their designers, who are extraordinarily powerful tastemakers. Most of the time, some opinion notwithstanding, this business influence on taste is for the good. Precisely because businessmen are so often at a loss to know just how public taste is going to shift, they tend to let their corporate and personal self-esteem line them up on the side of good, or at least professional, design. And for their part, even the most mercenary practitioners of the "We'll design you any damn thing you want" school would rather turn out something they regard as good than something pandering to bad taste. Most good designers, indeed, take the view that the public's frequent uncertainty about its taste offers the opportunity of turning out something better than they might if the public knew exactly what it wanted.

The preference of corporate executives for "good" design is sometimes a matter of self-esteem; perhaps goaded by their wives, they feel sheepish about making stuff their friends regard as cheap or junky. Frequently their preference is more sophisticated: they want to create a high-class image of their company and its products. As David Ogilvy of Ogilvy, Benson & Mather puts it, "It pays to give a product a high-class image instead of a bargain-basement image. Also, you can get more for it." Or executives believe that taste is changing for the better and the wise policy is to anticipate it. "We try to design just ahead of the market," says Arthur BecVar, manager of General Electric's Industrial Design Operation in Louisville, "so that when public taste advances we are ready for it."

The "Aspiration" Drive

The phenomenon that springs from these forces and at the same time strengthens them all, of course, is the old American urge for self-betterment and self-expression. The currently popular theory of how this urge works has been developed by what might be called the status-symbol school of sociologists, who hold that: (1) people constantly express their personalities not so much in words as in symbols (i.e., mannerisms, dress, ornaments, possessions); (2) most people are increasingly concerned about what other people think of them, and hence about their social status. Thus the taste of many Americans is expressed in symbols of various social positions.

Several sociologists, notably W. Lloyd Warner of the University of Chicago, have divided Americans into status groups, based chiefly on occupation and education, with more or less common traits and tastes. Such classifications have been useful to advertising and marketing men trying to draw an accurate bead on their markets. But the group boundaries, the status-symbol sociologists hasten to add, are not necessarily the boundaries of people's aspirations. The urge for self-expression and self-betterment, shared by nearly all Americans, takes the form of aspiring to higher status. Thus people tend to buy things that symbolize their aspirations—a certain make of car, a certain style of house, a certain mode of dress. Their very status aspiration, in other words, drives them to emulate "better" taste and so upgrade their own.

But this does not yet mean, says Dr. Burleigh B. Gardner, founder of the motivation-research firm of Social Research, Inc. (which pioneered the status-symbol concept in advertising), that a workingman's wife wants to emulate the wealthy matron far above her, or that a steelworker wants to emulate the chairman of the board. A beer advertising campaign featuring a fox hunter in a pink coat flopped because the hunter symbolized nothing relevant to the ordinary people who drank the beer. The brewer aimed too high. As a rule, the sociologists point out, consumers emulate tastes within reach.

The Shifting Symbols

Sometimes a product loses its efficacy as a status symbol; a good example, says Dr. Gardner, is the automobile. Because the U.S. motorcar industry has built its cars more and more alike, the old American custom of upgrading from one make to another is disappearing. Many consumers have taken to foreign cars not so much because they are cheap to operate but because they are different. What is happening, most status-symbol theorists agree, is that houses and furnishings are replacing motorcars as status symbols.

Nevertheless, the furniture industry has been having a hard time taking advantage of the shift in status symbols. The industry lost a seventh of its market, measured as a percentage of disposable income, between 1948 and 1957, and saw its sales sag 4 per cent in prosperous 1957 and 7 per cent in 1958. So Kroehler, the largest U.S. furniture maker, hired Social Research to find out what the trouble was. The American housewife, Social Research observes, obviously does not choose furniture as she chooses can openers. She wants furniture she likes, but she also wants furniture in good taste—furniture that will proclaim her family status. The trouble is that she does not know for sure what good taste in furniture is, and the furniture industry has confounded her with a plethora of styles. Consequently she spends too much time just "looking around" at furniture instead of buying it. Many stores have professional decorators to help customers with their frustration. Whether they have helped is hard to say, but furniture sales have turned up.

The "High Mobiles"

Who are the people who first adopt the tastes that others follow? The evidence is strong that these innovators are not necessarily the people with the most money. As a group, they are the "new suburbanites," a status with an obviously strong appeal. A Chicago *Tribune* survey recently gave respondents a choice of twenty-one characterizations of themselves and their lives. Most of them, even some tenement dwellers, identified themselves with the "new young suburbanites" and indicated that they aspired to their kind of life.

It would be foolish, of course, to say that all young suburbanites are pioneers in taste, but the group apparently does contain the important innovators. Opinion Research Corp. of Princeton, New Jersey, trying to identify the dynamic Americans, made a study of 105 suburban households. The "early adopters," it found, included about a quarter of the suburban families it interviewed. They are people who are moving upward in economic status, who are moving around geographically, who are active intellectually, who have acquired a good deal of education, and whose work and play throw them into contact with a wide variety of people. Opinion Research calls them "High Mobiles." The High Mobiles were the first to buy electric blankets, low-calorie beverages, dining credit cards, food freezers, colored sheets, wall-to-wall carpeting, and other things that later became popular. Opinion Research, naturally, argues that business can get a reliable indication of the future trend of consumer tastes by watching the preferences of the High Mobiles.

A "Differentiation" Trend?

But even when emulating others, consumers do make innumerable choices in which status symbol plays little or no part. Although the American urge for self-expression and self-betterment is as strong as ever, its manifestation in the form of status seeking actually may be declining. In *Housing Choices and Housing Constraints,* soon to be published by ACTION, sociologist Nelson Foote suggests that even occupational and educational differences in the future will carry less and less weight, and people will bother less with proclaiming status.[1]

Foote reasons that rising discretionary income will force people to "differentiate" as well as emulate. Just as the newly rich in time become prudent and discriminating buyers, so ordinary Americans who suddenly find themselves with more money to spend will become more discriminating about the way they spend it. They will tend to expand their individuality, says Foote, and will begin to regard life as "a pursuit of meaning." The theory seems fortified by group income trends: the disposable income of the lower income groups is rising faster than that of the upper income groups, and the lower income groups may be confronted with so many more opportunities for emulating the upper groups that emulation itself will become pointless.

At all events, Foote predicts that people will "differentiate" mainly in their leisure pursuits—in such activities as travel, theatregoing, gardening, crafts, participation in public affairs and voluntary associations. To put it another way, people will achieve status by being different—or by being themselves. Or as Dr. Ernest Dichter, president of the Institute for Motivational Research, has remarked, "social status is coming closer to self-realization."

Something of the sort, as a matter of fact, can be observed among Americans whose social position or self-esteem is so secure that the thought of striving for status amuses more than it worries them. Their tastes are diverse, and dominated by no authority, traditional or contemporary. They casually install a Victorian love seat and a Barcelona chair in the same room. They do not try to emulate or surpass their neighbors, but, if anything, go out of their way to be a little different from their neighbors. And they do not rush out to translate a salary rise into a status symbol.

---

[1] *The Status Seekers,* the bestseller by Vance Packard, gives the absurd impression that almost every human reaction in the U.S. is heavily, not to say totally, conditioned by status and status symbols. Packard comes to the sensational conclusion that class lines in the U.S. are growing more rigid, although much of the evidence he himself brings forward actually argues the other way.

The Lower Mobiles

But most of these people, so far, are probably the High Mobiles. Meantime, what is happening to the taste of the ordinary American consumer? Few designers of rank would be willing to argue that it is fine, but most would grant that it is improving measurably, if sporadically. To be sure, some designers and architects are depressed by "Cinderella" or "Hansel and Gretel" houses— essentially simple dwellings decorated with atavistic gimcrackery like scallop-trimmed gables, "leaded" windows, and garages with artificial haylofts. But these confections seem to be prized most by people whose incomes have been rising faster than their taste standards; and anyhow they seem to be better to look at than the bleak bungalows of forty or fifty years ago. More important, the dwellings being built by the High Mobile taste setters usually meet the approval of the experts.

Automobiles, reflecting changing taste, seem headed for simpler, "cleaner" lines, with much less superfluous ornamentation. Appliances, despite such aberrations as clothes washers with instrument panels more dazzling than those on autos, are moving toward better design. "You can no longer design a thing so 'bad' it will sell," says Donald L. McFarland, head of General Electric's small-appliance design division, "or so 'good' it won't sell."

Furniture given to gross stylistic excesses seems actually to be growing scarce. "The broadening of consumer credit has helped a lot," says J. Chalmers O'Brien, vice president of Carson Piri Scott & Co. in Chicago. "The only place many people could afford to buy a bedroom suite fifteen years ago was one of the "Borax" houses. Now they can buy good furniture on time at the better stores."

"She Must Be American"

Improvements in Americans' taste show up strikingly in their choice of food and clothes. American food preferences are becoming astonishingly sophisticated. Dishes that could be found only in the *haute cuisine* of New York and a few other cities thirty years ago are now fairly common in millions of middle-class homes. Small-town hotel dining rooms and restaurants whose victuals were once an ordeal to even an undiscriminating drummer now turn out food that is not only edible but even appetizing. And the sale of dry table wine has increased no less than 64 per cent in the past decade.

And by the almost unanimous consent of all who pretend to know anything special about the subject, no women in the modern world have ever been so tastefully dressed as American women are today. "When you see a *really* well-dressed woman abroad today," says David Ogilvy, "you think, she must be an American." Precisely because women's clothes can be copied quickly and mass-produced cheaply, the general level of taste in clothing is high and still rising. What is more, all this mass production and style imitation, far from stifling individual expression, have actually encouraged and enabled the American woman to exercise it to a greater degree.

Here may lie a lesson for those who deplore the fact that so much of the advance in American taste amounts to imitation of others. To a considerable extent, of course, all taste must be learned. Even a genius must usually absorb a great deal of conventional knowledge before he can express himself with genuine originality. Yet American women and their clothes demonstrate that ordinary people can discriminate when they have learned enough.

From Extreme to Extreme

The elevation of American taste, however, is surely not a gradual, even process. Business can look forward to frequent and extreme changes in style and fashion, probably to an endless and rapid series of fads. (Sociologists distinguish fad from fashion as something with a touch of the unexpected or irresponsible.) Such changes, of course, are an old story. Fashions in women's clothes have often been carried to faddish excess, whereupon they disappear quickly—as did the hoop skirt, the leg-of-mutton sleeve, the Empress Eugénie hat, the sack dress. Architectural and industrial fashion, which cannot be so quickly imitated as clothes fashion, does not change so rapidly, but even it tends to run from extreme to extreme. The two-story house gives way to the ranch house, the ranch house to the split-level, the long low look in the motorcars to comfort, commodiousness, and perhaps even an upright look, the ornamented public building to the starkly simple one, the starkly simple one to the "subjective" style of Edward

Stone. "American taste," says William Snaith, managing partner of Raymond Loewy Associates, "is probably now going into a vigorous kind of romanticism—an effort to escape from starkness."

Extremes of fashion, far from being reprehensible, are both natural and psychologically useful. They are the result of money and leisure, and the desire to express or achieve status, sometimes complicated by a yearning for notoriety. They enable people to revolt from custom discreetly, to participate in extremes of taste they would be embarrassed to indulge in all by themselves. "Fashion," says sociologist Edward Sapir, "is custom in the guise of departure from custom."

The American people, with their rapidly rising discretionary income and leisure, seem likely to humor their "sideline" impulses more than ever, and so will intensify and accelerate the swings of fashion and fad. The lesson for business is clear. In an article in the *Harvard Business Review* last year, Dwight E. Robinson of the University of Washington wrote that "all of the fame and bulk of a leading textile, appliance, construction, or automobile company will not save it from fashion's dust-bin. . . She [fashion], and not the so-called fashion dictator . . . is the true autocrat; and only in a totalitarian state, where the consumer's taste is legislated by government edict, does she meet her match." She bids fair to be a power in the U.S. of the 1960's, and the designers who can intuitively divine what people want before they are fully aware of it themselves will come into their own.

Kitsch Culture

A good many intellectuals, as already noted, take a dim view of American taste. Consider *Mass Culture*, a recent anthology of essays on current American culture. Of its forty-nine articles, only seven were favorable to or optimistic about U.S. taste. Ernest van den Haag, professor at the New School for Social Research, for instance, argues that mass production, creating more leisure and wealth, is at the root of the trouble. Not that business aims at the lowest common denominator of taste, he says, but the trouble is that a mass-produced article or service, while reflecting everybody's taste to some extent, is unlikely to embody anybody's tastes fully. This matters particularly in education and entertainment, van den Haag goes on. Moreover, all culture is becoming homogenized by catering to the masses, and mass culture drives out high culture and folk culture because it tends to suck in the talents that might produce good things.

In the same volume Dwight Macdonald argues even more strongly that what the Germans call *Kitsch* or junk culture tends to drive out high culture. Because mass culture is so easy to produce, he says, it overwhelms by its very quantity, and people's taste sinks to that of the least sensitive and most ignorant: "There are just too many people." The future of high culture is dark, Macdonald concludes; the future of mass culture is even darker, and we will be lucky if it doesn't get worse.

The Audience Is There

The main defect common to such talk is that it disregards social and economic forces such as those described in this article, and so underrates the nation's capacity both for self-criticism and for high culture. The U.S., indeed, probably gives ear to more criticism of its culture than any other nation in history. Although it does not automatically guarantee a large income to anyone who cries its shortcomings, it will endure and even reward name-calling and invective provided that they contain some sense and are rendered in clear and vivid English.

And it is merely recording the obvious to say that high culture in the U.S. is not only very much alive but is growing fast. The American artistic output, as the whole world testifies, is both sizable and respectable. American writing, painting, sculpture, architecture, and music were once merely imitations and extensions of European culture; today they influence the culture of the rest of the world as much as it influences them.

If, as Walt Whitman once observed, it takes great audiences to produce great art, the U.S. should very soon be launching a great new era of musical composition. There are today forty-two major American symphony orchestras, against six in 1905 and thirty-two in 1956. Counting those in colleges and smaller communities, the total is more than 1,100, and at least 275 of them were formed between 1951 and 1957.

A growing number of Americans are not put off by "difficult" listening. Alban Berg's atonal opera *Wozzeck*, which was expected to be a flop at the Metropolitan Opera last season, played to sold-out houses. When it was put on the air on a Saturday afternoon, several out-of-town newspapers assigned their music critics to review the broadcast. One reason for this broadening of U.S. musical taste is that the sale of serious music on records is increasing at least as fast as the sale of all records. The fact is that many Americans with a record player today listen to more musical works in a year than even professional musicians once could in dozens of years.

The Rising Demand for Books

Although Americans may not read as many books per capita as the British, Scandinavians, and French, the astonishing fact, considering the competition of other diversions such as radio and television, is that they read as many as they do, and that many of them are as good as they are. Americans are buying some 630 million books a year (including paperbacks and juveniles but not textbooks), up from 330 million ten years ago. The success of the paperbacks, which are selling several hundred million copies a year, is enormously significant. A large percentage of the total is trash, but paperback versions of *The Iliad* and *The Odyssey* have together sold more than a million copies. So has J. D. Salinger's *The Catcher in the Rye* and George Orwell's *1984* (which argued, ironically, that the mass media of today will pave the way for the "double-think" of 1984). "The paperbacks," says Clifton Fadiman, "are democratizing reading. They are conferring upon it the simple, healthy status of a normal habit."

What is also relevant, one of the most successful newspaper columns of recent origin is Mortimer Adler's feature dealing with philosophical questions suggested by readers. Inaugurated October 19, 1958 (in the Chicago *Sun-Times*), it has been syndicated in eleven newspapers.

Radio and television, which have received their share of criticism, cannot be excluded from any inventory of American cultural media. Although they thrive on mass production, they also cater to special audiences. One can sometimes see or hear on them works one might never have seen or heard in a country with an aristocratic high culture and no mass media, such as Britain and Germany fifty years ago.

All this, of course, does not mean that the masses, for the first time in history, are rushing to embrace high culture. What is significant is that millions of the kind of Americans who make the nation's tastes have clung to or taken up the values of high culture voluntarily, uncoerced by state or other cultural authority, in a tolerably free market, and in the face of powerful competition by a multitude of mundane leisure activities. What millions have thus found good, millions more, if past behavior means anything, will almost surely find good.

More Quality and Variety

Taking everything together, then, it is reasonable to say that the forces changing American taste are changing it for the better. Thus business can look forward to a demand for "quality," for more choice and fashion, and for the uncommon or unusual. The large mass producers will probably have to provide more variety —as indeed the auto industry is doing today. And the small businessman with a product that isn't geared to the average will doubtless have a bright future.

Business will still be able to sell junk to a lot of Americans. But it surely will be able to make more money operating on the assumption that people want something "better" not only functionally but aesthetically.

Industrial production—chemicals, machinery, paper, textiles—is the bedrock on which the whole economy rests. Industrial output is the ultimate source of the country's strength and well-being: the market behind the market, responding to changes in consumer taste and actively shaping demand through new products and materials. During the present decade, industrial production is expected to expand by 60 percent, to better than $260 billion, but growth rates will vary widely from one industry to another.

The Market behind the Markets*

"When not kept back by bad institutions or a low state of the arts of life," wrote John Stuart Mill, "the produce of industry has usually tended to increase." In terms of the U.S. economy, this is surely one of the understatements of the industrial age that Mill, a century ago, was analyzing. The U.S. economy has more than "tended to increase;" it has grown to a level that Mill could never have imagined. And more exciting is the fact that industrial production, which provides the underpinning for the whole economy, is growing even faster. The prospective increase in U.S. manufacturing and mining output over the next decade is almost as large as the whole of that output just twelve years ago. In 1947 industrial production amounted to $105 billion (in 1959 dollars); this year it will come to $164 billion, comprising one-third of the nation's total output

by Todd May
and
Sanford S. Parker

* Vol. 60, December 1959, pp. 110–113, 242–257.

of goods and services. And by 1970 industrial production probably will come to more than $260 billion, 35 per cent of the $750-billion G.N.P. that *Fortune* has projected for that year.

This 60 per cent, or 4.4 per cent a year, expansion of U.S. industrial production over the next decade is not guaranteed. It could be interrupted by a number of unforeseen factors—e.g., intensification of the cold war, malfunctioning of the domestic or international credit system. Yet the fact that the economy has the potential for such an enormous industrial expansion is clearly important. It explodes the notion that the U.S. is becoming a "soft economy" largely devoted to the output of services rather than goods. Industrial output, after all, is the ultimate source of the country's strength and well-being. In previous articles, the probable needs of consumers have been detailed, as well as the needs for capital spending, and for defense and other government spending. It is the industrial machine that must meet these needs; the industrial process is the market behind the market, responding in depth to the most subtle changes in consumer taste and in investment requirements. But the industrial market does a lot more than just respond to these changes; it actively shapes demand through the proliferation of new products and materials—e.g., antibiotics, plastics—and the discovery of new production processes. Indeed, the growth of industrial research and development has served to accelerate the pace of innovation, hence to increase industry's role as a source of change.

The fact that industrial production both shapes demand and responds to it means that the rate of growth will vary widely from industry to industry in the 1960's. The textile industry, for example, will continue to shrink relative to industry as a whole, as it has been doing for sixty years. Total textile production will go up only one-third, with synthetics like nylon and Dacron gaining at the expense of cotton, silk, wool, and rayon. Steel production probably will expand 40 per cent, to 175 million ingot tons a year; output of stainless steel will rise half again as fast. Machinery production should double, with output of transistors going up tenfold, that of computers more than tripling, but production of farm machinery barely rising. And while output of some individual chemical lines—e.g., viscose rayon, ammonium sulfate, and soap—may actually decline, the chemical industry as a whole

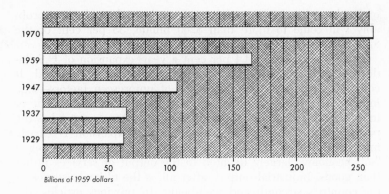

Billions of 1959 dollars

FIGURE 4. The Expanding Volume of Industrial Production. Despite gloomy predictions that United States' economic growth is
lagging, the output of its mines and factories continues to sweep
ahead. As the bars above indicate, industrial production in 1947
was 70 percent above 1929, and in 1959 output was 55 percent
above 1947. In the next decade, there will probably be another
60 percent expansion, to better than $260 billion.

probably will expand its output more than two and one-quarter
times, with even faster gains for polyethylene, polypropylene,
steroids, and other "wonder drugs" and plastics.

We Were Where Russia Is

These dynamic changes in the structure of industrial production and in its relation to the whole economy will continue a
process that has been going on for many years. At the turn of the
century the U.S. was still shifting from agriculture to industry,
and in the cities themselves factories were taking over functions
that had always been performed in the home—e.g., the baking of
bread, the making of clothing. Hence, during the first three
decades of the century, industrial production grew much more
rapidly than the economy as a whole. (See Fig. 5.) Thereafter,
with the shift from farm to factory slowing down, the lines of the
two growth rates tended to draw together. Since 1947, industrial
production has grown by 3.8 per cent per year or some 10 per
cent faster than G.N.P. In the Sixties, owing to increasing productivity and the expansion of the labor force, both will accelerate.

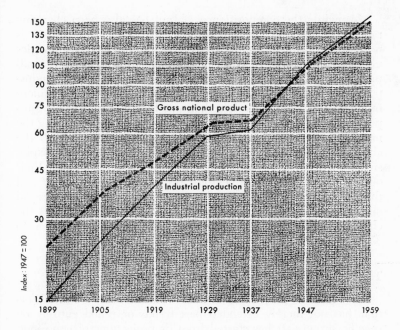

FIGURE 5. Comparative Growth Rates for Six Decades. As an "underdeveloped country," the United States enjoyed a faster rate of industrial growth than it does today. And even between 1899 and 1929, industrial production (solid line) expanded by 4.7 percent per year as opposed to 3.8 percent following World War II. But the economy as a whole (broken line) has been growing faster in the postwar period than it did earlier in the century, thanks to an acceleration of productivity gains. In the 1960s, on *Fortune*'s projections, G.N.P. will grow by 4.2 percent a year and industrial production by 4.4 percent.

Meanwhile the composition of output has also been changing radically. The first big shift—similar to that which Russia is now experiencing—was the rise of the durable-goods industries vis-à-vis soft goods. In 1899, for example, the textile and food-processing industries accounted for nearly 40 per cent of industrial output, while the metal and metal-fabricating and machinery industries accounted for less than one-fourth. By 1929 the proportions had been almost exactly reversed, a big reason being the meteoric rate at which the auto industry grew. Since 1929 the chemical and machinery industries have displayed more explosive growth trends. These two industries have expanded their output fortyfold and sixteenfold, respectively, since 1899, and they now account for more than one-fourth of total industrial output, compared to under 12 per cent in 1899. By 1970 the chemical and machinery industries' share will have risen to 35 per cent.

The Investment Push

In making its projections of industrial markets, however, *Fortune* has not merely extended past trends or relied entirely on specific surveys. It has started from its projections of consumer, investment, and government spending for the 1960's and calculated the probable impact of this spending on each major industry. *Fortune* has analyzed industrial markets, therefore, from the two viewpoints of final demand and individual industry output. In terms of demand, this year's industrial output of $164 billion will be divided as follows: consumer goods account for about $85 billion, or slightly more than half; $50 billion of final output goes into the investment stream, in the form of machinery and other capital goods and the materials used in building factories, stores, houses, schools, and roads; government takes $23 billion, mostly for planes, missiles, tanks, and other defense goods; and $7 billion goes into inventory accumulation and export trade.

In the 1960's production of consumer goods will rise a handsome 60 per cent, to $136 billion, which is faster than the 50 per cent rise in 1947–59. But investment will provide the largest stimulus, for the accelerated rise *Fortune* has projected in G.N.P. and in industrial output will require an even faster expansion of productive capacity. Thus, production for investment purposes—

capital goods and materials for private and public construction —will expand by 75 per cent (vs. a 25 per cent rise in the last decade) to $88 billion. Defense and other government purchases, on the other hand, will provide a much smaller boost than in the past decade, rising less than 50 per cent compared to a quadrupling between 1947 and 1959. Defense spending will not rise as much as it had to from the demobilization levels of 1947, and the new military technology requires relatively fewer planes and missiles and relatively more investment in research and development, only part of which goes for hardware. There will be some slight stimulus to production, too, from inventory accumulation —a concomitant of expanding sales—and from export trade.

Progress as a Product

This changing pattern of final demand will, of course, affect individual manufacturing and mining industries in radically different ways. The most immediate beneficiary of the investment boom of the 1960's will be the machinery industries, which produce the principal tools of production for all industries, not just for manufacturing. Mechanization, after all, is the principal (or at least the most direct) source of productivity gains. And the growing complexity of consumer products requires more and more fabrication relative to materials—though it requires far more sophisticated materials as well, e.g., chemicals and plastics. In the last twenty or thirty years, moreover, business firms have tended to use more and more machinery per square foot of plant space. In the Sixties, machinery output will be further stimulated by both expansion of capacity and the unending search for new ways to cut costs. Consumers as well as producers will demand new tools; there is no end in sight for the attempt to mechanize personal services that are irksome or expensive, and to use mechanical devices (such as home air conditioners) to provide more comfortable living conditions.

All this seems fairly obvious. And yet it may come as something of a surprise to businessmen, who generally regard machinery as primarily a feast-or-famine business, to learn that after chemicals and transportation equipment, machinery is the fastest-growing industrial sector. Machinery sales are volatile, rising more in booms and falling further in depressions than those of other industries. Over the long term, however, the trend of machinery production is sharply and inexorably up, and the increases have been greater than for industry as a whole. In 1929 machinery was only the fourth-largest U.S. industry. Eighteen years later, in 1947, it had become the largest industrial sector, accounting for 15 per cent of all output. The share rose as high as 16.7 per cent in 1957, at the top of the capital-goods boom, to $26 billion. Roughly 70 per cent of machinery output represents business machinery in the broad sense; 15 per cent is military production, and about the same proportion consumer appliances and TV. Output will roughly double over the next decade to $52 billion, and so by 1970 machinery will be accounting for almost one-fifth of all industrial output.

It is the skyrocketing sales of electrical and electronic equipment, of course, that make machinery a growth industry. Output has more than doubled since 1947, and former General Electric Board Chairman Ralph Cordiner predicted once that output would swell to $90 billion a year by 1976, compared to about $20 billion now. A big factor both past and present is the heavy purchase of electric generating, transmission, and distributing equipment and other types of electrical apparatus by the utilities, whose own output has been expanding by about 9 per cent a year compounded—i.e., an increase of 190 per cent since 1947.

The prospects for electronics are still brighter. Production reached about $9 billion, or one-third of total machinery output, in 1959. It has increased two and a half times since 1950, thanks to a sixfold increase in equipment for the armed forces and a tripling of industrial and commercial equipment, e.g., computers, instruments, controls, etc. These tremendous growth rates are bound to slow down somewhat, of course, but even so, production will expand two and one-half times by 1970. The sharpest rise will be in computers and other business equipment (presently 17 per cent of total electronics output), which will triple. Output of defense electronics—54 per cent of the total now—will go up less rapidly than in the past decade, but still will nearly triple. Production of consumer goods—TV and radio sets and tubes and other spare parts—should rise by 60 per cent (vs. only 15 per cent in the Fifties) as the result of replacement needs and some improvement in color-television sales.

Production of non-electrical machinery has expanded only 40 per cent in the postwar years but is likely to speed up somewhat in the Sixties. Farm machinery, to be sure, has been barely holding its own and is not likely to enjoy any vigorous growth in the near future. There have been sharp gains, however, in cost-cutting machinery—fork and lift trucks, conveyers, and other types of materials-handling equipment made by firms like Clark Equipment, Yale & Towne, etc. Output of metal-fabricating machinery like lathes and drills has also risen handsomely, if sporadically.

Cars, Trucks, and Planes

No industry has ever grown so spectacularly or had so large an impact on the whole economy as "transportation equipment," the heading under which the government statisticians lump the production of cars and trucks, planes and missiles, diesel engines, freight cars, and ships. The most fabulous gain occurred early in the century, of course, when the auto industry grew overnight from a few small shops to the largest mass-production industry in the world. In 1900, for example, only about 4,000 cars were produced in the U.S. By 1914, production passed the 500,000 mark, and only nine years later output of cars and trucks exceeded four million. As a result of this rise, the transportation-equipment group increased its share of output from 2.3 per cent in 1899 to 8.3 per cent in 1929, and in the postwar it has jumped again to 11.6 per cent.

This latter rise has been largely due to the spectacular sixfold expansion of aircraft production under the impetus of rearmament; aircraft now accounts for roughly 40 per cent of total transportation equipment, compared to just 16 per cent in 1947 and less than 2 per cent back in 1929. (See Fig. 6.) But production of cars and trucks—half of all transportation equipment—also expanded handsomely in the postwar years, i.e., by 69 per cent, or considerably faster than industry as a whole. One reason, of course, was that auto production in 1947 was abnormally low, owing to shortages of steel and other materials. Another reason was the trend toward "more car per car," which expanded the value of production faster than the number of cars and trucks themselves.

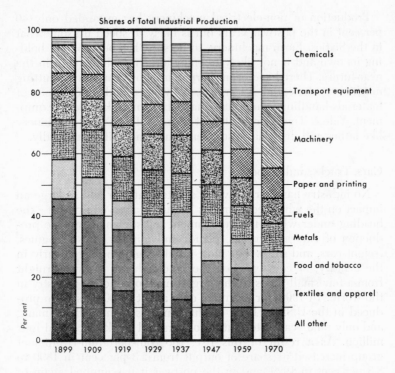

FIGURE 6. The Dynamics of Industrial Production. As industrial production has grown, its composition has changed quite radically. The chart above breaks total industrial output into nine major industrial groups and shows how each group's percentage share of total output has been changing.

The composition of total output has been changing more rapidly in recent years than at the beginning of the century. The chemical industry's share of total output has quadrupled since 1899, from 2.5 to 10.8 percent, but the fastest growth has been since 1929. Since the total output is ten times the 1899 level, that means a fortyfold increase for chemical production. And the share will rise to 15 percent by 1970. The transportation-equipment group has grown even faster, from 2.3 percent to 11.6 percent of total industrial output.

The 1960's will continue to be profitable for Detroit. Cars and trucks will expand in line with total industrial production, i.e., by 60 per cent, with trucks going up less, cars more. The value of auto production will rise nearly two-thirds, compared to a 50 per cent rise in unit sales, for the rise of the "compact car" will only slow, not halt, the "more car per car" phenomenon.

For the aircraft industry, on the other hand, the outlook is somewhat gloomy. To be sure, jet passenger planes have a rosy future, though output may taper off for a while after current orders are filled, and a large new market may open if the industry can develop an economical jet cargo plane. But sales to airlines and other private buyers account for only a small fraction of the aircraft industry's output, and aircraft will be very much less important in defense procurement in the Sixties than in the Fifties. Firms like General Dynamics, Lockheed, Boeing, and Martin, of course, assemble missiles as well as aircraft. Even so, the industry's total output will rise only very moderately. For most of the rise in procurement spending will go for electronic systems to control the missiles or warn of enemy missiles; for construction of underground bases; and for expanded research and development.

New Hope for the Rails

The rest of the transportation-equipment industry, however, should have an easier time in the Sixties than in the Fifties. The private merchant marine, for example, which consists largely of ships built during World War II, is becoming obsolete and will have to be replaced over the next decade or so. And the government is committed to subsidizing much of this replacement in U.S. shipyards. The potentials are even larger for railroad equipment. If U.S. railroads had the earnings, they could profitably invest $2.5 billion to $3 billion a year on new freight cars, automatic signaling equipment, electronic traffic control, freight-yard switching equipment, etc., as against $750 million of actual expenditures in 1958 and $1 billion this year. It's doubtful whether profits will rise that much in the near future, of course, but even so, the prospects for a revitalization of the railroads are brighter now than in several decades. The reason is not the imminence of legislative reform but the rapid growth of "containerization."

This is a system in which freight is carried in standard-size containers, e.g., truck-trailer bodies without wheels, and moved by rail, water, or highway—whichever is the most economical means for each part of the route. The economic logic of containerization seems irresistible; by the end of the 1960's, therefore, it's likely that containerization will have forced a reorganization of the entire freight-transportation industry—not just of the rails.

Steel's Mature Growth

The primary metal and metal-fabricating industries will enjoy a favorable climate in the 1960's, thanks to an investment boom and rising consumer purchases of cars and other durables. To be sure, metals will go up less than industrial production as a whole —as they have since 1929. (See Fig. 6.) Even so, production of primary metals and metal products probably will expand more in the next ten years than in the past twelve, i.e., by nearly two-fifths compared to less than one-third in the postwar.

For a "mature" industry, the metals group is subject to a surprising number of crosscurrents. Of the $19 billion of metal production this year, about half consists of so-called "fabricated-metal products": i.e., structural materials, heating and plumbing equipment, metal stamping and coating, tin cans, cutlery, and hardware. There has been a tendency in recent years for auto and appliance manufacturers to make their own stampings. This doesn't restrict total output, but it does shift the production from "fabricated-metal products" to "motor vehicles" or "electrical machinery." Competition from polyethylene is cutting into sales of metal containers, and foreign manufacturers have taken a substantial share of the hardware and cutlery markets. On the other hand, the growth of "curtain-wall" construction of offices and factories is enlarging the market for porcelain enamel and other structural materials. As a result of all these cross-currents, fabricated-metal products have been keeping pace with primary-metals output all through the postwar; the same probably will be true in the 1960's.

The prospects for steel continue strong, despite the active competition from aluminum and plastics. Steel producers are predicting only moderate growth: Armco, for instance, thinks ingot production will rise from a rate of 125 million tons in the first half of 1959 to 144 million tons in 1970. *Fortune* believes expansion will be much more rapid, owing to the growth of the whole economy. On its estimates, ingot production by the end of the 1960's will be in the neighborhood of 175 million tons—a 40 per cent advance over pre-strike levels. The value of steel output should rise by about the same amount—i.e., from $7 billion to $9.8 billion.

There are a number of factors, to be sure, that may tend to push up the average value of a ton of steel, e.g., the shift from carbon to stainless steel and from heavy to light structural shapes, and the demand of auto manufacturers and others for steels of ever greater strength and lighter weight. But these tendencies are being offset by metallurgical innovations that vastly improve carbon steel itself, e.g., heat-treated carbon steels that perform as well as steel alloys. The result is a standoff so far in the ratio between dollar and ingot output.

Aluminum's Golden Future

Output of nonferrous metals—$3 billion this year—should rise by about a third in the decade of the Sixties. Production of copper, lead, and zinc has been relatively stagnant and copper and lead, in particular, have shown little ability to find new markets or to recapture old ones. In the next decade, however, zinc may break out of this pattern because of the rapidly growing demand by business for corrosion-resistant materials. The 1960 cars, for example, use much more zinc than last year's models. Armco and other steel companies are making an improved zinc-dipped galvanized steel sheet that competes with stainless steel in many uses. But the dynamic factor in the nonferrous group is, of course, aluminum, which provides a classic example of how constant attention to market development, combined with product improvement, can produce an exponential sales curve.

Aluminum, indeed, exemplifies what the late, great Professor Joseph Schumpeter called "imitation," as distinguished from "innovation." Though improvements are always being made, the basic, technological innovations in primary aluminum were completed fifty years ago. Yet aluminum remains one of the real growth industries. To be sure, output did level off in the past several years, because of cutbacks in aircraft production and in the government's stockpiling. As a result, the industry is plagued

with considerable excess capacity—perhaps 20 per cent above
this year's output of 2,300,000 tons, counting plants now under
construction and several whose construction was suspended
shortly before completion. But the aluminum companies probably will have to start a new round of expansion in just a few
years, for they expect to be turning out at least four million tons
a year by 1965.

It's easy to see where this growth will come from. The home-
building industry, for example, now consumes only forty pounds
of aluminum per house, on average. But National Homes, largest
U.S. prefabricator, is using 1,200 pounds per house in its new
aluminum prefabs, indicating a large potential ahead. The auto
industry uses an average of only sixty pounds of aluminum per
new car (up from six pounds just eleven years ago). But Chevrolet is using about ninety pounds per car just for the aluminum
engine in its new Corvair, and if the aluminum engine became
general, the industry would triple its purchases of aluminum overnight. And after fourteen years of sales effort, Reynolds has just
cracked the railroad-equipment market with an order from the
Southern Railway for 1,200 aluminum hopper and gondola freight
cars.

The Fuels: Sickness to Health

The prospects for the fuels—coal, oil, and natural gas—are also
bright. In the postwar years, the statistics of industrial production
showed a very small expansion of the fuels. The reason is that gas
production, which was rising rapidly at the expense of coal and
oil, is largely reflected in the output of utilities rather than in
mining and manufacturing. Now this displacement is slowing
down, and as a result the industrial contribution of the fuel group
will tend to rise. In addition there will be increasing demand for
all fuels, and so production—now at about $15 billion per year—
may go up as much as 50 per cent.

Coal, for example, will again become a growing rather than a
declining industry. There will be no further loss of markets from
dieselization of the railroads or conversion of homes to oil and
gas burners, simply because these shifts are now virtually complete. More to the point, sales to the electric-utility industry will
be rising handsomely. Output of electric power, as mentioned be-

fore, will rise faster than industrial production, and coal's competitive position vis-à-vis gas has improved. Development of more powerful transmission lines, for example, makes it economical to "ship coal by wire," i.e., to locate generating stations near a coal mine and transmit electricity over a long distance rather than put the generators near the consumers they serve, which requires hauling coal a long way. Indeed, American Electric Power has built a generating plant that receives the coal by conveyer belt directly from a coal mine four and a half miles away. The utilities, therefore, are rapidly becoming the principal market for coal. The one cloud on coal's horizon—and a large one—is the possibility that the steel industry may turn to direct reduction of iron ore in the 1960's. This would mean some displacement of coal by natural gas in steelmaking—and steel takes 18 per cent of coal production. But this loss could be offset by several processes now being developed to manufacture gaseous liquid fuels from coal.

Some Slowdown for Oil

U.S. consumption of oil, meanwhile, which has been growing by 6 per cent a year, should rise by at least 3.5 to 5 per cent a year in the 1960's, according to such oil experts as John Winger, vice president in charge of the Chase Manhattan Bank's Petroleum Economics Department. Whatever effect the new economy cars have on gasoline consumption will be offset by Americans' tendency to drive their cars a little further each year. Natural gas will continue to make some inroads in the home-heating, industrial, and utilities market, but the almost vertical sales curves of the past decade simply cannot continue. Nor will imports keep expanding their share of the U.S. market; they may even rise less than total consumption, for whatever the wisdom of the present national oil policy, the chances are that it will not be changed radically in the near future. Hence, domestic production should expand in line with final consumption.

Chemicals' Busy World

No major industry, of course, save electronics, has a future or a past as resplendent as the $18-billion "chemical and allied products" group. Indeed it has its own special tone and atmosphere, as may be judged by the fact that a senior executive of Union Carbide, second-largest U.S. chemical firm, carries on his person a little booklet titled "Compound Interest Tables for Determining Growth." The booklet shows the effects that various annual growth rates would have if compounded over time—and the rates go as high as 50 per cent a year. In a list of about 100 "growth products" (products growing by 7½ per cent a year or faster)published a few months ago by the Department of Commerce, for example, forty were chemicals of one sort or another.

The chemical industry seems to defy the traditional "law" of production, which holds that as an industry matures, its growth rate must slow down and ultimately decline. Chemical production has been growing faster than total industrial output for as long as detailed figures are available—i.e., since 1899, when chemicals accounted for only 2.5 per cent of industrial output. And the growth has been accelerating, not slowing down. Thus chemicals accounted for only 4 per cent of total industrial output in 1929. By 1947, however, the share had climbed to almost 7 per cent, and it jumped to nearly 11 per cent in 1959, as chemical production expanded at a compound rate of nearly 8 per cent a year. Growth should continue at this rate even if chemicals should slow down a little relative to the economy as a whole, for the latter will be growing faster. By 1970, therefore, chemical output probably will come to nearly $40 billion—15 per cent of the value of all industrial production.

When chemical output is broken down by product, of course, the "laws" of production do seem to apply; the industry as a whole keeps growing—in large part because it keeps proliferating new products like polyethylene, penicillin, nylon, etc., which grow at rates of 15 per cent a year and up. Chemical firms spend more of their own funds on research and development than any other industry. But research also keeps opening up new uses for old chemicals like ammonia, formaldehyde, sulfuric acid, etc.—more often than not as a "building block" for some new and more glamorous chemical product. This tendency for almost any chemical to serve as a raw material for some uses and an end product for others is what makes the industry so bewildering to the outsider.

Plastics represent the most dramatic growth market within chemicals as a whole. Only ten years ago, in 1950, production of polyethylene came to barely 30 million pounds. This year output will top one billion pounds—the first plastic to achieve this long-time industry goal. And the growth is by no means nearing a plateau: new applications are being added all the time in packaging, wire and cable coverings, coatings for paper and other materials, etc. The future seems equally bright for a number of other plastics just being brought to market. Production of polypropylene, for example, is still on a pilot-plant basis, but Paul Mayfield, vice president of Hercules Powder, its leading developer, confidently expects output to pass the billion-pound-a-year mark by 1965. Mayfield may be a trifle over-optimistic—but Dow, Eastman Kodak, Humble Oil, and du Pont are all building plants. And there are even more dramatic possibilities for so-called "high performance" plastics, according to such experts as Francis Williams, president of the Chemical Fund. These are plastics that offer unique operating characteristics which outweigh their high cost. Du Pont's Teflon, for example, has the lowest coefficient of friction of any known material, which means it can be used to make a greaseless bearing. Teflon bearings are already being used in the British Comet and du Pont is developing Teflon bearings for a greaseless automobile. Hercules' Penton and G.E.'s Lexan have many possible uses as a substitute for metal, because of the ease with which they can be fabricated.

And an enumeration of new plastics hardly exhausts the list of growth products in the chemical group. Hardly a month goes by without announcement of a new oxygen plant at Air Products, Union Carbide's Linde Division, or some other oxygen producer, as a result of the steel industry's mushrooming use of oxygen in basic-steel production. And hardly a week goes by without the discovery of some new wonder drug—anti-cholesterol drugs, psychic energizers, improved steroid compounds, synthetic penicillin, to mention just a few. Hence output of the major drug firms is bound to keep shooting ahead. Indeed, pharmaceuticals comprise 15 per cent of chemical output—twice as much as plastics—and they are growing almost as fast.

The older branches of the industry are also doing very well. The fact that farmers lose an estimated $5 billion a year from crop and cattle pests and diseases, for example, offers a huge and tempting market for producers of insecticides and other agricultural chemicals and drugs. Even so familiar a chemical as chlorine has an expanding sales curve, thanks to its growing use, among others, as a bleaching agent to improve the quality of paper. Taking everything together, therefore, *Fortune*'s projection of a 125 per cent expansion in chemical output during the 1960's seems tolerably conservative.

The Other 40 Per Cent

The five broad industry groups analyzed so far—machinery, transportation equipment, metals, oil and coal, and chemicals— are contributing roughly $100 billion to national output this year. That leaves about $65 billion, or 40 per cent of total industrial output, to be accounted for. About $17.5 billion consists of the conglomerate of stone, clay, glass, and wood products (including furniture) lumped together as "all other" in Fig. 6. Their output is fairly closely correlated with construction activity, and so should rise about 50 per cent over the decade.

Three rather clearly defined market groups account for the rest of industrial output. Textiles and apparel—$20 billion this year—are tied more closely to population than to income growth. Rising discretionary income will of course provide some stimulus —especially to apparel, which accounts for about half of all textile usage—and output will rise faster in the Sixties than in the Fifties. Even so, the group will not keep pace with industry generally, and the share of output will fall, from 12.2 per cent now to perhaps 10.5 per cent in 1970.

The $15-billion food-processing industry is also affected more by population than income. But the population factor will be more favorable toward growth of food production in the Sixties than in the postwar. Teenagers, for example, consume 27 per cent more calories than the average adult, and the teenage population will be growing more than twice as fast as population as a whole. The amount of processing, moreover, will increase relative to food consumption in the 1960's as a result of rising demands for baby foods, diet foods, frozen foods, etc. Hence food processing should go up by nearly 40 per cent, compared to only 24 per cent since 1947, which would, however, lower its share.

Paper and printing—$15 billion this year—have been growing as fast as industry as a whole during the postwar and have held to a remarkably stable 9 per cent of total output. The share probably will hold steady in the 1960's, too, which means a 60 per

cent expansion. Publishing and printing, which is closely correlated with personal consumption expenditures, will rise less
than that; paper production more. Several factors account for
paper's rapid expansion, among them the continued emphasis on
packaging of consumer goods; changes in product mix, which raise
the value of output more than actual tonnage; and the growth of
domestic pulp and newsprint production vis-à-vis imports. New
uses are also being developed, e.g., as a raw material for disposable non-woven fabrics. Scott Paper is already producing disposable sheets and towels for the Army on an experimental basis;
it may be cheaper to throw away the linens than to launder them.
And Kimberly-Clark recently formed a joint subsidiary with
J. P. Stevens to exploit new markets in this area.

The Overrated Import Threat

Adding up the separate markets, therefore, industrial production is likely to rise from nearly $165 billion this year to better
than $260 billion in 1970, or by about 60 per cent. These projec-
tions, it should be noted, take into account the probability of increasing competition from abroad, which has been a growing
source of concern to many businessmen. In the past, U.S. industrial expansion was closely associated with rising exports of manufactured goods. It came as a shock, therefore, when exports
dropped sharply last year and then failed to rise along with
domestic output in the first half of this year. Since imports continued to rise, our usual large export surplus, which is necessary
to cover private foreign investment and foreign aid, evaporated,
and this year the U.S. may have a $3-billion to $4-billion gap in
its total balance of payments. Exports are now picking up and
will keep rising faster than imports, hence the gap should close
in 1960. Nevertheless, a persistent over-all deficit on foreign accounts is serious, involving the most far-reaching questions of
domestic and international monetary policy.

It is well, however, to emphasize that this problem is monetary
and to keep foreign trade in perspective so far as U.S. industrial
output is concerned. And here the fears of some manufacturers
seem to be exaggerated. To be sure, imports of manufactured
goods have nearly tripled over the course of the postwar. Even
so, such imports come to only $8 billion in an industrial market of

$165 billion. Nor can imports keep rising indefinitely, without a comparable rise in the exports needed to pay for them. To exaggerate just a bit in order to clarify the principle that's involved, it would be manifestly impossible for the U.S. to import everything it needs; it simply couldn't pay the bill. This need to pay for the goods one buys abroad places a stringent limit on the possible expansion of net imports. The fact is that foreign competition cannot seriously impair the growth of total output. This may be small comfort to individual textile and pottery manufacturers who are being affected by low-priced imports. But given reasonable monetary stability, foreign competition stimulates the transfer of capital and labor from low to high-productivity industries.

The New World of Industry

Such competition, however, will be only one and indeed a minor cause of industrial change; the great changes in the pattern of industrial production will continue to come from within. The burgeoning research outlays of industry and government— larger in the next decade than in the sixteen decades of U.S. history to date—should lead to continuing breakthroughs in electronics, metallurgy, chemistry, and power generation. Markets that do not yet exist may spring up overnight, and old and powerful markets may atrophy in the wake of scientific and technological innovations.

It is this prospect of accelerated change, no less than the prospect of a 60 per cent expansion of total industrial production, that is heartening in terms of the future. So much of late has been made of Soviet growth statistics that the dynamics of America's free economy have been all but overlooked. No projection, of course, can be more than a statement of probabilities; the future has to be earned. But the U.S. economy has certainly not lost its capacity to grow, and perhaps more important, it has not lost the adaptability and capacity for innovation that flow from competition and private initiative. Indeed, acceleration in the rate of change will be the hallmark of the industrial market of the 1960's.

part II

PRODUCTS

In the decade of the 1960s $120 billion will probably be spent for research and development. This sum exceeds substantially the total investment in science and technology in the 185 years from 1776 through 1960. While there is no guarantee what this huge investment will produce, it is likely to bring a torrential flood of new products for consumer and industrial use. Ultrasonic clothes washers, solid-state refrigerators, fuel cells, communications satellites, and a host of other exciting developments will help shape future living patterns.

The 1960s:
A Forecast of the Technology*

In the decade of the Sixties man will finally soar beyond the thin film of the earth's atmosphere in which he and all his ancestors have been imprisoned for a billion years or more. The next target will be the moon. Whether anyone lands there before December 31, 1969, is relatively unimportant. Men will build the great moon rocket as soon as their technology permits and take off as soon as their curiosity drives them to it. No one can believe that the machinery or the desire will long be lacking.

by Francis Bello

Meanwhile, throughout the Sixties, space technology will keep feeding back a wealth of engineering ideas that can be put to use in hundreds of unforeseen ways throughout industry. Like the atomic-energy quest, the space venture will confront scien-

* Vol. 59, January 1959, pp. 74–78, 190–200.

tists and engineers with a host of new and baffling problems. The effort to solve them will broaden and deepen man's understanding of nature and extend his control over the materials and forces of the physical world.

It is this growing mastery of energy and matter that gives the American market such a prodigious variety of products and so much thrust. And it is for this reason that this article provides an appraisal of the scientific and technological advances that the next decade could bring. Some of the matters to be discussed may seem remote from the market place, but the gap between a laboratory achievement and commercial application is getting shorter and shorter.

The market's future vitality is guaranteed by the huge sums—federal and private—being invested in research and development. In 1950 the nation's R. and D. (Research and Development) expenditure was less than $3 billion. By 1958 R. and D. spending had zoomed to $10 billion, with half the funds provided by the government. For the entire Fifties, the R. and D. expenditure will add up to $60 billion. In the Sixties the U.S. will easily spend twice that sum. This is exponential growth in precisely that area of human activity that exerts the greatest impact on the economy and on society as a whole.

The nation's R. and D. outlay has grown so huge, indeed, that one leading economist, Fritz Machlup, has recently suggested that part of the money might more profitably be spent elsewhere —on education, for example. There is no doubt, in any case, that the division of the total expenditure between basic research and development has become inexcusably lopsided. Out of 1958's $10 billion, no more than $750 million went for basic research in all fields—and even this sum was heavily skewed in the direction of nuclear and subnuclear physics. Meteorology, geophysics, oceanography, and the various life sciences (e.g., biochemistry, genetics, psychology) have all been seriously underfinanced. Leading American scientists are determined to see that U.S. science develops in a much more balanced fashion over the next decade than it has in the past. This determination was expressed in a report conveyed to the White House by the President's Special Assistant for Science and Technology, James R. Killian, Jr. The report offered thoughtful recommendations for strengthening U.S. science.

If fundamental research is indeed pursued more diligently in the years immediately ahead than in the past, the Sixties can scarcely fail to produce more scientific surprises than the Fifties. Both science and technology, however, present a curious mixture of the predictable and the unpredictable. The business of science is discovery, and discovery requires penetration of the unknown. But as Table 1 indicates, basic science also includes "discovery" of such things as the antiproton, the antineutron, and the neutrino, which had been predicted to exist. On the other hand, technology is not easily predictable just because it rests on the application of established science. As the chart also shows, the technology of the Fifties—both commercial and military—contained many surprises. Ten years ago few scientists expected a U.S. thermonuclear explosion as soon as November, 1952, and the U.S. was totally unprepared for a Soviet duplication of the feat less than a year later.

In nonmilitary technology, some developments moved faster, others slower than expected. Ten years ago it was clear that electronics was on the threshold of great advances. The transistor had just been announced in 1948, and the first electronic computer—the ENIAC—two years earlier. On balance, the transistor came along at just about the rate that cautious engineers would have predicted—meaning the transistor had its troubles—but the commercial and industrial demand for computers outstripped all sober estimates. In 1949 anyone could have predicted color TV in the Fifties, but many experts were betting on the wrong system and the impatience of the public for color was grossly overestimated. Ten years ago few U.S. airline executives foresaw that the jet age was so close at hand, and that jet transports making scheduled flights in 1958 would have greater range and payload than any prototype jet bomber flying in 1949. And in 1949 only science-fiction fans—and a few scientists—were prepared for artificial satellites in the Fifties. Russia's launching of Sputnik I on October 4, 1957, was the most stunning technological news of the decade.

On retail shelves there was nothing so unexpected as Sputnik, unless it was the tranquilizers, which suddenly appeared in drugstores in the mid-Fifties. The tranquilizers were first reported in medical journals in 1954 and within three years had been used by at least twenty million "normal" Americans—with precisely what benefit no one will ever know. Some anxieties, no doubt, were al-

	1950–52	1953–54
Basic Science	*Discovery of colliding galaxies ('51) Discovery of radio emission from cold hydrogen in space ('51) *Total synthesis of cortisone ('51)* *New estimates doubling size and age of universe ('52) *Discovery of brain's arousal mechanism ('52)	*Total synthesis of oxytocin, pituitary-gland hormone ('53)* *Proposed structure of DNA, key genetic substance (U.S.-U.K., '53)* *Detailed structure of insulin (U.K., '54)* *Discovery of reward centers in brain ('54)
Inventions and Experimental Achievements	Junction transistor ('51) *"Area rule" for design of supersonic aircraft ('52) *Bubble chamber for tracking elementary particles ('52) Heart-lung machine used on a human ('52)	Bevatron in operation ('54) Solar battery ('54) *Maser, ultrasensitive electronic amplifier ('54)
"Practical" and Commercial Achievements	Orlon ('50) Extensive cloud seeding ('50) *Antibiotics used to stimulate animal growth ('50) Coast-to-coast TV ('51) Large electronic computer delivered to Bureau of Census ('51) Start of "automation" in auto industry ('51) Zone-refining of metals ('52)	Dacron ('53) Wide-screen movies ('53) Chemical "milling" of metals ('53) Color TV ('53) *Tranquilizers ('54) First large computer delivered to industry ('54) Silicon transistor ('54)
Nuclear Technology	First electric power from U.S. reactor ('51)	First demonstration of fuel "breeding" ('53) Boiling-water reactor ('53)
Military and Space Technology	*First U.S. thermonuclear explosion ('52)*	*First U.S.S.R. thermonuclear explosion ('53)* Nike missile ('53) First supersonic flight by a military aircraft ('53)

TABLE 1. Scientific and Technical Triumphs of the 1950s . . . and a Prospectus for the 1960s. Two fabulous decades of science and technology, the one closing and the one rapidly approaching, are charted here in retrospect and prospect. In the two pages above, the chart records, primarily, the more memorable American achieve-

1955–56	1957–58
*Further upward revisions in size and age of universe ('55; revisions continuing) Creation of antiproton ('55) Creation of antineutron ('56) Confirmation of neutrino's existence ('56) *Total synthesis of reserpine, hypotensive and tranquilizer ('56)*	*Fall of parity principle ('57) *Discovery of cold fusion ('57) Creation of element 102, nobelium ('57) *Discovery of intense radiation zone in nearby space ('58)
VTOL (vertical take-off and landing) jet aircraft ('55) First "proof" of rainmaking ('55) *Cryotron, low-temperature electronic switch ('56) *Experimental use of oral contraceptives ('56)*	Thermionic (heat to electricity) converter ('57) VTOL jet "tail-sitter" ('57) Sun photographs from unmanned balloon ('57) *Test-tube creation of DNA-like molecules ('58)* *VTOL flying "jeep" ('58)*
Mass use of Salk polio vaccine ('55) All-transistor radios ('55) First turboprops in U.S. ('55) Polyurethane foams ('55) Weather forecasting by computer ('55) Transatlantic telephone cable ('56) *Television tape recording ('56)*	*Linear polyethylene ('57)* *Synthetic diamonds ('57)* Use of giberellin in agriculture ('58) Stereophonic records ('58) Super insulators for storing liquefied gases ('58) *Transatlantic jet service ('58)*
First nuclear power to a U.S. utility ('55) *Disclosure of U.S.S.R. research to control thermonuclear reactions ('56)*	Portable package power plant ('57) First U.S. underground nuclear explosion ('57) Large Shippingport power reactor in operation ('57)
Nuclear-powered submarine ('55)	Completion of DEW Line ('57) First U.K. thermonuclear explosion ('57) *First Russian ICBM; Sputniks I and II ('57)* *First U.S. satellites and ICBM ('58)*

ments of the 1950s, but also includes several foreign accomplishments of outstanding significance. In all, 14 of the achievements listed (asterisked) were totally unpredictable; 19 (italicized) were achieved sooner than most experts would have expected.

	Early 1960s (including 1959)	Mid-1960s
Basic Science	Total synthesis of chlorophyll	Radiotelescopes probe "edge" of observable universe
Inventions and Experimental Achievements	Completion of 25-bev accelerators at Brookhaven and Geneva Completion of super computers Animal kept alive with internal artificial heart Machine translation of languages Predetermination of sex in humans	Borehole to "Moho," boundary between earth's crust and interior
"Practical" and Commercial Achievements	Electronic telephone exchange Portable battery-operated television sets Ultrasonic dishwasher Applications of fuel cell Appliances using thermoelectricity	New family of ultrahigh-capacity computers Significant advances in weather forecasting Panel lighting for homes Gas-turbine trucks and buses Introduction of irradiated foods VTOL or STOL aircraft for short-haul routes
Nuclear Technology	Nuclear-power merchant vessel, aircraft carrier, and aircraft	Experimental use of nuclear explosives for nonmilitary purposes Demonstration of 100-million-degree fusion temperatures
Military and Space Technology	Flight of X-15 (3,600 mph) Unmanned probes to moon, Mars, and Venus Satellites as navigation and meteorological aids Operational ICBM's Million-pound-thrust rocket engine	Man in satellite and return VTOL military aircraft Anti-missile missile

TABLE 1 (*con't.*). **Scientific and Technical Triumphs of the 1950s ... and a Prospectus for the 1960s.** On these two pages the chart attempts a forecast for the 1960s, but as the 1950s have proved, the

Late 1960s	Long Shots for the Late 1960s
Total synthesis of insulin	Comprehensive theory of elementary particles Test-tube creation of a living cell Detailed understanding of the aging process
Controlled mutations in plants and animals	Computers with brainlike attributes Substantial control over tornadoes and hurricanes
Major advances in treating atherosclerosis, cancer, mental illness Major advances in structural materials: polymers, metals, ceramics Electronic safety devices for cars and highways Mural television	Cure for cancer 2,000-mph VTOL airliner Small VTOL flying car Accurate ninety-day weather forecasts Fresh water from sea water at acceptable cost
Direct conversion of nuclear energy to electric power (experimental)	Nuclear power competitive in most of U.S. Atomic explosives in practical use Fusion power technically feasible
Communications using satellites Man in flyable space ship	Man on the moon Rocket mail and freight service

hazards of prophecy are formidable. It is predictable, however, that a tremendous R. and D. effort will be aimed at reaching the goals listed at the far right as "Long Shots for the Late 1960s."

layed, but the greatest impact of the new drugs seems to have been in the mental hospitals, where the number of patients has now declined for the third consecutive year.

In consumer goods of the more tangible sort, the Fifties held few surprises. In 1949, Americans could already buy TV sets, air conditioners, dishwashers, clothes dryers, power lawn mowers, high-fidelity phonographs, LP records, tape recorders, Polaroid Land cameras, and automobiles with automatic transmissions. It is true, of course, that the Fifties added power steering (1952) and power brakes ('53) to the automobile, and stereophonic sound ('58) to phonograph records, but these were relatively modest accomplishments, from a technical point of view.

The Invisible Frontier

It would be wrong to conclude, however, that the R. and D. billions of the Fifties did little more than polish existing products and produce new military weapons. What has been happening is that industrial technology has been deepening its insights and changing its emphasis from the obvious and macroscopic to the subtle and submicroscopic. Manipulation of the invisible has always characterized research in chemicals, drugs, petroleum, and electronics, but even these industries have found exciting new frontiers at the level of precise molecular and interatomic design.

Advances at this deep level have already had a profound effect on the market and will have still more in the future. In 1949 there was only one wholly synthetic fiber of consequence, nylon. Today there are a variety of synthetics: the acrylics Orlon, Acrilan, Dynel, Verel, Creslan, Darvan, and Zefran, and the polyester Dacron, soon to be joined by Kodel and Teron. These fibers have transformed whole industries. In the Fifties, polyethylene (first produced in volume in World War II) became a household word. Latex-based paints, introduced in 1949, ran off with the do-it-yourself market; fiberglass revolutionized pleasure-boat building; and handsome, long-wearing vinyl plastics cut sharply into the market once dominated by linoleum and asphalt tiles.

The transistor provides a similar example of what to expect as technology deepens its insights. By itself, the transistor does nothing that could not be done before. But because of its tiny size, ruggedness, and low power consumption, its influence has now extended to every corner of electronics. All-transistor hearing aids were on the market by 1953 and all-transistor radios by 1955. In the Sixties there will be more and more transistors in the home, in the family car, and elsewhere, doing jobs for which vacuum tubes are hopelessly impractical.

The lesson in all this is immensely reassuring. Manufacturers of consumer products enjoyed a fabulous decade in the Fifties without a single innovation comparable to the automobile (which became commercially important about 1910), the radio (early 1920's), mechanical refrigerator (mid-1920's), automatic washing machine (late 1930's), or home air conditioning and TV (late 1940's). The Sixties may fail to bring forth any single new consumer product (none is in sight) of impact comparable to the automobile, radio, or TV, and still be a decade of huge economic growth.

Meanwhile, during the Sixties, Americans may show an increasing desire for technological advances other than the kind that can be bought at retail. Indeed, most Americans doubtless would prefer for 1969 a cure for cancer rather than a family flying car; clean air to breathe rather than a Picturephone, carrying images as well as speech; many might even prefer a "push button" in Washington to prevent tornadoes and control hurricanes, rather than a push button to perform every imaginable household chore. And, in fact, the first choice in each pair may represent the more readily attainable scientific or technological goal in the light of present knowledge.

The Ultrasonic Kitchen

The Sixties should make crystal clear to every industrial research laboratory—if any are still in doubt—that there is no way to isolate technology from basic science. The two form a continuous spectrum ranging from the most prosaic product engineering to the most esoteric basic research. In the pages that follow, we shall work our way backward from the consumer market to basic technology, thence to outer space and basic science, and conclude with the outlook in health and medicine.

In the Sixties the technological subtlety of synthetic polymers and transistors will begin to be felt in a wide variety of consumer products. There will be home appliances using ultrasonics, refrigerators with no moving parts, and lighting systems without heated filaments or glowing gases. Most of the big electrical and electronics firms are working intensively on one or more of these developments, and there should be important commercial results in the Sixties.

Ultrasonics—the use of sound vibrations above the audible range—is already at work in industry solving difficult cleaning problems. Westinghouse indicates that an ultrasonic dishwasher —employing an ultrasonic generator or vibrator immersed in a detergent bath—will appear in the Sixties, and presumably other firms are working toward the same goal. Ultrasonic clothes washers should follow soon after.

Hot and Cold Light

"Electronic" or "solid-state" refrigerating devices should reach the market within the next year or two. They will exploit the fact that an electric current will force heat to flow from one side of a metallic junction to the other, if the junction is formed of suitable materials of the semiconductor family. In this way heat can be driven out of a box that is to be cooled. Both R.C.A. and Westinghouse have built experimental electronic refrigerators with capacities of four to ten cubic feet. But the method's immediate usefulness should lie in smaller special-purpose cooling units—possibly portable and battery operated.

Last fall Westinghouse demonstrated a simple, plug-in wall panel that could heat or cool and also provide light, using electroluminescence. This lighting method employs special phosphorescent substances that glow when energized by electricity. The three-way panel may be many years off, but panel room lighting should be moving by the mid-Sixties. By the late Sixties, electroluminescence should lead to mural TV screens of almost any desired size for both black-and-white and color.

Electronic Highway Safety

Here are a few other commercial developments that look reasonably certain for the early and mid-Sixties:

• All-electronic cooking ranges. (In early models, the penetrating radar waves cooked the inside of the roast without browning the surface. Hotpoint says it has this problem licked.

- Fully portable TV sets operating from batteries that can be recharged from an electric outlet.

- Tiny high-fidelity speakers of exceptional range and brilliance.

- Electronic safety devices for automobiles. The devices may warn of cars approaching from behind or that a car ahead is being overtaken too fast. Automatic car guidance on an electronic highway is also being studied, but its appearance in the Sixties seems unlikely.

- Gas-turbine trucks. But unless Detroit is engineering a massive ruse, enthusiasm for a gas-turbine automobile has seriously waned. Reason: too costly.

Perhaps the mid-Sixties will also see the appearance of foods that have been either sterilized or pasteurized by gamma rays or electron irradiation. The Army Quartermaster Corps expects progress to be sufficiently rapid so that it can start use of irradiated meats by 1963. While the food industry seems generally cool to irradiation, a successful Army demonstration—with full FDA approval—might whet commercial appetites.

Plastics That Produce Water

During the Sixties much research will go into methods for obtaining fresh water from saline waters, either from sea water itself, or from brackish waters of lesser salinity. Last year Congress authorized the Department of the Interior to spend up to $10 million building five experimental desalting plants, two of which will have a capacity of a million gallons a day.

Last year Coalinga, California, ordered the first desalting plant to provide municipal water in the U.S. The 30,000-gallon-per-day plant, to be built by Ionics, Inc., Cambridge, Massachusetts, will use plastic membranes that let fresh water pass through but not salt. The plant input will be brackish water from wells. Coalinga now pays $7 a thousand gallons for fresh water carted in by truck. Ionics says the new plant will produce water for about 50 cents per thousand gallons. However, neither the Ionics process nor any other yet tested will desalt sea water for much under $2 per thousand gallons. Price of most municipal water in the U.S.: under 25 cents per thousand.

Electricity without Wheels

While municipal water companies are watching the progress of desalting, electric utilities will be following closely the progress being made in thermoelectricity. This process turns heat directly into electricity by exactly reversing the principle of the electronic refrigerator.

Westinghouse has developed special alloys and ceramic-like materials that convert heat into electricity with claimed efficiencies of 10 per cent and with 15 per cent in sight. While 10 per cent is only one-quarter the efficiency achieved in large steam-power plants, it compares favorably with that of small prime movers and auxiliary power plants. Westinghouse expects to show in the Sixties that thermoelectricity will be economic as a standby power source in large power plants. Almost certainly the new techniques will be used within the decade to obtain power directly from a nuclear reactor.

G.E. does not share Westinghouse's enthusiasm for thermoelectricity, but has conceived a rival principle embodied in a "thermionic converter." In this device, electrons "boiled out" of a heated metal surface provide an electric current.

Still a third method of generating electricity from a device containing no moving parts is under development in the "fuel cell." A clean fuel such as hydrogen or alcohol is passed over a catalytic surface where combustion occurs with a direct yield of electric current. Union Carbide has built cells of 1-kw output that have the remarkable efficiency of 75 per cent. Possible early application: supplying electric power at remote military bases.

The efficiency of the fuel cell is so high that it could serve as the equivalent of a very-high-capacity storage battery. The British have suggested that electric-generating stations might produce and store hydrogen (by decomposing water) during periods of low power demand. The peak power demands could be met by burning the hydrogen in fuel cells. Such possibilities will be carefully explored in the Sixties.

Meanwhile, U.S. utilities will be participating in the nation's costly atomic-power program. Proof that the atom can compete with fossil fuels in most of the U.S. is no better than a long shot for the late 1960's.

When Will the Atom Pay?

After years of optimistic speeches and press releases, the AEC disclosed in November that it had begun an "agonizing" reappraisal to learn why the nuclear-power program was lagging.

Modern steam plants, even those not especially favored by nearby coal supplies, can produce power for 6 to 7 mills per kwh. Estimated cost of power from the most efficient nuclear-power plants now building in the U.S. is 50 to 100 per cent higher, with large uncertainties as to actual fuel and maintenance costs. The principal uncertainties are two: how much power can actually be obtained from a given type of reactor, and how long will the fuel last? The Sixties should answer these questions for the several types of plants now building and under design.

"By any scheme now in sight," says W. E. Shoupp, technical director of the atomic-power department of Westinghouse, "6-mill nuclear power is just not in the cards. Eventually, conventional power and nuclear will cross in the region of 8 to 10 mills."[1]

The "agonizing" reappraisal of nuclear-power progress is being accompanied by a similar appraisal of the outlook for early harnessing of fusion or thermonuclear energy. The Second Conference on Peacetime Uses of Atomic Energy, held at Geneva, brought out a spectacular display of U.S. apparatus for fusion research. But the conference papers on fusion disclosed that Russian, British, and U.S. scientists are all up against thorny problems for which no answers are in sight. The basic difficulty is that the plasma—a hot rarefied "soup" of dissociated deuterium nuclei and electrons—resists heating to fusion temperatures by undergoing oscillations that radiate energy away from the plasma at a high rate. "We'll be lucky now," says one fusion expert, "if we can just get some 100-million-degree plasma to study, without worrying whether we can get any net energy out of it."

Edward Teller, credited with the stroke of invention that made

---

[1] The outlook in Britain is considerably different, according to Sir John Cockroft, of the U.K. Atomic Energy Authority. His forecast: "We expect nuclear power to cost about 10 per cent more than coal power in 1960, to reach parity about 1963, and to be 30 per cent cheaper than coal power by 1970." The predicted 1970 cost of U.K. atomic power: 5½ mills.

the U.S. H-bomb feasible, has recently said that the only way he sees to get useful power from the fusion reaction in the near future is to explode an H-bomb underground. The heat released into the earth could then be extracted in the form of steam and used to generate power. Teller also suggests using nuclear explosions to create new harbors, to release oil from shale and tar sands, and even to create vast aquifers to serve as underground reservoirs for river water that would otherwise flow to the sea. The AEC is exploring such possibilities in Project Plowshare.[2] Routine use of nuclear explosives can be considered no more than a very long shot for the late 1960's.

Needed: Better Metals

If any one factor were to be singled out as holding back progress in atomic power and other advanced technologies, it would be lack of suitable engineering materials—particularly, metals and alloys. The materials situation is regarded as so serious that a number of worried scientists are urging that the government establish a major new research institute wholly devoted to the problem. The proposal is being studied by the President's Science Advisory Committee. There are, however, serious objections to the institute concept, the chief being that faster progress could be made by supporting more materials research in universities, in existing institutes, and in government laboratories.

The problem in metallurgy is easy to state: there has as yet been no major breakthrough in metals comparable to the transistor in electronics, nylon in high polymers, or nuclear fission in energy creation. The quest for newer and better alloys goes on in empirical fashion, with relatively little scientific understanding

---

[2] Harry Wexler, director of meteorological research for the U.S. Weather Bureau, has recently proposed a method of changing the world's weather by "the explosion of ten really 'clean' hydrogen bombs" in the Arctic Ocean. This would throw enough steam into the air to produce a vast "quasipersistent" ice cloud that would blanket most of the arctic north of latitude 65°. The result: melting of the arctic icecap; milder winters from latitude 35° to 50°N (the northern two-thirds of the U.S.) ; but heavier winter snows—reminiscent of the ice age—between latitude 50° and 65°N (meaning much of Canada, Europe, and Russia) ; and a rise of two to five degrees Fahrenheit in equatorial regions. Wexler's conclusion: "The cure [may be] worse than the ailment."

to quicken the search. The result is that each year alloys get a little stronger and tougher, a little more heat resistant, and sometimes a little lighter, but no sensational advance can be expected until development is guided by deeper scientific understanding.

There is good evidence that the Russians are seeking this understanding more diligently than anyone else in the world. In the U.S. the metallurgical industry has never felt inclined to support very much basic research. As a result, some of the country's most promising metals research is going on at General Electric, Westinghouse, du Pont, Union Carbide, and at a few government laboratories, notably those of the AEC. Out of this, eventually— though perhaps not in the Sixties—will come the science needed for some real metallurgical progress. Better metals would lead to cheaper electric power, to lower capital costs in oil and chemical plants (which use lots of pressure vessels), and to wholly new processes using high pressures and temperatures.

In the field of high-polymer chemistry, another aspect of materials technology, the U.S. has relatively great strength. The Fifties are closing with the tough new linear polyethylenes in volume production, and with polypropylene not far behind. These two plastics derive their strength and toughness from new principles of molecular ordering discovered in the U.S. and Europe within the last half-dozen years. Polymer experts believe that the full impact of these discoveries will not be felt until the Sixties, when plastics will take over more and more jobs now performed by metals.

Computers: No Limit in Sight

It is safe to say that few technical programs in the Sixties will be held back by lack of suitable electronic mechanisms. Solid-state devices (transistors, diodes, cryotrons, masers, magnetic amplifiers, and memory devices, and new "parametric" amplifiers) will increase the speed, sensitivity, reliability, and versatility of electronic equipment of all types. At the same time the urge— and the means—to make everything smaller and smaller will continue unabated.

R.C.A. has a sizable Signal Corps contract to build electronic circuits in the form of "micro-modules," built up from "micro-wafers" 0.3 inch square and 0.01 inch thick. A cubic-foot box would contain 600,000 circuit parts, or enough to build 1,000 television sets. Pilot lines making micro-modules should be running in 1962. Looking further ahead, R.C.A. is working on methods for packing the equivalent of six million circuit parts into a cubic foot.

At M.I.T., Dudley Buck, inventor of the cryotron, useful for switching and memory storage, hopes within the Sixties to produce cryotrons that are no bigger than a grain of photographic emulsion. If successful, he will be able to lay down several million cryotron elements within a square centimeter, and a stack a centimeter high might contain billions.

Such fantastic concentrations, inconceivable a few years ago, make it realistic for the first time to speak of a computer rivaling in complexity the human brain, with its ten billion switching and memory units called neurons. Against the day when such a computer may become available, information theorists and neurophysiologists are cooperating in an effort to unravel the brain's own "wiring" diagram and programing scheme so they can endow computers with brainlike attributes. This is a mind-numbing long shot for the late 1960's.

Perhaps equally startling is the growing belief of some physicists and mathematicians that information theory and computer theory will shed new light on human behavior. "The effort to translate languages by machine," says E. R. Piore, I.B.M.'s director of research, "is forcing us to a deeper understanding of language and its meanings. Since language and human behavior are so profoundly associated, better understanding of language should have important implications for the social sciences."

The New Tools of Research

The point where technology leaves off and science begins—the distinction between applied and basic research—has become increasingly fuzzy. In the Sixties it will become fuzzier yet, for the great research tools that will dominate physical science in the years ahead will be engineering marvels first and research tools second.

Three prodigious new research instruments are now taking shape, and like Galileo's telescope they cannot fail to provide sights and insights impossible to predict in advance. The powerful new tools are: the 25-bev (billion-electron volt) accelerators now under construction at Brookhaven, New York, and at the CERN laboratory in Geneva; the huge new radio telescopes being built at several sites in the U.S.; and, finally, the satellites and space probes that will be launched by the dozens in the coming decade.

During the Fifties, scientists reaped a rich harvest from earlier counterparts of each of these three tools: from the Brookhaven Cosmotron (2.5 bev) and Berkeley Bevatron (6 bev); from the 200-inch optical telescope on Palomar, and early radio telescopes; and from high-altitude rocket and balloon flights.

The bevatron produced, on order and as predicted, the previously unobserved particles of antimatter, the antiproton and antineutron. And it provided a rich profusion of puzzling K-meson tracks that led, in 1957, to the overthrow of the physicists' sacred principle of parity. (See "Physics: The Magnificent Riddle," *Fortune*, January, 1957.)

The great Palomar telescope, in less than ten years, has doubled and redoubled the estimated size and age of the universe. And, in collaboration with radio telescopes, it has produced the first evidence of galaxies meeting in titanic collision. Finally, the pre-Sputnik rockets carried measuring instruments to the edge of the earth's atmosphere for the first time. They provided brief tantalizing glimpses of a new frontier of discovery.

Peering toward Infinity

The 25-bev machines, scheduled for operation in 1960, should help to establish whether the inventory of elementary particles is now complete at thirty, or whether still more remain to be discovered. The machines, acting like supermicroscopes, will also provide clearer "images" of the elementary particles and thereby guide theorists to a new understanding of the baffling subnuclear universe. Out of the interplay between experiment and theory may come new concepts upsetting all present notions of time and space. But many thoughtful physicists believe that a comprehensive theory of the elementary particles—comparable to quantum theory of the Twenties—will still be eluding man's grasp ten years from now.

Most astronomers are confident, however, that powerful new radio telescopes will be probing—and, perhaps, defining—the "edge" of the observable universe by the mid-Sixties. Astrophysical theory holds that the galaxies in the universe are rushing outward in all directions, and that the more distant the galaxy the faster it will appear to be receding from the earth. Presumably there are galaxies receding so fast that their light (or radio emission, which is the same thing) can never reach the earth. Thus there is an "edge" to the universe beyond which man cannot hope to see.

The discoveries that will be made in the Sixties by satellites and by unmanned space vehicles probing to the moon, Mars, Venus, and to the vicinity of the sun are truly impossible to predict. Whether the probes will detect life of any sort, even the most primitive, is a matter of speculation.

When the satellites are big enough to carry telescopes, of perhaps twenty-inch aperture, they should provide stunning celestial photographs, having a clarity unattainable from the earth. And the first view of the earth itself—suspended in space, radiant in the sunlight—will provide the most breath-taking scene ever photographed. It will be hanging on classroom walls in 1969.

The Payoff for Earth

The space vehicles should have an impact almost immediately on daily life. Equipped with simple radio beacons operating on solar batteries, satellites will soon be serving as navigation aids. Their precisely calculated orbits will be handily available in almanacs. Equally soon, satellites will keep the whole world's weather under surveillance. They will transmit to earth simple pictures of shifting cloud patterns, together with a detailed energy survey, showing how much of the sun's heat is absorbed and how much is reflected back into space. Once information of this sort has been correlated with the earth's weather, meteorologists should make dramatic improvements in their forecasting techniques. A target for the late 1960's: accurate ninety-day weather forecasts.

How great a role satellites may play in worldwide communications is the subject of vigorous debate among experts. Some regard the satellites as the cheapest, most effective means for achieving high-capacity international transmission of radio and TV programs, along with private telephone and telegraph messages. They point out that the first transatlantic telephone cable (1956) cost $40 million and could carry only thirty-six conversations (though this will soon be raised to seventy-two). To establish a satellite radio-relay network—consisting of three to a dozen satellites—might cost anywhere from $100 million up, but it could have a capacity of 500 to 1,000 phone conversations, plus several FM channels and a TV channel or two. Communications experts who are not impressed by this vision point out that the radio spectrum is already crowded and that filling the air with messages to and from satellites would only make matters worse.

TV round the World

The placing of an 8,700-pound Atlas missile into orbit dramatizes the high priority being given to satellite communications experiments, especially by the military. In the present experiment the satellite does not act as a simple reflector or instantaneous repeater of messages, but serves instead as a high-speed message carrier. A message beamed to it from, say, Los Angeles is stored on tape and then played back to earth on command. Thus a message could be delivered, with high reliability, halfway around the world in fifty minutes. While short-wave radio could carry the same message almost instantaneously, transoceanic radio is notoriously unreliable and easily jammed—and, of course, could not carry TV. With only modest miniaturization a TV tape recorder could be placed in orbit and could carry short (five-to-ten-minute) programs to any part of the globe.

The Atlas engines that launched the big satellite almost certainly had to make some use of high-energy fuels. The booster rocket engine of one million to 1,500,000 pounds' thrust, now in early development, will be able to put seven to ten tons into orbit with standard fuels, and twice that mass if high-energy fuels are used in the upper stages. Finally—still within the decade—a cluster of million-pound boosters could be used to launch as much as 100 tons into orbit. By that time, a nuclear-powered rocket may be contending for weight-lifting honors. "Depending on luck and the budget," says Herbert York, director of research of the Advanced Research Projects Agency, "we may get a man to the moon and back by 1970."

What Budget for Health?

There seems little likelihood that space technology will be starved for funds in the years ahead. One of the biggest unknowns for the Sixties will be the level at which the U.S.—especially the government—will support basic research in medicine. By every criterion, the U.S. ought to be spending a great deal more on biological and medical research than last year's estimated $400 million.

It would be rash to predict for the Sixties fundamental cures or prophylaxis for any of the outstanding medical problems—coronary and atherosclerotic disease, cancer, or mental illness—but the decade should certainly see major advances. And it could well see a substance to control essential hypertension, as insulin controls diabetes.

Cancer, in all its various manifestations, is still a deep mystery, but basic research on the process by which DNA (deoxyribonucleic acid) controls cell growth might suddenly clarify the whole problem of unrestrained cell and tissue growth. Meanwhile, on a less fundamental level, the intensive search for drugs that will disable specific types of cancer cells could have important results in the next few years.

Mental illness, like cancer, appears to consist of a host of disparate ailments that would be unlikely to yield to a single therapy, but again the diversity may be more illusory than real. It may be that the greatest value of the tranquilizers and "psychic energizers" (mood raisers) discovered in the Fifties will have been to open the eyes of psychiatrists generally to the importance of biochemistry in mental health and illness.

The Uses of $120 Billion

If, as seems likely, the U.S. spends approximately $120 billion on R. and D. during the Sixties, this will substantially exceed the nation's total investment in science and technology in the 183 years between 1776 and the present date. There is no guarantee that the money will produce another Einstein, or even a Willard Gibbs. (And, more than likely, it will not.) It may not even guarantee the U.S. world leadership in science and technology if the $120 billion is used so that the Sixties—field by field and area by area—is simply the Fifties swollen to double size.

While the most recent recommendations of the President's Science Advisory Committee, headed by Dr. Killian, should help to prevent this from happening, government action can, at most, directly influence only half of the total R. and D. effort. It will be up to industry to reexamine its own R. and D. programs to see where they can be strengthened in the years ahead.

There is a clear need for more industrial effort in basic technology—as well as in basic science—to achieve greater productivity gains than the 2½ to 3 per cent typical of recent years. Experts may disagree on the seriousness of the Soviet "economic threat," but there can be no doubt that the U.S.S.R. has large cadres of well-trained scientists and engineers to assign to the productivity problem, undistracted by the need to turn out annual engineering refinements in cars and a host of other consumer products.

Should the cold war somehow be ended during the Sixties, there would presumably be a sharp reduction in the federal funds pumped into R. and D. It would then be imperative for scores of corporations to find nonmilitary outlets for their capabilities. The result could resemble the technological demobilization that followed World War II, which diverted into the civilian economy a torrent of ideas and techniques, and thousands of talented young people at the peak of creativity. Another such torrential release, if it came, say, by 1965, could have an unimaginable impact on industrial technology and on the market before the decade ended.

A New Age of Discovery

Short of an ending of the cold war—and barring the outbreak of a hot one—science will inevitably take on a more international character in the Sixties, following the pattern of the highly successful International Geophysical Year. Plans are already afoot for an International Public Health and Medical Research Year. Such cooperative ventures can themselves do something to reduce international tension. If wisdom and forbearance prevail, the Sixties could be filled with wonders—not alone for consumers and businessmen, but for everyone who can perceive the beauty and excitement in the great voyages of discovery now going forward in every region of science.

There is no end to space. Man has hitched his wagon to the infinite, and this is bound to affect his life on earth. The space effort is already the size of the automobile industry; in a few years it may be a $20-billion business. The implications for 1970 and beyond are monstrous and the "fallout" of products promises to be fabulous. In the long run the space program could produce better products and ways of doing things from generating power to calculating probabilities, from packaging eggs to treating ailments.

Hitching the Economy to the Infinite*

There is no end to space, and so far as the U.S. economy is concerned, there will probably be no end to the space program. Man has hitched his wagon to the infinite, and he is unlikely ever to unhitch it again. A failure or two in the sky can be only temporary, a spur to the next success. And the next success will be merely the prelude to even greater triumph. As D. Brainerd Holmes of the National Aeronautics and Space Administration remarks, "The lunar program makes sense only if we go on from there." The space venture, in short, is likely to be more durably stupendous than even its most passionate advocates think it will be. It is bound to affect the nation's economy powerfully and in many ways.

by Gilbert Burck

During the next decade alone the U.S. will loft several hundred scientific satellites and dozens of lunar and planetary probes, and undertake upwards of forty manned space flights. By 1970, ac-

* Vol. 65, June 1962, pp. 123–125, 267–274.

cording to the most conservative initial estimates, NASA and the military will be spending around $15 billion a year on space, including $5 billion on missiles. But almost every space project so far has cost two to three times its conservative initial estimates. Mistakes are bound to be made, failures are bound to occur, and costs and ambitions bound to soar. The space effort (as it is coming to be known in official jargon) will very likely cost more than $20 billion a year by 1970.

Nothing is more fecund, industrially and socially, than large mobilizations of scientific knowledge and effort; and this is the greatest mobilization of them all. Precisely because the benefits it will bestow on the world will be incidental to the main effort, they may eventually come faster than man's capacity to use them economically. The space effort has already given man an immense psychological boost. Just as the Russian space successes have bolstered Soviet power internally by winning world power and prestige, so U.S. space projects are fortifying the old American optimism, confidence, and audacity. In thousands of offices and plants as well as in the endless anonymous corridors of Washington, prudent men who customarily discuss mundane prospects warily now talk with easy assurance of landing on the moon and exploring Mars. And they are even more sure of the benefits flowing from space techniques. Hundreds of American-made satellites will soon be buzzing the globe, guiding its navigation, mapping its impenetrable jungles, solving the cosmic riddles of its erratic weather, searching its hostile terrain, and relaying libraries of information and millions of photographs to receivers below. In the long run the space effort promises immense consumption dividends, a "fallout" of better products and ways of doing things from generating power to calculating probabilities, from packing eggs to treating ailments, real and imaginary.

A Military Thrust, an Inflationary Boost

Too often forgotten, however, is the fact that such pleasant rewards will be bought at a heavy price—a price that, all other things being equal, the U.S. might be reluctant to pay. This decade's program alone, which may be only preliminary, could impose unpalatable if not severe burdens on the nation. It will very likely kill all chances of reducing in our time the government's share of the economy. It will change, strain, and probably distort the distribution of the nation's resources. With all its emphasis on planning, both national and international, it could ultimately do violence to private enterprise itself.

Nor will the fabled practical benefits offset the cost of the program for a long time. Washington is teeming with lobbyists and other space partisans assiduously promoting the notion that space is the greatest surefire blue-sky investment ever, sure to pay off at 1,000 per cent almost immediately—as if the benefits were the primary aim of the program. Actually, the chief reason for allocating so prodigious a part of the national resources to an accelerated space program is the paramilitary necessity of being in space with the most and the best; and the fact that the U.S. has divided the effort into military applications run by the Department of Defense and general applications run by NASA does not alter the situation. (The Russians themselves regard NASA as a device for continuing space activities if an arms agreement is signed, which in a way it would be.) Although the space effort may realize a bonanza of practical benefits, it is hardly an efficient way of getting them.

By the time the satellites begin to pay off measurably, say 1970 at the earliest, the U.S. may have spent $75 billion to $100 billion on space activities, and another $50 billion on missiles. Annual interest on such sums, if reckoned at the prevailing government securities rate, will be around $4 billion, enough to pay the nation's yearly shoe bill; and what might be called the accumulated interest will come to another $20 billion by 1970, enough to run the whole U.S. railroad system for two years or to pay for most of the country's education for a year. The space program is right now giving the economy a powerful and potentially inflationary boost.

The implications for 1970 and beyond are portentous. Barring a genuine arms agreement—i.e., barring a revolution in the Soviet state religion—military costs other than missiles may well rise from their present $43 billion to more than $70 billion by 1970. So military and space outlays together could come to $90 billion or more a year. What could this mean? In its projections of the U.S. economy of the 1960's, *Fortune* estimated that G.N.P. (in 1959 prices) would rise from about $500 billion in 1960 to $750 billion a decade later, or at a compound annual rate of 4.2 per cent. So far, this appears a sound projection. *Fortune* also estimated that by 1970 defense outlays, including several billion a year spent overseas for military aid, etc., would not exceed 10 per cent of G.N.P., or $75 billion. But if defense plus space outlays rise to more than $90 billion, the growth of the rest of the economy will be correspondingly retarded unless people work longer or raise their output per hour. Only an industrially opulent country can mount a space effort worthy of the name. But even the most industrially opulent of all nations cannot take the imponderable demands of a huge space program in stride unless it uses its resources with sharply increasing efficiency.

Fewer and Bigger Contracts

The immediate effect of the space venture on the U.S. economy, besides pumping a lot of money into it, has been to change the pattern of much business profoundly. Space vehicles are the most complex structures ever built, running to thousands of components, subassemblies, and specialized devices; no single company yet has the immediate resources to manufacture whole vehicles. A given project is ruled by the prime contractor, which practices what is known as systems management: the integration of production and research and development, including its own and that of government and university laboratories, into a final working vehicle. Many companies handle more than one prime contract, but in addition they usually are subcontractors on several others, and thus no one company covers the biggest programs exclusively. The giant North American Aviation Corp., for example, is the prime contractor for the Apollo lunar spacecraft, but it is also a large subcontractor. McDonnell Aircraft estimates it has called in more than 4,000 subcontractors and suppliers on the $145-million Mercury capsule contract alone.

But even this pattern is changing rapidly as the central effort of the aerospace program shifts from missiles to propulsion and electronics. Missile production, after rising a little, may peak off at something above $5 billion. Other outlays by NASA (for such things as the moon program) and by the military (for such things as propulsion systems) are climbing toward the $10-billion mark, which they may reach as early as 1965. "Already," says Harry H. Wetzel, vice president of the Garrett Corp. of Los Angeles, which makes environmental control systems, "the aerospace business is a new game." As Wetzel and others see it:

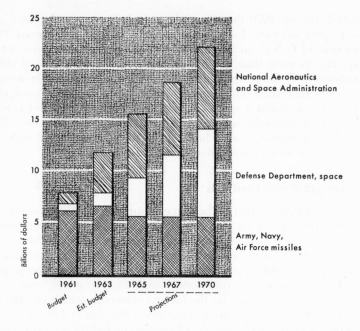

FIGURE 7. Growth Situation Extraordinary: The Space Market. Space outlays may well be pumping upwards of $20 billion a year into the economy by 1970. The "demand" for military missiles will probably level off after a year or two, but rocket motors and other forms of propulsion will rival electronics in eating up both military and civilian funds. These estimates are a compromise between the most conservative reckonings, based on work in progress and work scheduled, and informed guesses by government and industry experts, well aware that space programs always come to more than estimates. The conservatives set the 1970 total at around $15 billion. Many of the liberal estimates, by contrast, run to astronomical figures. Whatever the actual amount spent, it will be a big slice of the economy, creating a lot of complex problems—and doubtless someday returning a wealth of practical dividends. And 1970 will probably be only a prelude to many more and bigger decades in space.

1. There will be fewer and bigger contracts.

2. Production runs will decline steadily, and completely reverse the traditional four-to-one ratio of shop to engineering personnel. That is, companies will spend more on engineering and less on actual production; in fact, straight production capacity is already excessive. In 1960, Lockheed says, the company's R. and D. awards came to more than the whole nation spent on defense R. and D. in 1950.

3. The aerospace companies will need not only engineers, but physiologists, psychologists, space-medicine men, chemists, and systems engineers.

4. As the space program proceeds to moon shots and planet exploration, reliability will become increasingly more important, and will demand more research facilities that can simulate space environments, more control engineering, more surveillance of subcontractors' and suppliers' quality controls.

This trend may be hard on small business, and doubtless will result in many mergers—of small companies with big, and small with small. For the important contracts from 1965 on will be based on ground support and airborne guidance and control systems, which require large engineering organizations. "We can't exist without small business," cautiously explains Jack Parker, General Electric's vice president in charge of electronic and flight systems. "Yet as the emphasis on quality and complexity becomes greater, it is apt to reduce the amount of work small business may want." Says a blunter spokesman for another large company, in authentic space jargon, "Captive production will increase not only because companies will want to maximize dollar volume in-house, but because schedules must be met reliably. The need for specialized equipment and technical sophistication will inevitably reduce off-site work."

NASA is going out of its way to encourage little business; and the very nature of the space and missile program, with its demand for all manner of custom-made specialties, may continue to favor small firms devoted to electronic devices, engineering techniques, special research, and other relatively esoteric services and products. Small companies, as a matter of fact, can offer scientists unique advantages such as participation in top-level decisions; some offer higher salaries and more fringe benefits than big companies, a few offer more money than their own top executives get. T. F. Walkowicz, aeronautical engineer and associate of Laurance Rockefeller, who helped establish such Rockefeller-financed companies as Itek (information technology) and Geophysics Corp. of America (instruments for space research), concedes there will be a shake-out, just as there was in electronics, but argues that the brightest companies will survive and grow. "Brains are what count today, and nobody has a monopoly on brains."

Wanted: a Million More Scientists and Engineers

The space effort is the first paramilitary effort in history not accompanied by a demand for heavy hardware and mass-produced materials. Its great demand, instead, is for professional people, and it may relatively soon employ up to a million. Since more and more money will go into manpower, particularly engineers and other technical specialists, the well-worn question of whether the U.S. is producing enough professionals is no longer academic. By 1970, thanks in large part to the space venture, the U.S. will need more than two million scientists and engineers, or about double the number employed in 1959. A million more will be hard to find. NASA itself will have hired 4,500 specialists by the end of fiscal 1963; since, however, it has gone to a great deal of pains to get talent and also because many professional people would rather work where the big decisions are made at relatively low salaries ($8,000 to $20,000), it has managed to hire about 2,000 and expects no great trouble in corralling the other 2,500. Some experts argue that if engineers and high technical talent were used efficiently—i.e., not assigned to sales work and routine technical jobs—the shortage would not be so bad as it seems. But the majority agree that the shortage is already severe, and is bound to get worse as the space industry expands and R. and D. becomes more intensive.

The President's Science Advisory Committee hopes to make specific recommendations for stimulating the production of scientists, and many other authorities are discharging wisdom on the subject. So as the demand for professional and scientific personnel rises and is reinforced by incentives, the supply is certain to rise eventually, too. For a while it probably will not rise fast enough to meet the demand, and important civilian research and development may be temporarily deprived of talent.

In the longer run, however, the space effort will be the prime force in increasing the U.S. scientific and professional population. And in the process it will accelerate greatly the secular tendency for U.S. business to depend more and more on R. and D. This trend, in turn, according to a preliminary study made by Dr. Howard Vollmer of the Stanford Research Institute (sponsored by the Air Force), may eventually change the "organizational structure" of all U.S. industry. That is, it may make U.S. industry less bureacratic and more intellectually challenging, "with greater opportunity for professionals to participate in work-related decisions."

Mass Production in Space

The first large-scale matching of corporate enterprise with the commercial possibilities of space is taking place in the communication-satellite program. Possibly no invention will have ever jumped the rugged gap between concept and commercial application so quickly and dramatically as the communication satellite. Like much in the space effort, it has been overtouted. No less an authority than Lloyd V. Berkner, chairman of the space-science board of the National Academy of Sciences, has predicted that it could eventually earn $100 *billion* a year. Although such talk has already run aground on cruel reality, the principle of the communication satellite does make economic sense. What it amounts to is a device for the mass production of long-distance wireless communication; once it achieves volume and overcomes a host of problems, it could be nicely in the money.

The economic validity of the communication satellite rests on a genuine technical advantage. Because lower frequencies are overloaded, progressively higher frequencies are necessary to handle the growing volume of radio communication. But when frequencies attain thousands of megacycles per second, the waves travel in a straight line from the transmission tower, are blocked by hills or buildings, and cannot reach beyond the earth's surface or the horizon. Even in flat country, therefore, their optimum range is about thirty miles. There is no technical problem on land, where relay stations can be built at appropriate intervals; but it makes microwave radio impracticable over the ocean. Transoceanic communication is limited to submarine cables or relatively small capacity or lower-frequency radios. Hung high in the sky, satellites could relay a huge volume of traffic, including TV and data-processing signals, across the seven seas.

Essentially, there are two types of satellites: passive, which are merely metallic balloons that reflect or bounce back signals from the earth; and active, equipped with instruments that amplify and relay back the signals. Both active and passive systems could be orbited at altitudes up to 7,000 miles. To cover the world at such altitudes—i.e., to make sure a satellite is always visible to ground stations—twenty to thirty satellites would be needed. They would also require powerful ground transmitters and sensitive and expensive receiving equipment.

On the other hand, it would take only three active satellites to cover nearly the whole world if lofted 22,300 miles above and parallel to the equator; at this altitude and placement, they would appear fixed in the sky. But they would be expensive to build, hard to launch and hard to spot, and could be kept in place only by intricate controls. Most engineers tend to favor the high-altitude ("synchronous") system because, among other things, it would eliminate the need to switch from one satellite to another as successive satellites rise and set over the horizon. But they concede that complex and expensive launching facilities still have to be developed. And neither system could operate until frequency assignment and other international problems were solved.

In an analysis of the potentials of both a high-altitude system and a low-altitude system, William Meckling of Rand Corp. gets down to dollars and cents. The low-altitude system, with as many as 120 satellites in constant orbit (depending on the control system), would be subject to some interruption, says Meckling, as the number of operating satellites declines; the high-altitude system would work constantly until one of the satellites failed, whereupon it might take days or even weeks to restore service unless a spare satellite were kept handy in the sky. But given reliability, such systems would have enormous capacity. A worldwide low-altitude system would provide 7,800 transoceanic channels or about twenty times the number now serving the U.S., says Meckling, and a *single* twenty-four-hour satellite 4,800. Used at capacity, a low-altitude system (with an average life of two years) might cost $8,500 a year per channel, and a high-altitude system (with an average life of one year) $10,000 a year per channel—against $27,000 a year per channel for a new underwater cable system.

But, of course, no company could hope to start out at capacity. So assuming a fair advance sale and a growth of 15 per cent a year compounded—considerably more than the growth rate of international communications since World War II—Meckling figures that a company could achieve close to capacity operation in fifteen years. Meantime, its average annual costs per channel would be roughly three times as high as the capacity estimates, or about those of new submarine cables.

The big question: can the satellites generate enough business to operate at close to capacity? A satellite company, to get the volume that would enable it to realize its potentially low costs, would have to cut rates deeply—a familiar business situation, and one full of risks, including the risks in coming to terms on rates with foreign government-owned companies. Since companies now pay $240,000 a year for one voice channel in old, high-cost cables, however, there is plenty of margin for rate cutting. Nobody knows exactly what a system would cost, but experts think that $400 million or so would buy one, and that it could break even before the end of the decade and could be earning good money for its owners by 1975. No wonder that a good many companies not given to throwing money down holes are eager to get in space, so to speak, on the ground floor.

Whose C.S.C. Will It Be?

The American Telephone & Telegraph Co., which cooperated with NASA by building the ground stations for the first passive Echo satellite, favors a system of twenty to thirty satellites at 6,000 to 7,000 miles, owned and operated by FCC-authorized companies. The company is now launching its Telstar or active low-altitude satellite, which it hopes will provide enough know-how to put a whole communication system in operation by 1965.

But the Administration, on the grounds that A.T. & T. should not dominate the new industry and that the taxpayers, who will have invested $175 million in research on the system by 1963, should be allowed direct participation, proposed to charter a $1-billion Communications Satellite Corp., financed by Class A stock, selling at a minimum of $1,000 a share. The Class A shares of C. S. Corp., to be sold to both the public and the communication companies, would have voting privileges and get all the dividends. Communication companies could also buy nondividend-paying Class B shares, and would realize profit on them by including the cost of the shares in their rate base and so in effect get higher returns.

Almost everybody remotely concerned wants a role in shaping the relationship between space and private enterprise. The late Senator Estes Kefauver, not surprisingly, argued that the government should own and operate the project. Representative Emanuel Celler characteristically argues that "since it is almost impossible to regulate A.T. & T. on earth, we should need divine guidance to regulate A.T. & T. . . way above us." R.C.A. and Western Union, among others, are for the Administration proposal, even though R.C.A.'s General David Sarnoff has testified that investment in the satellite corporation would be speculative. (R.C.A. also has come out for a high-altitude synchronous system, which it probably would like to build.)

Since getting on with the job is important, FCC Chairman Newton N. Minow would limit ownership of the government-sponsored corporation to communication companies. However, the influential Senate Space Committee accepted the government plan in principle, and reduced the price of a share to $100; but it would give the companies a break by providing for only one class of stock, to be sold equally to the public and the companies, with foreign governments allowed to buy up to 10 per cent of the public shares. And it proposed that communication companies should be allowed to own some of the potentially profitable ground stations.

No More National Privacy

Probably the quickest space payoff will come from satellites like NASA's upcoming "orbiting observatories," which will carry telescopes and other astronomical and geophysical instruments. Such satellites could map the world as it has never been mapped before. "When it comes to mapping, the satellite is to the airplane as the airplane is to the ground surveyor," says Richard S. Leghorn, president of Itek Corp. and chairman of the National Planning Associations' Committee on Security through Arms Control. "The present proposal to map Antarctica with planes could be done with satellites for half the money and in a fifth of the time." All that needs to be decided, says Leghorn, is whether the government or private industry is to run them.

Once the decision is made, observational satellites could begin to earn money immediately, on jobs now scheduled. Itek itself stands to gain by an early decision, for as a specialist in information storage and retrieval it has developed a machine that can read diagrams and pictures and otherwise relay information graphically without programing—i.e., without reducing information to a machine code. "There's no such thing as backyard privacy if we orbit the world constantly," Leghorn likes to point out. "We're ahead on information satellites; we should take advantage of them to open up the Soviet Union to view. Great areas there are barred off, but what would be the use of barring them off if we know what's there?"

Probably the most broadly remunerative of the space vehicles will be the government-operated weather satellites, designed not only to predict short-term weather movements but to gather enough data to enable men to understand just how these movements are generated. Four R.C.A.-made and NASA-supervised Tiros (television and infrared observation satellites) were launched between April, 1960, and early 1962. Orbiting the world every hundred minutes or so, and equipped with two TV cameras apiece, they recorded significant new cloud formations over enormous ocean areas. All except Tiros I gauged solar energy reflected and scattered by the earth's surface and atmosphere as well as infrared radiation leaving the earth and its atmosphere. Relevant findings were analyzed promptly and passed on to weather forecasters here and abroad. Although Tiros IV missed the epochal east-coast "Ash Wednesday storm" last March—it was orbiting the Northern Hemisphere by night at the time—Tiros III tracked seventeen tropical storms, and gave advance warning of Hurricane Esther.

Within a year NASA plans to launch at least three more Tiros and an advanced Nimbus satellite, which will orbit the earth from pole to pole. It is possible that the Russians will cooperate in such a venture, perhaps by lofting a second Nimbus-type satellite. At all events, such satellites will enable the U.S. Weather Bureau to trace the progress of any disturbance anywhere. To view a large part of the world from a steady vantage point, moreover, NASA and the Weather Bureau are planning an Aeros high-altitude orb.

How much all this will save the world it is hard to say. A dozen or so years ago, when the Weather Bureau tried to determine the value of storm warnings and correct forecasts, "business and agricultural interests" suggested that such forecasts could save $3 billion a year in water resources and up to $2.5 billion a year in farm products, to say nothing of a hundred million in transportation (exclusive of air transport). But F. W. Reichelderfer, bureau chief, now feels such figures are meaningless. "Everybody benefits from better weather forecasting," he says, "so we're trying to value something we really can't measure. We know, however, the benefits are there. Just think how much could have been saved if Tiros IV had been around to forecast that east-coast storm last March." Accurate weather forecasting could make farm supports an even greater absurdity than they are. Underlying the whole support program is the assumption that farming, owing to the weather, is egregiously risky. With the risk eliminated, there would be less reason for subsidizing farmers than for subsidizing small manufacturers or storekeepers.

Despite the predictions of the space enthusiasts, it will be a long time before man can even attempt to begin to control the weather. First he must thoroughly understand it, and he still has a long way to go. But he will find out more about it in the next few years than he has in all history.

The Beneficent Promise

"In whatever direction our technology is moving," an I.B.M. engineer puts it succinctly, "the space program is advancing us faster." Thus the "fallout" of other kinds of benefits from the nation's investment in space research and development, though some will be long in coming, may be incalculable. To get space discoveries and inventions where they will help the civilian economy, NASA has set up an Office of Applications that will identify "inventive elements and apply them to industry while they are new." One of its first moves has been to hire the Midwest Research Institute of Kansas City to pick up potential applications, document them, and circulate news of the possibilities among industry people.[1] It has also retained the Denver Research Institute for a different kind of investigation: to find out whether industry is already making products and using processes originating in the space effort. After careful screening, Denver Research found 145 such examples, and thinks it will find more. But the big advances lie at some point in the future when the new techniques have had time to blend with the old and join the economy. When they do, space will be largely responsible for many new looks here below. Among the promising areas of development are:

Materials. Structural demands of rocket and spacecraft vehicles, the intense power requirements at takeoff, the sustained power required in flight, and the intense heat encountered on re-entry are making for a sharp advance in the strength and property of materials. In the area of metals and alloys this will lead to successful hypersonic planes, the development of simpler, more efficient aircraft and automobile engines, and, perhaps twenty years hence, to lighter and stronger building structures. The development of powerful new fuels is leading the chemical industry to use extreme-temperature, high-pressure techniques, one of which, indeed, is already being used to produce liquid hydrogen. A large array of entirely new metals and materials will be available for untold uses.

Reliability and miniaturization. Because space-vehicle machinery must be both small and absolutely reliable, industry's trend

---

[1] Business, however, has been complaining that it has been discouraged from adapting new products and processes developed while working on NASA contracts, because patent rights on those products and processes automatically become government property unless the administrator waives the government's rights. The Department of Justice has entered a strong plea to keep things that way. The issue, whose importance is obvious, seemed to be building up to major proportions when the patent subcommittee of the House Science and Astronautics Committee voted to revise NASA practices. If its recommendations are adopted, NASA could be brought more in line with the Defense Department practice of retaining license rights—but not title—to patents taken out on inventions and improvements made by companies while working on military contracts.

toward miniaturization and reliability, already illustrated by the development of transistors, diodes, etc., will accelerate. Computers will be among the first to profit by the new techniques; computers that used to fill large rooms will soon be housed in packages the size of a small TV set. The Burroughs D210 computer, designed to guide missiles, occupies less than ¼ cubic foot, uses less power than a 60-watt bulb, operates 50,000 hours without failure, and costs only $25,000 to $50,000, against more than $1 million for the present Atlas computer. Various forms of microcircuitry, developed for space vehicles, some already used widely, will probably result in miniature consumer goods, like radios, at reasonable prices.

Automation. Advances in guidance systems for space vehicles will improve and speed up automation techniques. "Everything we have learned about guiding the Titan," says one I.B.M. man, "will be useful in guiding machine tools." By way of humble example, Allied Research Associates of Boston has used space innovations to develop a machine that automatically sorts cigars for uniformity of color.

Bonding techniques. Because high vacuums are essential for space environmental test chambers, and because many of the specialty metals for space vehicles are being made in vacuum, high-vacuum techniques are being accelerated. Scientists of the National Research Corp., for example, have recently shown that certain metals, if cleaned and put into an almost perfect vacuum, bond together tightly and permanently as if welded. This demonstration will help industry make bearings that will not congeal and clog in the vacuum of space; on the other hand, it will probably result in new nonwelding techniques for bonding many metals here on earth.

Aerial observation. Interpretation of aerial pictures, now being used by Itek Corp. to advise grape growers of California on the quantity and quality of the crop and so to forecast market price, will be extended to hundreds of uses. The problem of storing and retrieving vast amounts of technical information, brought into being by the space age, will be solved by digital graphic systems such as Itek's EDM machine.

Klimps and Kudl-Pacs. Space components are easily damaged, and must be handled a lot, so new packaging techniques have been developed for them. North American Aviation's subsidiary, NAVAN Products Inc., has invented an L-shaped wire fastener it calls a "Klimp," which is replacing nails in packing boxes, and "Kudl-Pac," a thermal-plastic, polyurethane-lined case that adapts itself to a variety of shapes and can be used over and over again. NAVAN has promoted this product by sending prospects a real live egg enclosed in a Kudl-Pac.

Packaged power. Probably the broadest area of practical development will grow out of the new, compact, self-contained sources of power needed by satellites and spacecraft to operate their equipment and to maintain men and their environment independently in space. Already being developed by private and government research for eventual commercial use, they include: (1) Silicon solar cells, converting sunlight directly into electricity, which are being used to power such disparate things as portable radios, railway crossing lights, and community radio receivers in Indian towns. (2) Thermoelectric materials, which can convert low heat directly into electricity, or electricity into heat or cold by reversing the direction of the current. (3) Thermionic tubes, which convert high heat directly into electricity. (4) Fuel cells, converting chemical reactions directly into electricity. (5) Highly compact atomic-power packs, tapping electricity directly from the atom through a converter. (6) Magnetohydrodynamic generators, which convert the movement of a very hot and ionized gas stream ("plasma") into electricity by passing it through a magnetic field. Such a device will make possible high-efficiency power stations: Avco Corp. and a group of eleven electric utilities led by American Electric Power Service Corp. are supporting a research program on MHD generators, which may turn out to be 40 per cent more efficient than the most modern power generator. As a result of its work in plasma, incidentally, Avco is marketing a "PlasmaGun" or high-heat gun using a tungsten electrode and water-cooled copper nozzle for applying such coatings as tungsten, molybdenum, titanium carbide, and tantalum carbide to metallic and ceramic surfaces. Achieving temperatures up to 30,000°F., the gun can also be used for flame cutting and materials studies.

Compact power packages will probably be developed to the point where they can generate electricity on the spot for home lighting, appliances, and industrial processes. The natural-gas industry is financing a research program on fuel cells, reacting natural gas with an oxidizer to make gas the sole source of domestic energy—heat as well as electricity. Thus walls for homes and buildings may be designed with their own built-in, self-contained heating, cooling, lighting, and electrical systems, feeding on fuel cells, or free energy from the sun. These and other devices, already being carried over from the space industry by such giants as General Electric and Westinghouse, may revolutionize the generation and distribution of power on earth.

Solution to overpopulation. Gazing far into the future, some scientists believe that the greatest benefit the space effort will confer on the human race is to enable man to migrate to other worlds. Theoretically, atmosphere can be created on planets where it is nonexistent or very thin, perhaps by seeding the planets with a catalytic substance to release oxygen now locked up there in compounds like carbon dioxide. "If you want to look ahead a hundred years or more," says Murray Zelikoff of Geophysics Corp., "I think the real purpose of the space effort is to colonize the planets. How else can we solve the population problem? It's not only politics that moves men, but social and biological factors. Subconsciously these are moving men to outer space."

Feet on the Ground

Such a prospect is still far out, but it no longer belongs in the comic strips. The space project is surely enlarging man's notions of the potentialities of the universe, and is accustoming him to think in terms of longer periods of time. Engineers look ahead at least twenty years in planning a space program, and to the extent that business is involved, its scale of thinking is correspondingly enlarged. As General Electric's Ralph Cordiner has remarked, when business deals with space it deals with a technology that needs a planetary scale to stage it, decades to develop it, and a much bigger investment to cross the threshold of return than is customary today.

Private enterprise is not disdaining the challenge. As we have seen, it is stepping into the communication-satellite business; and if other jobs, such as launching operations, can be put on a paying basis, it may gradually take them over. With its own money, industry is already constructing space-simulating facilities, such as G.E.'s laboratory at Valley Forge, Pennsylvania, and R.C.A.'s space center at Princeton, New Jersey.

Nevertheless, the great space effort is primarily dependent on government planning, national and international. Consequently, it is boosting the ardor and ambition of those who believe the world is headed for more state planning, and that the scope of private decision is inevitably narrowing. They "observe" that planning for space will train men to plan ahead in other fields, that the idea of government and free enterprise as distinct entities is no longer adequate. For them the great implication of space is that it will somehow free man from his preoccupation with profits and losses and other sordid things that tyrannize him here on earth.

But alas for the idealists, it is precisely this tropism of worldlings for minding their business that has enabled the space program to be created. Only this mundane preoccupation can carry the great program along, world without end. Contemplating the starry heavens above, as Immanuel Kant once did, even a normally reflective person finds it easy to muse on the shortcomings of mankind. But it should also be obvious that the space program, no matter how abundantly it pays off, will be a big and growing investment, and that, like all investments, it cannot be made until people first produce something to invest. To rise in the sky, the U.S. will have to keep its feet on the ground.

One of the largest treasure hunts in science today involves a device with the odd name *laser*. The laser (an acronym for Light Amplification by Stimulated Emission Radiation) can carry vast amounts of information, make superaccurate measurements, perform delicate surgery without cutting, weld microscopic wires, and burn through any known material. Here is a roundup of how lasers work, who is developing them, and how they are likely to be used in the future.

The Laser's Dazzling Future*

It is only three years since Theodore H. Maiman, a physicist then working for Hughes Aircraft Co., first succeeded in making a ruby rod emit coherent light— a narrow, intense beam whose waves are all nearly parallel, in step, and of the same wavelength. Maiman's ruby rod,

by Lawrence Lessing

as nearly everyone now knows, came to be called a laser (for "light amplification by stimulated emission of radiation"). Recent as its discovery is, its development is moving forward with something of the speed of its own light.

The principle upon which the ruby worked went down into the depths of atomic physics or quantum mechanics. When the atoms of certain materials are excited to a high energy state, they subsequently drop back to their normal state, ejecting the excess energy as photons of light. The ruby device was so formed that it caused the photons to be emitted as coherent light. By now this principle has been extended beyond the familiar ruby into four

* Vol. 68, June 1963, pp. 139–142, 151–166.

or possibly five distinct families of lasers, involving solids, liquids, and gases. More than twenty elements, from argon to xenon, have been found to lase—a new verb added to the language since 1960, to the anguish of purists. Over 400 company and university laboratories, as well as the Army, Navy, and Air Force, are engaged in some kind of laser research; the total expenditure in the field this year is estimated at some $30 million, about half of which is military.

The possible applications of lasers—from communications to computers, fine measurements to medicine, plasma physics to chemistry, radar tracking to range finding, welding to weaponry —seem to stretch out in a variety almost as endless as that of the devices themselves. Already, laser range finders of new speed, compactness, and precision are in experimental production for the Army. Laser beams have been used in delicate eye operations, and are also delicately welding and cutting difficult metals. This spring a laser optical radar was scheduled to track a 600-mile-high satellite with a beam of light, and experiments to impress voice messages and television pictures on a beam of light are getting seriously under way.

Room for 80 Million TV Channels

Earlier this year the third international Conference on Quantum Electronics, devoted mainly to lasers, drew about 1,000 scientists to Paris from some twenty countries, including Soviet Russia. The conference attracted so many scientific papers that they had to be presented in double shifts. No technical development in recent times has moved so fast and with quite so much basic promise.

Basically, the laser opens to highly controlled use and development a huge new region of the electromagnetic spectrum, many times more commodious than all the regions now devoted to radio, TV, radar, and microwave services combined. Light is simply another term of electromagnetic wave energy, related to all these, and differing only in its much higher frequencies or shorter wavelengths. In the narrow band of visible light alone there are frequencies enough to contain 80 million TV channels of the present bandwidth. And this is to say nothing of the bands of infrared and ultraviolet light stretching out on either side. Until the laser came along, light could not be exploited for these purposes because it was incoherent, radiating out in all directions in random phases and mixed wavelengths.

Laser light has inherently unique properties. It is an extremely fine radiation whose wavelengths are measured in microns, or only a few tens of millionths of an inch, from crest to crest. (Standard radio waves are measured in hundreds of yards, FM and television waves in feet, and microwaves have lengths of about one to a fraction of an inch.) Its beam is so nearly parallel that with a lens system it may spread as little as one-third of an inch per mile, about 10,000 times more concentrated than the best searchlight. And it is so intense it can be focused down at short range, as in a burning glass, to densities a billion times hotter than the surface of the sun.

Laser beams also have limitations. Chief among them is that, like ordinary light, they are absorbed or obstructed by atmospheric conditions, such as fog or rain, and, like TV, are limited on earth to line-of-sight operations. (Neither of these limitations, of course, is a problem in space.) In addition, much associated circuitry remains to be developed or invented before the basic principle can be applied to most major uses. But, for the first time, the laser provides an instrument to generate and control light waves—the radiation that has given man nearly all his perception of the world—as precisely and coherently as radio waves. The full consequences of this basic discovery can hardly yet be foreseen.

The laser's economic potential is currently a matter of some heated division of opinion. The more enthusiastic proponents estimate that by 1970 lasers will be a business of over $1 billion a year. Recently, however, some more determinedly hardheaded analysts, reacting against the dazzle, have taken a dimmer view. They tend to regard lasers as merely an extension and competitor of microwave devices. They see no immediate, large commercial prospects, and think that some of the more touted applications will take years to develop—"if ever," adds the staid London *Economist*. And they are right insofar as it takes some time for a three-year-old to grow.

But much the same dour view was taken of the vacuum tube about 1910, three years or so after its invention. It was regarded as just another and not very satisfactory detector of wireless telegraphy signals; all the circuitry required to make it work as the key generator and amplifier of radio waves was yet to be invented; and radio-broadcasting itself was not even to be thought of as a business until 1920. The laser is at much the same stage as the vacuum tube in 1910. But research is progressing much more rapidly today from a deeper, more sophisticated level of physical knowledge, not always fully comprehended by economists.

From Maser to Laser

Like so much of modern technology, the laser was no simple invention but a development out of rather remote physical theory. In 1951, Charles Hard Townes, a young professor at Columbia University who was studying the absorption of microwaves in gases, conceived of a new, more sensitive, and almost noise-free device for greatly amplifying very weak microwaves. Instead of using a flow of free electrons, as in all electronic devices, he used as an amplifier the natural vibration of the electron shells of atoms and molecules bound in matter. He first separated into a tube a stream of ammonia gas whose molecules had been excited to a higher energy state than their neighbors. Then, when he prodded the molecules with a microwave, they swiftly dropped back to a lower energy state, emitting their excess energy in a cascading effect as a much strengthened replica of the triggering wave. Townes called this two-level quantum-energy system a maser (for "microwave amplification by stimulated emission of radiation"). And it soon led to more compact and more efficient solid-state masers, including one using a ruby, developed by Bell Telephone Laboratories and others. But such masers generated so much heat they had to be cooled by liquid helium, and most electronics engineers considered them quite far-out, long-haired devices. Slowly they found specialized uses as atomic clocks, and in radio astronomy, radar, and, more recently, the ground receiver for Bell's Telstar communication satellite.

All along, however, it had been clear that the maser principle might work at much higher frequencies and achieve the amplification of light. Indeed, a light amplifier was suggested in principle some thirty years ago, long before its full implications were recognized, by a German physicist, F. G. Houtermans. In 1958, Townes, who had become a consultant at Bell Labs, wrote a historic paper in collaboration with his brother-in-law, Arthur L.

Schawlow, putting forth a theory and a proposal for building an optical maser. Townes and Schawlow did not know exactly what materials might work most easily, but they suggested that the effect might first be achieved in a gas, as in the first maser. Major U.S. laboratories, including those of Bell, G.E., Westinghouse, and M.I.T.'s Lincoln Laboratory, as well as some institutions abroad, promptly sent groups off on an intensive hunt.

One of the hunters was Maiman, who had been working with masers on military radar applications at Hughes Aircraft. He came in first with a solid-state ruby device that was an entirely different piece of apparatus from the ruby maser. Ruby, in fact, had been almost written off in a leading technical paper as a suitable laser material. Theories abounded as to why it would be much too inefficient to work properly, and most researchers were looking elsewhere. But Maiman calculated that in experiments on ruby as a possible laser material, it simply had not been driven at high enough power. When he managed to drive it hard, suddenly a threshold was crossed, and from the pink heart of the ruby darted the first telltale burst of brilliant, coherent, red light.

Applying the maser principle, Maiman used a high-powered flash lamp to excite or "pump" the active atoms in the ruby crystal —chromium—to a high energy level, from which they then dropped back to emit light. To get the cascade or amplifying effect, opposite ends of the ruby were made optically flat and then silvered, with one end semitransparent, so that the emitted light bounced back and forth through the crystal structure between these mirrors, stimulating more chromium atoms and building up the effect, until a coherent beam burst forth through the semi-transparent end. The first crude device operated in pulses in the visible red, at room temperatures, and delivered beams of only a few kilowatts in power, not wholly parallel or coherent, because crystals of the required purity and near-perfect homogeneity were lacking. Still, this was unexpectedly high power. In a few weeks the feat was excitedly repeated in dozens of laboratories over the world, and the laser was on its way.

Even Plain Air?

The next big strike was at Bell Labs. As the laboratory that had fostered the original Townes-Schawlow paper and from the beginning had mounted the biggest research effort, Bell had a right to feel chagrined by the coup at Hughes Aircraft. But within six months, in January, 1961, it had a first of its own at least as great as Maiman's. A group, led by a Persian physicist named Ali Javan, succeeded in making the first gas laser—a long tube of helium-neon with mirrors mounted at both ends, which is excited by an electrical discharge instead of light, much like an ordinary neon tube, and gives forth an exceedingly pure, continuous-wave beam in the near (invisible) infrared. By mid-1962, Bell had got this type of laser to work in the visible red, had developed two oxygen lasers, and in one fell swoop demonstrated laser action in five pure gases—helium, neon, argon, krypton, and xenon—each at different wavelengths.

All together, these gases, and others that have come along since, provide the widest bracket of different wavelengths—from 0.6 to 28.1 microns—so far available. "I expect any day now," says one Bell Labs worker, "to hear that someone has got a tube of plain air to lase." Though they have had much less publicity than the ruby, and are much more limited in power, with beams down in the range of a few thousandths of a watt, the gas lasers are highly significant as a group. At room temperatures, they put out continuous waves, with a choice of frequencies extending deeper into the visible band than any other type. And their beams are the narrowest, most monochromatic (pure in color), and most stable in frequency so far obtained—qualities of the greatest importance for communication uses.

Meanwhile, Bell Labs, along with others, had launched into the investigation of ruby lasers, to understand and improve their performance. In January, 1962, Bell succeeded in getting a ruby into continuous-wave operation in a complicated combination with sapphire. Bell also announced an important new solid-state laser—neodymium in calcium tungstate crystal—that reached continuous operation in the infrared more simply and with much less input power than the ruby. The fluorescent possibilities of other solid materials attracted many other researchers. As early as December, 1960, International Business Machines Corp. got a foot in the field when a team led by Peter P. Sorokin developed two pulsed solid lasers in calcium fluoride, one with samarium, the other with uranium. Both operated, however, at liquid-helium temperatures (about $-270°$ Centigrade). And in April, 1962, Radio Corp. of America announced a calcium flouride laser with divalent dysprosium, working at liquid-nitrogen temperatures (about −196° Centigrade). All together, over a dozen different solid-state lasers have been discovered so far, of which the ruby is still the star.

The Versatile Glass Rods

A strong challenge to ruby arose, however, in October, 1961, when Elias Snitzer and a group at American Optical Co. came up with a whole new class of lasers in glass. The major advantage of glass is that it may be formed more perfectly homogeneous than ruby or similar crystals, and molded to almost any size or shape. A special high-quality optical glass is simply infused with different fluorescing elements. The most prominent one is a pale-violet neodymium glass, heretofore used chiefly as art glass. Like ruby, it operates at room temperature in short pulses, though recently it also has been made to perform continuously. It is more fragile than ruby, but cheaper and more efficient. So far, however, glass lasers have operated only in the invisible infrared.

The versatility of glass soon became apparent. By developing a method of coating neodymium glass rods with clear glass to increase their light-pumping absorption, for instance, American Optical was able to draw them down into long slender fibers and get them to lase along their full lengths, for possible applications in fiber optics. At the same time, rods can be made so big that they have the highest energy of any lasers thus far. For this reason their development is receiving sizable support in military research contracts. Corning Glass, Eastman Kodak, and Bausch & Lomb are also briskly at work in this field.

Still another round of new developments crowded in late last year. Simultaneously in November, G.E. and I.B.M., followed closely by M.I.T.'s Lincoln Laboratory, announced the first of an entirely new family of semiconductor lasers resembling transistors. These work in an entirely different way from all other lasers. The semiconductor laser is a tiny crystal of gallium arsenide, an exotic metallic compound, with a positive and a negative region created in it, as in a p-n junction transistor. Instead of being "pumped" by light or by gaseous discharge, this crystal is simply excited by an electric current, which causes it to emit, from one edge of the p-n junction across the crystal, a tiny, coherent, continuous beam of invisible infrared light. (G.E., substituting phosphorus for some of the arsenic, also got it to emit in the visible red.) As this was going to press, I.B.M. announced another semiconductor in the infrared—indium phosphide.

The semiconductor's beam is still very low powered—about a tenth of a watt—and is about as coherent as that from a ruby laser, but much less narrow and coherent than that from a gas. And it works well only in the freezing cold of liquid nitrogen. But it is the most efficient laser so far. Where most other lasers convert only a small fraction of the light or energy pumped into them into coherent light—for an efficiency of only about 1 to 2 percent—gallium arsenide converts most of the injected electricity into light for an efficiency of 20 to 50 percent. And since it works on an electric current, its output may be controlled more easily than that of other lasers. This ease and efficiency, plus cheapness and compactness, make the semiconductor laser an important addition in the building up of laser systems.

In December of last year, Hughes Aircraft was back with a first approach to another new family of lasers—a series of organic liquids, from benzene to toluene. Laser action was achieved in these liquids by using a high-powered pulsed ruby laser in place of a flash lamp. They then emitted, through an effect called "stimulated Raman-scattering," coherent light beams at various frequencies lower than the ruby-beam light source. By applying this method with other laser light sources, dozens of additional wavelengths may be opened to laser action and study.

Early this year, R.C.A. came up with the first plastic laser. Chelates or clawlike molecules containing europium, dispersed in a clear Lucite-type plastic—like chromium in ruby—act as the lasing medium. Pumped by flash lamp at liquid-nitrogen temperatures, the europium-plastic laser emits intense pulses in the visible red. Chelates incorporating other elements may lead to a large family of plastic lasers in the widest visible range, capable of being easily formed into rods, fibers, and sheets of any size or shape.

Gaps in the Spectrum

The first stage of development—exploring the range of possible laser materials—may now be drawing to a close. So far there are four broad family types: the solid light-pumped lasers, such as ruby or glass; the gaseous lasers, such as helium-neon or xenon; the solid injection or semiconductor lasers, mainly gallium arsenide; and the liquid or plastic lasers. A fifth type, yet to be achieved, though Ali Javan thinks it a good possibility, is the flame laser, in which coherent light may be generated by the pyrotechnic reaction of two chemicals brought together in a tube.

The reason for the scramble to find materials that will lase is that, unlike electronic devices, each laser emits light only at or near the natural frequency of its particular atomic structure. To get markedly different frequencies, the engineer must go to different materials. There is now a strong possibility, however, that present laser beams may be shifted up or down in frequency by special techniques. In 1961, Peter Franken and a group at the University of Michigan discovered that when a ruby laser's beam was passed through a quartz crystal, a small part of the emerging beam was doubled in frequency by the nonlinear character of quartz to yield a second harmonic wave in the ultraviolet. This technique has since been greatly extended by a group at Ford Motor Co., which used other nonlinear crystals and liquids to get not only more voluminous second harmonics, but also third harmonics. And the use of nonlinear materials has led to other important manipulations of light waves, which will be seen later on in this article. But more immediately, by this and other means, it may be possible to generate from present laser beams almost any frequency needed to fill gaps in the spectrum.

One of these gaps lies in the frequencies between the near infrared and microwaves, which is known as the far infrared. Another lies in all the frequencies from orange-yellow in the visible band on up through the invisible ultraviolet. The latter are important for possible special applications—for instance, lasers that emit beams in the visible blue-green are being avidly sought by the Navy, which thinks they will be particularly suitable for underwater transmission.

This is another reason for the development of many forms of lasers. Not only do the various blocks of frequencies seem to be aimed at specific applications, but the various types of lasers themselves tend to fall into functional groups. There is, for instance, the high-powered group led by ruby and glass, and the low-powered group led by gas and semiconductor lasers. Each of these has its own properties, advantages, and disadvantages that point the group toward specific applications.

Burning Holes in Diamonds

The lasers most likely to find immediate applications are the early, pulsed, solid-pumped variety, ruby and glass. This is because more work has been done on them; it is easier to get very high peak power in pulses than in continuous waves; and pulsed transmission, leaning heavily on microwave radar experience, is simpler to use. Most of the early stunts with lasers took advantage of these easily generated, intense, short pulses. The most famous one, performed jointly by M.I.T. and Raytheon Co. last summer, was to bounce and receive a coherent light pulse off the moon, through a telescope, from a six-inch ruby rod that emitted a beam so narrow that it circumscribed a cone of light less than two miles across on the moon. This is at least one hundred times narrower than the best radar beam. Nearly everyone has been demonstrating, at the drop of a hat, the intensity of such beams by burning holes in razor blades, diamonds, and other hard materials.

Meanwhile, the crystals and techniques have been intensively improved to get even narrower beams, more rapid pulses, and still higher powers. The peak power put out by a laser is measured in watts, while its energy or heat-producing ability is measured in joules—one joule equaling one watt for a second. Hughes Aircraft early developed a method in which emission was delayed and energies were allowed to build up within the ruby, then released in one giant pulse, for a thousandfold increase in peak power. By this means and others, the ruby's output was soon raised from a few kilowatts to megawatts. Meanwhile, the energies have also climbed—from less than one joule to about 350 joules in the ruby, and upwards of 1,000 joules in neodymium glass. Recently, Theodore Maiman, who left Hughes soon after he built the first laser and eventually formed his own company, Korad Corp., got a new ruby generator-amplifier up to a peak of 500 megawatts. Maiman is confident that this ruby system, which he expects to have on the market this summer, can eventually be driven up into the billion-watt range. Actually, there is no limit in sight to the powers obtainable from solid lasers; all that remain are engineering problems, chiefly in the dissipation of heat. These are still formidable.

The most obvious and immediate use for such powerful pulses is in an optical form of radar, a pulsed device. The laser's advantages are that its ultrafine radiation can pinpoint objects, define their range and velocities more rapidly and accurately than ordinary radar, and the size of antennae and other apparatus can be dramatically reduced. Laser antennae may measure only a few inches. Little over six months after the first laser, Hughes incorporated it in the first, crude, experimental optical radar system, which it called Colidar. This Hughes has now refined down to a forty-five-pound, gunlike range finder and backpack, requiring no motors. It is accurate within five yards on a target seven to fifteen miles away. R.C.A. is producing nine somewhat similar battlefield range finders for the Army, and Raytheon, Sperry, and others have working models.

This spring a more complex optical radar built by G.E. was scheduled to start experimental tracking of NASA's S–66 beacon satellite, orbiting over the poles at 600 miles up. Optical radar promises to determine orbits and trajectories faster and more precisely than previous methods. In space itself, optical radar has an even more promising role, as a highly accurate guidance, control, and range-finding instrument in satellites and spacecraft, and as an instrument to reconnoiter and map, down to the finest detail thus far obtainable, such celestial bodies as the moon.

The next most immediate use for these heavy pulses is in the welding and cutting of metals or other materials. This should become a commercial possibility within a year. Dozens of companies are experimenting—mainly with rugged ruby lasers—and many of the most active firms are already offering packaged laser units. The laser's forte is that its beam can be concentrated to a fine point, with an electric force of up to 10 million volts per centimeter, in a flash ten billionths of a second long or less—so fast and hot that unwanted side reactions have no time to take place. In addition, beams from compact, hand-held units can cut or weld objects through glass or in inaccessible places.

The main problem in welding has been to develop shaped pulses and controls so that the beams do not punch straight through materials, but this is now being solved. Glass lasers may have an edge here because they can be so easily formed to any configuration and mode of operation. The first uses will probably be in the electronics industry itself, for micromachining and precise welding of very thin, exotic metals. Here the laser will compete strongly with electron-beam welding, which can be done only in a vacuum. For larger-scale uses, such as in the aerospace industry, the laser's ability to compete against present welding methods will depend on how much its efficiency can be raised; it is still low in terms of energy consumption. Here, too, the glass laser has an edge on ruby because it starts from a higher level of efficiency.

Translating Information into Light

The use of lasers in communications is at a somewhat more rudimentary stage. Bell Labs, M.I.T., General Telephone, R.C.A., and others have demonstrated in the laboratory the feasibility of putting voices, images, and other intelligence on light beams, and these experiments are rapidly being extended. Most of this activity turns now upon the gas lasers, for communications do not need the extremely high peak powers put out by ruby and glass, but rather require extremely sharp, stable, continuous beams—not pulses. Bell Labs, which has led in gas-laser development, has refined the first, long, cranky fluorescing tubes, difficult to keep in adjustment, down to pencil-thin tubes only a few inches long, rugged and exceedingly stable. Though some more power is needed, the main beam transmitter is now here in one form at least. But many problems still remain in developing and putting together all the associated components needed to make such a transmitter work in a communication system.

For a laser beam to carry intelligence, it must first be varied or modulated in some way to take on the coded pattern of information being transmitted. Then, at the receiver, it must be detected, amplified, converted, and demodulated to bring the information back into useful form. All this is now easily done in radio circuitry. The vacuum-tube transmitter is electrically modulated to vary either the amplitude (power) or frequency of its carrier wave, and at the receiver the job is done by the well-known superheterodyne circuit. But light beams present quite different problems and cannot yet be so readily or reliably modulated. (The semiconductor laser can be electrically modulated simply by varying the current injected into it, but it is still much too low powered and its beam too spread out.)

Many schemes for modulating lasers are boiling in development. One that is being actively investigated is to modulate the beam as it leaves the laser by passing it through a nonlinear crystal of KDP (potassium dihydrogen phosphate) or certain organic liquids. These materials have the peculiar property of varying their polarization as signals (from a microphone or television camera) are put through them, thus varying the phase frequency or amplitude of the laser carrier beam. A more direct method is to use a magnetic field to modulate the laser crystal itself. R.C.A. has recently announced a successful device of this kind.

On the receiver problem, considerable activity is going into the development of phototubes, photomultipliers, photodiodes, and other light-detecting, amplifying, and demodulating devices to convert the modulated light beam into microwaves or electrical current. One experimental technique, again employing nonlinear crystals, promises a receiver circuit that will do for light what the superheterodyne has done for radio. Two light waves are simultaneously passed through a nonlinear material, such as KDP, where they are mixed or "beat" to yield a single wave that is the sum or difference of the two input frequencies. In effect, this allows the frequency of an incoming modulated light wave to be translated down into microwaves, where it can then be handled by regular electronic means. On all these devices much work still needs to be done, and no one yet knows for certain what their final configurations will be, but Bell Labs is convinced by their rapid development that a working communication system is now within sight.

Pipelines for Light Beams

The first uses of such a system will undoubtedly be in space. The laser, like so much new, uprushing technology, seems to be made ideally for the exploration of space. There a continuous laser beam, unhindered by air, can reach out to calculated distances in the billion-mile range—for interplanetary communication, for better communication between spacecraft, satellites, and between spacecraft and earth, particularly on re-entry. Laser beams, unlike radio waves, can go through the hot ionized gases or plasmas surrounding spacecraft that black out communications at this critical juncture.

Closer to earth, laser beams offer the ideal, high-capacity links between communication satellites, particularly of the high-altitude, synchronous variety. And still closer in, laser beams could provide new, highly secure military communications between aircraft, and between air and ground, even though they would be washed out at times by bad weather. No one outside the beam's narrow cone of operation—which may be only several yards across at 1,000 miles—could break in to eavesdrop or jam signals.

On the earth itself, weather is the big obstacle to the laser's use in full-time commercial communications. But ways may be found to get around this limitation. Bell Labs already has been experimentally sending light beams through long pipes. And International Telephone & Telegraph Co., which has been making similar studies, calculates that a 2-watt gas-laser beam (still to be developed) could travel sixty-mile lengths of such a pipeline before needing a boost and refocusing. The pipe would have to be evacuated or filled with an inert gas, such as nitrogen, to keep out condensation; and corners would have to be turned by mirror arrangements, which earth tremors could throw out of adjustment. But these problems are not much more difficult or fantastic than those solved in Bell's new transatlantic underwater telephone cables.

Actually, the limitations upon developing a laser communication system within a very few years are not so much technical as economic. The laser beam is essentially a great trunk-line carrier of extraordinary capacity, and the traffic is not yet big enough to make use of it. However, with the enormous growth of communications predicted by 1970, on which the whole satellite communication scheme is based, the laser's great additional bandwidths will be needed and will be ready.

Chemicals, Computers, and "Death Rays"

Other more speculative laser applications stretch out into the future. One that is getting some attention from major chemical companies is the use of laser beams to effect a new range of highly controlled chemical reactions. By using intense, coherent light of a precise frequency, some reactions may be selectively initiated, or single molecular bonds may be broken or welded to create entirely new materials. No one has yet achieved this. And the latter type of reaction is dependent upon finding lasers in the ultraviolet range—the extremely short waves necessary to intervene accurately in tiny molecular affairs. So far there have been only a few, unconfirmed reports of lasers emitting in the ultra-violet. But the laser as a tool in chemical production is a distinct possibility, for it can transmit very precise high energies, which is what makes chemical reactions go. Coherent light beams may also fit readily and precisely into other industrial processes and control systems.

Several laser applications in computers have been proposed. The first is simply to use the beam's huge information-carrying capacity as a swift, private communication link between computers—e.g., to transfer whole memory stores from one to another—and between data-control and information-retrieval centers. This is the evolutionary use of lasers that currently interests I.B.M. the most. Another, more speculative approach is to use light beams between units within computers to speed up the transfer of information, cut time between computations, and eliminate wiring, perhaps the single biggest problem in growingly complex computers. But since the light will probably have to be conducted around through glass-fiber optics, the system might grow as complex in the end as any wiring.

Farthest out of the computer ideas is a wholly optical computer that would be built on an entirely different principle from the conventional electronic type. At the input of such a computer, information-carrying light beams would trigger laser actions in networks of long glass or plastic-fiber optics, which would do the actual computations. Such fibers act a good deal like nerve fibers in their transmission of pulses, and the whole scheme is based upon simulating the action of neurons in the brain and nervous system to carry out data processing at the fantastic speed of light. R.C.A., which showed in theory that a complete computer logic might be built of such "neuristor" fibers, has a contract from Rome Air Development Center to attempt to put it in some tangible form. No one, including R.C.A., knows whether it will work. Or, if it works, whether its speed and logic will give it sufficient advantage over present electronic computers. But if it really works, the optical computer will move closer than any other man-made device to the lightning processes of learning and even of thought.

On the bare fringe of the possible is the idea that has gen-erated the most public speculation: the use of lasers as a kind of "death ray," incendiary beam, or radiation weapon to destroy missiles at long range. Military attention is warranted even if there is a 1 percent possibility—and it is probably no more than that—of finding such a defense against weapons for which no really effective defense is yet in sight. There is no doubt that a laser beam is already energetic enough to be destructive and dangerous at short range. At about 1,000 joules, the highest energy so far reported, a single pulse, concentrated by lenses, could set wood, paper, and other easily flammable materials ablaze at a distance of about two miles. Conceivably there may be some military uses for this more modest kind of incendiarism. But this is still far short of the fantastically high concentrations of energy needed to knock out missiles 500 to 1,000 miles up.

Scientists who are not working on the program freely speculate on the difficulties. To get enough energy out there from the earth to destroy a missile would require upwards of 10 billion joules, with banks of capacitors as big as a large building to store and supply the energy. More energy would be needed to get the beam to burn its way through the atmosphere than to melt a missile. Less energy would be required if the beam were focused to a small spot, simply to incapacitate or divert the missile. But this would still leave the problem of accurate aiming. The precise position of the missile at a given moment would have to be known, and someone would have to be out there holding a focusing lens close enough to make it effective. Alternatively, the beam might be generated from a satellite above the atmosphere; this would require still less energy. But energy-storage facilities would still be an extremely heavy burden for any foreseeable satellite. And this is to say nothing of tremendous heat generation in the laser and other problems. Unless a way can be found around such difficulties—and not everything is yet known about manipulating coherent light—a laser anti-missile weapon will remain in the realm of Buck Rogers.

A Look inside the Living Cell

Much greater and more promising new powers are likely to come out of the use of lasers in basic scientific research. This aspect is usually overlooked by the practical-minded because such discoveries as may turn up here cannot even be conceived as yet. Light is one of the great constants of the universe, and it has always played a large role in all its forms—visible, infrared, and ultraviolet—in the instruments of science and technology. With the laser's ability to manipulate light at precise frequencies, the whole science of optics is suddenly in a high state of rejuvenation. And similar effects are rippling through the study of materials, astronomy, chemistry, biology, physics, and other sciences.

Ali Javan, the laser pioneer, says: "You punch a hole in a diamond or razor blade—so what? . . . Let's wake up and do some physics. . . . We can now measure length to an accuracy of one part in 10 trillion to 100 trillion by detecting a tiny shift in the light's frequency traveling the distance of a meter. . . . We can see a variation in length that's less than the nucleus of an atom! . . . Now if we could measure time as well as length in optical frequencies, by closing the gap in the far infrared, we could tie time, length, and mass together as one." Even now it is possible to check more accurately various aspects of relativity. In addition, the laser beam's energy may be focused down to so small a spot, about one micron in diameter, that with it scientists will be able to observe what is going on within a living cell, measure its constituents, or pick off a single protein molecule in a chain for biological experimentation.

Already the gas laser's very fine beam is revolutionizing spectroscopy, which no longer requires diffraction gratings to get even higher precisions than ever before. It is entering into interferometry, microscopy, and very high speed photography. It offers the first precise instrument for penetrating, measuring—and perhaps even generating—high-temperature plasmas, the key to controlled thermonuclear power and other advanced power technology. It has been experimentally built into an optical gyroscope, by Sperry Rand Corp., operating entirely on revolving light beams, which determines position to much greater accuracy than mechanical gyros. And the ruby laser has been developed into a surgical instrument. It was first used in 1961 by a Columbia University and American Optical team to burn a tumor out of a human eye. It is now being developed by various groups into an instrument for rapidly and cleanly "welding" detached retinas. And the development of long, thin fiber lasers opens the prospect of using them through body orifices for very precise microsurgery.

Into the Future on a Light Beam

Meanwhile, the laser rushes forward in industrial development. The alacrity with which the electronics industry picked it up has put the U.S. clearly ahead, where it is likely to stay, along with the major companies—such as Bell Labs, Hughes, R.C.A., G.E., I.B.M., American Optical, Westinghouse, Raytheon—that leaped in first. Many smaller specialized companies have sprung up, in the pattern of the day, to carry the laser energetically forward. Among them are Technical Research Group, Inc. (military systems specialist), Perkin-Elmer Corp. (scientific-control instruments), Spectra-Physics, Inc. (advanced gas lasers), Lear Siegler, Inc. (laser systems), and Maiman's Korad Corp. (recently acquired as a subsidiary by Union Carbide Corp.).

In circles intimate with electronics there is no doubt about the laser's future. For nearly a century, on one instrument after another, men have been climbing the electromagnetic spectrum. As each level of frequencies was opened, new services rushed in to fill them, so that there has been a continuous effort to push upward in frequencies for more space and more channels. The same pressures are at work even more insistently today. And the laser opens to settlement the greatest swath of frequencies so far.

Stimulated by a discovery in basic science, du Pont needed ten years of product and process development to create the new plastic—Delrin. It also required $42 million and some daring decisions by management. Here is the exciting story of how du Pont develops "Better things for better living . . . through chemistry."

Delrin: du Pont's Challenge to Metals*

As the summer began, process engineers of E. I. du Pont de Nemours & Co. were pushing themselves to tune up a novel addition to the company's complex of plants at Parkersburg, West Virginia. This highly automatic unit is to produce a novel, versatile engineering plastic

by Herbert Solow

called Delrin. Made more than 50 per cent of oxygen, it is chemically by far the airiest stuff ever proposed for applications that specify real strength. Delrin's oxygen is embodied in a giant molecule of formaldehyde that has been created by du Pont scientists.

Formaldehyde, a common, simple, organic compound, is sensationally active; it is always trying to mate with something else or to engender something new out of itself. The griefs of start-up that attend any new large-scale process are multiplied when formaldehyde is in the pipes. Clogging in those pipes, discoloration of the normally whitish product, and other frustrations were hampering the engineers in their race. Since du Pont had put into the new venture a total of $42 million, including $15 million for

* Vol. 60, August 1959, pp. 116–119, 160–164.

the Parkersburg plant, which can produce about 15 million pounds annually, without getting a penny back, the prospect of a delay in the first commercial production of Delrin was dismaying.

Delrin need only approximate its advance billing as a competitor of earlier plastics, wood, glass, ceramics, hard rubber, and, above all, metals, to produce important changes in a whole range of industries. About three-quarters of the applications that du Pont is now promoting for Delrin would be competitive with metals. Metals are already being pressed by earlier plastics to some extent, but Delrin may be the first man-made substance to challenge them in applications that require the whole armamentarium of metallurgical properties—strength, toughness, dimensional stability, and so on—or at least a goodly number of them together.

Delrin will appear in some consumer goods of the hardest kind, but it will probably be more widely used in industry, most interestingly for mechanical parts. End uses immediately envisioned include gears, cams, bearings, bushings, and springs, as well as hardware, containers, and fittings for all sorts of appliances, from refrigerators to washing machines. Thus Delrin may finally kill the once widespread notion that a plastic product is primarily a cheap second-best to something else, soon to break and be discarded.

And its challenge, if du Pont's top management is not way off base, will be more than technical, for the historic price trend of metals, though erratic, has been generally upward, while that of plastics has been steadily downward. Consequently, Delrin embodies rich commercial promise.

Radicalism in Wilmington

Bringing Delrin to market required daring. It necessitated decisions that were radical even for du Pont. Increments of big money had to be invested over a decade of wearisome development work. Recurrent technical surprises and setbacks had to be overcome. There has been nothing comparable in the company's one hundred and fifty-seven years of chemical operations except the pre-commercial commitment of $60 million for Orlon. The development of nylon, for example, took only four years and

$27 million. And nylon may have been a smarter bet than Orlon has thus far proved to be. It remains to be seen whether, in terms of profits, Delrin is another Orlon or another nylon. Whatever the outcome, it has already been an exciting gamble. Some highlights:

• Starting in 1948, a venture into truly basic science: the first extensive study of highly purified monomeric formaldehyde (the simple molecule), which for a century had largely evaded chemical sleuths, plus an imaginative grasp of the possible practical implications of this basic work.

• One of the boldest decisions in the history of the chemical industry: to leap in 1952 from a level of five investigators to sixty at an average annual cost of close to $2 million for what turned out to be an additional seven years of effort.

• A direct scaling up from bench testing of the process to a full-sized plant. A small, makeshift "semi-works" at Belle, West Virginia, was inadequate for piloting a novel, fussy process, but it did, in du Pont lingo, "horse out" some product for field testing at a date earlier than would have been possible for a pilot plant.

• An intensive market-development program, carried out with the help of some 250 corporations, which gave Delrin the most elaborate pre-commercial testing any new plastic has ever had. It was partly the lack of a comparable program that resulted in some confused and expensive drifting for linear polyethylene after it was introduced in commercial quantities in 1957. Delrin will enter the market with well-documented fabrication and performance specifications.

Already customers representing many U.S. industries are pressing for supplies, while would-be foreign licensees of the basic chemical process are making eager inquiries at Wilmington. For automotive parts alone, under the hood and elsewhere, du Pont hopes within five years to sell about two pounds per U.S. car. To reach this goal should not be hard, since the average car now contains about 120 pounds of die castings made from aluminum and zinc, major targets for Delrin competition.

General Motors has been studying Delrin seriously ever since January, 1957, when it sent thirty-five engineers to du Pont's Sales

Service Laboratory at Chestnut Run, Delaware. G.M. may put some Delrin parts into its cars next year, and Ford, Chrysler, and American Motors also are considering early adoption. Considering the Detroit multiplier, two pounds per car would be a sizable business in itself. In brief, quite apart from any metals shortage that war or other political disturbances might produce, Delrin seems sure to go far. Du Pont certainly thinks so. Even as the Parkersburg crew extended itself to tune up, Wilmington was considering adding some equipment to the plant in order to double capacity.

A Triumph with a Difference

If du Pont does as well with Delrin as it hopes to, it will have a new kind of triumph. A century and a half ago it won leadership of the U.S. explosives industry with its black powder. A generation ago it won leadership of the manmade-fibers industry with nylon. In between those triumphs it had others of comparable moment—e.g., moistureproof cellophane, which revolutionized packaging, and Duco lacquer, which revolutionized car-body finishing. But du Pont's plastics men have never enjoyed the prestige that has, from time to time, marked the men in explosives, film, and fibers, though du Pont has, of course, made money with a variety of plastics.

To understand why Delrin may win a new, prestigious leadership role for its plastics men, as well as profits, it is necessary to know something of the new material's particular nature. To chemists Delrin is superpolyoxymethylene. Du Pont's generic name for it is "acetal resin," a reference to its oxygen-carbon-oxygen linkage, typical of acetals. Delrin is one of many possible polymers (giant molecules) of formaldehyde. An opaque, whitish solid, it will be marketed in the form of tiny pellets that the company calls a powder. Delrin weighs less than any die-casting alloy (1.42 specific gravity as against 8.5 for brass, 1.81 for magnesium). Like a metal, the new polymer has a well-defined melting point (347° F.) and high crystallinity. It is one of a young group of plastics whose crystallinity is "controlled." The crystallinity is partially built into these plastics by the ingenious chemists who produce the polymer, rather than being largely inherent, as in metals.

100,000 Miles at 110 mph

Delrin does not have one or two sensational properties that would make it salable at almost any price for a few special uses. Instead it boasts a remarkable battery of properties that may enable it, at the right price, to fight its way into many applications. Its tensile strength, dimensional stability, and fatigue endurance are high. Hard to bend, when bent it recovers like spring steel. It is among the most solvent-resistant of organic compounds. It resists abrasion better than some metals. Its friction coefficient is not only very low but also constant for starting and operating motion. Because electrically it is a nonconductor, circuits can be "printed" on it. Despite its formaldehyde origin, it is odorless, tasteless, and nontoxic, and it is pleasant and smooth to the touch.

Many Delrin parts have survived two or three years of testing in diverse environments (e.g., air, water, and various solvents), even at high temperatures. Here are some performance records:

• A Delrin speedometer shaft ran against a steel gear for the equivalent of 100,000 miles at 110 mph with practically no wear.

•Aerosol bottles of Delrin under pressures thirteen times greater than normal were stored at room temperature for over two years, others at 130° F. for three months, and the contents remained fully dischargeable.

• Water at 150° F. was run continuously for three months through a Delrin shower head with so little wear as to suggest a twenty-year service life.

• Delrin gears in a standard household food mixer stirred a bowl of heavy grease for 700 consecutive hours, showed no measurable wear even after the motor burned out.

Delrin is a thermoplastic like nylon or polyethylene, rather than a thermoset like the phenolics. Any fabricator of a thermoset must use several components to create his resin by chemical action during fabrication, and after that he cannot return to the original state of his material. But the thermoplastic fabricator merely heats, shapes, and cools the resin. If he wants to, he can remelt the product and refabricate it. Like other thermoplastics, Delrin acetal resin can be injection- or blow-molded or extruded in almost any shape, and machined to close tolerances on standard equipment. Parts made of Delrin can be joined by mechanical fasteners, including self-tapping screws, or by a variety of welding techniques, or they can be snap-fitted. The resin can be extruded as a coating of almost any thickness onto film, paper, or fabric, which can then be cut or folded. It can be textured, integrally colored, painted, or metal-coated.

Poor Man's Metal?

At the outset Delrin will sell for 95 cents a pound in truckload lots, three to seven times higher, in other words, than such common metals as copper, zinc, and aluminum. Nor is the cost of molding Delrin much lower than the cost of casting metals from dies. But when the relative weight-volume ratios are taken into account, the price advantage of metals tends to diminish. Moreover, a molded Delrin product is close to being a finished part, while die-cast metal parts require substantial finishing—anything from flash removal, facing, reaming, and tapping up to chrome plating and complex machining with jigs or fixtures. It is this that makes Delrin competitive. For example: Even allowing for differences in the ratios of weight to volume, Delrin resin costs twice as much as zinc. But, assuming a production run of at least 50,000 units, forming and finishing costs may add only 100 per cent with Delrin, as against 200 to 400 per cent when zinc is used. Delrin's advantage over brass is even greater. It can also compete with steel in some applications. Union Chain & Manufacturing Co. of Sandusky, Ohio, will substitute Delrin for stainless-steel and carbon-steel plates in brewery and food-processing conveyers that must encounter hot water and detergents. Its lighter weight and superior bearing surface give it three times the service life of steel—at a third to half the cost.

Delrin is not simply a poor man's metal. It promises success in applications that, price aside, defy metal. Because of fabrication problems, many metal gears are sturdier than need be for service. Delrin gears could help to miniaturize whole assemblies. Because

Delrin is highly resistant to corrosion, it is more successful than metals in aerosol containers. Again, in long runs of a decorative application, Delrin tooling is likely to be less subject to minute cracking or dimensional change than dies for metal casting.

There are other advantages over metal. Delrin can be constantly in a salt-water environment without ill effect. One fabricator that is eagerly awaiting the resin is Zebco Co. of Tulsa, Oklahoma, world's largest maker of closed-face spinning reels for fishermen. Delrin parts will give the Zebco reel new durability, even in the hands of the careless. Each reel will use one-third of a pound of Delrin, and the estimated market potential is 35 million U.S. anglers.

The elimination of considerable subassembly work is a major reason for a shift to Delrin by James Kilburg, San Mateo, California, manufacturer of an automatic device for dialing telephone numbers that is offered to subscribers by Bell and other telephone systems. When designing with Delrin, Kilburg can replace fifty-nine metal parts by twelve, all produced in a single "shot" in a twelve-cavity mold. Also, by tossing a dye into the boiling water used to relieve stress in molded parts, he can color-code his parts and thus employ less skilled labor for assembly and wiring.

Thus Delrin will open markets because of its particular properties and fabricating advantages. All told, formaldehyde seems ready to assume an industrial importance that it never had in the century that has elapsed since some of the resinous polymers startled a Russian organic chemist, academician Alexander Mikhailovitch Butlerov, by appearing spontaneously in his laboratory vessels as he tried to study the protean monomer. In a sense, the story of Delrin acetal resin began then.

Butlerov's polymers, low in molecular weight, melted at 302° F. and were soluble in dilute acids and bases. They were puzzling and nobody showed much interest in them for a long time. In the 1920's a German chemist, Nobel prizeman Herman Staudinger, began to study formaldehyde in the course of working out his polymer or macromolecule theory. Polymers spontaneously formed in his laboratory vessels when he dissolved monomeric formaldehyde in ether, and he concluded that they were long chains rather than rings, the structures that most contemporary theorists favored. But Staudinger's formaldehyde polymers were unstable and he concluded that they could have no practical use.

And Incidentally—Nylon

While Staudinger was at work, du Pont was embarking on its celebrated program of basic scientific research. In 1929, as part of this program, one of Wilmington's great chemists, Wallace H. Carothers, began research that established the Staudinger theory beyond serious challenge. And in 1935 he "incidentally" discovered the polymer now known as nylon.

Not until late in 1947, however, did there appear on the project list of du Pont's Chemical Department (now known as Central Research) a proposal to study the properties of monomeric formaldehyde. Of course du Pont, being in the business of money-making rather than monomer studying, was entertaining a normal, if remote, hope that such a study might eventually pay off. But at the time nothing could have seemed more academic. For that very reason, however, the project appealed strongly to one of the department's scientists, Archie E. Barkdoll Jr., then thirty-two years old. He had come to du Pont in 1942, soon after taking his Ph.D. at Harvard. Here was a chance to do what he had always wanted to do—some pure organic-chemistry research. In this case it meant studying a substance so little known that no one could give him even a small sample to start off with.

First Barkdoll had to purify the monomer, which happens to be a highly reactive gas, in quantities adequate for study. To do this he had to liquefy it by passing it through a series of cold traps, kept at temperatures below −19° C. He got a pure monomer, which, however, now and then spontaneously polymerized. The polymer had interesting properties—strength, resilience, and resistance to solvents. From this information, and from what he incidentally learned about formaldehyde polymerization factors, the company was to benefit after Barkdoll ended his project in June, 1949.

Within a few months Central Research set up a new project on formaldehyde. This one was undertaken by Robert N. MacDonald, a Ph.D. from Yale, then thirty-three, under the sponsorship of (that is, at the expense of) the Polychemicals Department. Polychemicals, one of du Pont's major industrial subdivisions, was a newly formed union of the old, stagnant Plastics Department and the Ammonia Department, learned in the lore of high-pressure chemical processes, including those for conventional polyethylene. Top management was hoping that the new unit would go somewhere in plastics, and Emil D. Ries, its general manager, was anxious to start. By leaving control of the new and still quite basic project to Central Research, Polychemicals buffered MacDonald against overeager promoters; by financing MacDonald, Polychemicals sought to accelerate practical application. (This kind of dual-purpose arrangement is characteristic of du Pont.)

With Barkdoll's findings to give him a start, MacDonald set out to develop a controlled method of producing a tougher, more stable formaldehyde polymer. He introduced dry, gaseous formaldehyde rapidly and continuously into an agitated reaction medium such as heptane, which is chemically inert to formaldehyde, in the presence of such a catalyst as triphenylphosphine. The resulting fluffy, white polymers were insoluble in the medium, and MacDonald was able to draw them away as rapidly as they formed. And MacDonald's polyformaldehyde was thermally more stable than any produced by prior art.

What Dr. Williams Smelled

Polychemicals now backed up MacDonald with four departmental chemists. Polyformaldehyde, however, remained just one of half a dozen plastics possibilities under investigation by Polychemicals, until the department got some fatherly advice in 1952 from a company official assigned to dispense precisely that. This was Roger Williams, then a vice president and member of the executive committee with the portfolio of company-wide research adviser. Dr. Williams, who had managed du Pont's wartime atomic effort, including the Hanford plutonium works, was also a former Ammonia Department research chief who could talk to the Polychemicals research men bluntly. Reviewing their program and prospects, he smelled not only formaldehyde in the polymers produced by MacDonald, but also a combination of unusual promise;

- The stuff had good mechanical properties.

• It could be made from a material, methanol, that du Pont was already producing cheaply.

• It was novel and might therefore do jobs beyond the range of plastics developed from traditional materials.

• It was in an area that was patent-free as far as processing was concerned, and, far more important, basic composition of the product.

The End of Monkeying

Dr. Williams' advice was to "quit monkeying with a lot of things" and concentrate on formaldehyde polymers. Thereupon, late in 1952, Polychemicals put sixty men to work—chemists, process engineers, product-development men, etc.—with about $1 million budgeted to support them for six months. There are still about sixty at it, even as the Delrin plant in Parkersburg is being tuned up, though the mixture of skills in the team has been repeatedly altered.

The problems seemed infinite, and of infinite variety. At first the Polychemicals team could produce only a few grams of Delrin a day. These they used for property tests. Then the smell of formaldehyde—gaseous emanation from polymers that were still somewhat unstable—was tackled.

The material had to be stabilized at temperatures adequate for many industrial uses. Moreover, it had to be made stable at even higher temperatures, so that it could be fabricated under normal commercial conditions. When this was achieved, there was still the problem of discoloration, the product often being light brown instead of white.

Anybody with a new plastic tries it out in combs because they constitute a nice test of molding characteristics, and eventually some Delrin combs were made, tested, and found good. Some machine gears made of Delrin showed up well, too. But while sales engineers were canvassing U.S. industry for opinions on Delrin, moods on the Polychemicals team varied widely. A given application would look promising one day, seem impossible the next, come back strongly on the third, as problems were posed, struggled with, finally solved.

Selling the Salesmen

Late in 1956, Jack Manning, an experienced du Pont salesman, became product manager for Delrin. Now it was up to him to sell the new idea to all of du Pont's plastics salesmen, each of whom handles the company's full plastics line. Soon afterward, Polychemicals' Sales Service Laboratory at Chestnut Run near Wilmington began the education of potential customers in Delrin fabrication methods and engineering design. Delrin resin was given to 250 companies for fabricating and in-service testing in 500 different applications. These companies ranged from small ones like Gries Reproducer Corp. of New Rochelle, New York, which has unique automatic molding equipment, to giants like General Electric.

Meanwhile Robert Hershey, who early in 1956 had succeeded Emil Ries as head of Polychemicals, had asked du Pont's Engineering Department for a preliminary estimate of the investment that would be required for a production plant. With this and an estimate of other major cost factors in hand, he asked du Pont's Executive Committee for what Wilmington calls a "Part I authorization"—that is, permission to spend money on a firm estimate and engineering design for a plant. He got it on November 2, 1956, three days after the Delrin patent was granted, whereupon du Pont announced that it was preparing to manufacture the new plastic.

Now Engineering went to work under forced draft, the Parkersburg site was chosen, and many other details were brought into line. On October 21, 1957, du Pont's Finance Committee granted Hershey's request for "Part II," the money with which to build the plant. Ground was broken at Parkersburg next morning.

The trade had thus far been puzzled by Polychemicals' failure to produce important news during its seven years of activity. Du Pont had passed up the opportunity to get into linear polyethylene, to which the first U.S. producer, Phillips Petroleum, committed itself in 1955. Today eight U.S. companies are making linear polyethylene, but few have used their full productive capacity. Currently du Pont is building a plant for a specialized grade of linear polyethylene, after having made its usual detailed market studies. But the breaking of ground at Parkersburg in 1957 made the trade sit up and take notice.

No one at du Pont regards Delrin as a "miracle" material. The patent covers the use of the new product as a fiber or a film, and tests have shown it to be promising as an industrial fiber (for belting, bagging, etc.), but the du Pont departments concerned admit no more than an experimental interest.

Mustard Yes, Coffee No

Even as a plastic, Delrin has limitations. It is not going to put out of the running all the metals-replacement applications so far achieved by other plastics. Delrin products cannot be prudently used with strong acids or strong alkalies. Though Delrin is not affected by mustard, ketchup, or most foods, it is stained by very hot coffee. It cannot be easily cemented. It is subject, as are most plastics, to discoloration by ultraviolet rays. Consequently it has limited outdoor durability, except when darkened by an admixture of carbon black, or painted or otherwise made weather-resistant—at a price. It takes printing no better than molded polyethylene, which is not too well. In gaskets for spark plugs, where heats of over 400° F. are encountered, it has been a total flop. Though it burns slowly in contact with flame, it is not self-extinguishing, as nylon resin is. While it can be used for industrial pipe, a growing field for plastics, its ability to compete for flexible-pipe application with cheaper resins is dubious. It is still uncertain whether Delrin will be practical for very large shapes; the largest thus far successfully fabricated and tested is a garbage-can liner.

A Bane in the House?

Delrin could be a bane to another du Pont product. This is Zytel, also a highly crystalline, strong plastic made from nylon's expensive raw materials, hexamethylenediamine and adipic acid. Zytel is an excellent plastic for cable jacketing and mechanical and other parts, and du Pont was doing a thriving business with it at the time it began to spend important money to create Delrin.

At first, Wilmington talk about Delrin was that it might be "a poor man's nylon." But taking weight-volume ratios into account,

Delrin is to come on the market at .02 cents more per pound than the current price of Zytel. Since Delrin has greater dimensional stability, and greater water- and solvent-resistance than Zytel, it might, in fact, be salable for some applications at a higher price. On the other hand, Zytel has more impact strength, abrasion resistance, toughness, and resilience than Delrin, so that for other applications it should be able to command a better price. The price of Delrin can easily progress in the pattern of Zytel, which has dropped 25 per cent since 1955, thanks to technological progress and expanded production of nylon resins by du Pont and its competitors. Moreover, du Pont can pretty much dictate Delrin's price provided it stays within range of the prices of the common metals that are its main competitive targets, and so long as du Pont has exclusive proprietorship of Delrin. Its U.S. patent will expire in 1973, but du Pont, in the light of Antitrust Division policy, will probably license a competitor even earlier.[1]

Delrin may in the end prove to have more significant advantages over Zytel than vice versa. But in any case, this must have been clear to du Pont long ago: were Zytel to be protected against Delrin by price, Delrin sales volume would be restricted, and the recouping of the $42-million investment would be delayed; on the other hand, were Delrin's price set materially below Zytel's, the better to compete with metals, it might seriously cramp Zytel before new markets could be developed for the older product.

Did it make any sense for Zytel's proprietor to develop Delrin at all? Well, the man who had to reckon most seriously with the problem of a Zytel-Delrin battle was Hershey, who formulated Polychemicals' policy on the matter. "I never had any doubt," he says. "If anybody was going to knock one of our products out of the market, we wanted to be the one to do it, and not leave it to our competitors."

To be sure, there are always surprises when new materials come on the market. Orlon, for example, has had its big development in sweaters instead of in awning fabric, which was thought to be a sure bet. Perhaps Zytel and Delrin will find largely sep-

---

[1] Badische Anilin of Germany has recently done some work on formaldehyde polymers, and it may be that some "prior art" argument has thus far prevented du Pont from getting a German patent.

arate markets. And perhaps the du Pont "stable" may do as well with Zytel-Delrin as an "entry" in plastics as it did with nylon-Dacron in fibers. So confident is du Pont of its plastic strategy that last year, with the Parkersburg plant abuilding and plans to produce linear polyethylene also under way, it decided in addition to expand Zytel capacity by 60 per cent.

The Strategy of Bigness

Having brought Delrin to the brink of the market, after 300 man-years of R. and D. effort, the Polychemicals Department has justified the 1949 reorganization that created it. It now faces an altered world, however. When announcing in May that Delrin would soon be available commercially, du Pont also announced that some traditional Polychemicals missions—e.g., the production of ammonia, urea, and methanol—have been transferred to a new department, which also has absorbed the old Grasselli Chemicals Department. The newcomer is the Industrial and Biochemicals Department (sulfuric acid, fertilizers, pesticides, etc., plus the Polychemicals transfers).

Now Polychemicals has "nothing" to do but produce and sell Delrin, Zytel, Teflon, Butacite, Alathon, and a few other items—and get busy on something that will win it new laurels in 1965 or thereabouts. It is doubtful, however, that Polychemicals will be able to produce a better example of the company's fundamental strategy than Delrin.

This strategy *Fortune* once defined (October, 1950) as follows: to "seek out fields where it can make a unique technical contribution," concentrating "on big jobs that call for long-range investigation and the willingness to risk heavy sums." It is this strategy, du Pont maintains, that justifies its bigness. In the face of the $42-million gamble on Delrin, it is not easy to disagree.

As new products are developed and accepted, new conditions are created in the market. For the first time in recent history, the nation's steel industry faces real competition from plastics, nonferrous metals, concrete, and imported steel products. As a result steel companies are developing new pricing policies, new marketing methods, new technology, and new products to meet the challenge of changing markets.

Steel: It's a Brand-New Industry*

by

Charles E. Silberman

The fact that steel production has declined since 1955 while the gross national product has been rising suggests that steel is no longer the bellwether of the whole economy that it once was considered to be. It does not necessarily mean that steel itself has become a declining industry. On the contrary, it is far too early to relegate steel to the industrial scrap heap. When the reasons for the decline since 1955 are analyzed, it appears that the industry was buffeted by a number of adverse economic trends that happened to coincide. In a more fundamental sense, steel has been the victim of the general slowdown in economic growth that has occurred since 1955. But the industry retains the potential for substantial growth. Indeed, if *Fortune*'s projections for the whole economy are realized—if the G.N.P., that is to say, expands to $750 billion by 1970—then steel production *could* rise to 158 million to 169 million ingot tons.

* Vol. 62, December 1960, pp. 123–127, 249–264.

But steel will never realize these projections if it merely sits back and waits for the rest of the economy to grow, for the fundamental assumption on which steel companies have conducted their business has now been shattered. Until very recently, as one critic puts it, steel firms have acted on the assumption "that there will always be a market for steel—that in the long run people will have to come buying steel." Their energies, consequently, were directed toward obtaining as large a share as possible of the available steel business—a market whose total size they regarded as given and in any case beyond their control.

This approach and the assumption underlying it have been made obsolete by the fact that steel, for the first time in its history, finds itself in serious competition across the whole spectrum of its markets. Steel production is being threatened by concrete, aluminum, and plastics—not to mention foreign steel. More important, perhaps, it is being threatened by the development of new engineering and design techniques that reduce the use of steel even in the absence of competing materials. Steel, in short, is now just one more material—though still the most important, by far—and the industry's central problem is how to capture as large a share as possible of the total market for materials of all sorts.

To do so requires a fundamental change in the industry's outlook—and a whole new conception of its relations to customers and to the economy. The industry must recognize, as Bay E. Estes, Jr., vice president for marketing of U.S. Steel, puts it, "that our customers owe no permanent loyalty to steel as a material. Their loyalty must be to the markets they serve if they are to succeed. They will use in their products whatever material serves their markets best."

And the industry is beginning to change; under the pressure of competition, steel companies are developing new price and wage policies, new marketing methods, and new approaches to research and development:

• After having raised the price of steel 90 per cent since 1947 —two and one half times as fast as industrial prices in general— steel companies are now trying to reduce the price of steel relative to other materials. Thus, they have hardened their attitude at the collective-bargaining table, and they failed to raise prices when the last labor contract was signed, for the first time in recent memory. Nor are they likely to raise prices in the foreseeable future, despite the recent railroad-freight increase and a wage increase.

• Steel companies are experimenting with a host of new marketing and selling techniques at the consumer as well as the industrial level, designed to create new markets for steel as well as to hold on to old ones. Example: a recent full-page ad in *Life* by U.S. Steel, telling all about "The Wonderful, Wacky World of Sleep," and designed to induce consumers to choose steel innerspring mattresses in preference to foam rubber.

• They are stepping up their comparatively laggard research and development activities in an effort to improve the technical properties of steel—for example, to impart more strength per pound and to reduce the metal's tendency to corrode—as well as to create new types of steel aimed at specific markets, e.g., colored stainless steel.

All told, U.S. Steel companies are making strategic decisions as momentous as any they have ever faced. Some of the decisions, while certainly not easy, are nonetheless dictated by the competitive situation in which they now find themselves—e.g., the decision to hold the price line. Other decisions which flow from this one, require painfully difficult choices between competing alternatives,—for example, whether to spend large sums for cost reduction now, in effect committing the company to present technology, or to stall for time in order to capitalize on a new and perhaps far superior technology that may be available in a few years. It is with the whole range of decisions now facing the industry that this article is concerned.

Consumption vs. Production

Before describing the new strategies in any detail, however, it is necessary to separate the short-run forces that have crippled steel production in recent years from the longer-run factors that may be at work. The first thing to note is the familiar fact that steel *production* has declined far more than steel *consumption*. Indeed, while production dropped 13 per cent between 1955 and 1960, consumption fell off only 2 per cent. There are two reasons for this discrepancy. The first is a swing from inventory accumulation to inventory liquidation by steel users, the second a sharp rise in imports, which eliminated the industry's substantial export surplus.

Of the two, the inventory change is by far the more important. In 1955, steel users bought four million "product tons"[1] more than they actually used, thus building up their own steel inventories by that amount; this year they consumed two million to three million tons more than they bought—the fourth year in a row of inventory reduction. This swing from accumulation to liquidation amounted to six million to seven million tons— enough to cause an 8,500,000 to 10-million-ton drop in ingot production between 1955 and 1960.

Fortunately, inventory liquidation is nearing its end. Steel users cannot keep cutting inventories indefinitely; sooner or later, production will have to move back up to the level of consumption. To be sure, steel economists have been predicting an early end to inventory liquidation for three months or more. But there *is* a limit to how low stocks can go without making production impossible; that limit is in sight, whether this month, next month, or six months from now. Steel inventories held by steel users and warehouses now come to the equivalent of only 11 million to 12 million product tons, compared to 14 million at the start of the year and 15 million at the lowest point during the 1958 recession.

The second reason production dropped more than consumption was the sharp rise in steel imports. In 1955 imports of finished steel came to only 1,100,000 tons, as against exports of 4,200,000. This year, however, imports will come to roughly 3,250,000 tons —about the same as exports. This shift from a large export surplus to a rough export-import balance meant the loss of roughly 3,100,000 tons of finished steel—the equivalent of 4,400,000 tons of ingot production.

---

[1] Since a lot of steel is "chewed up" in the finishing process, i.e., converting the raw ingots into sheet, plate, structural shapes, etc., one ton of finished steel —what steel economists call a "product ton"—represents the equivalent of 1.4 tons of ingot steel, the unit in which production is usually measured.

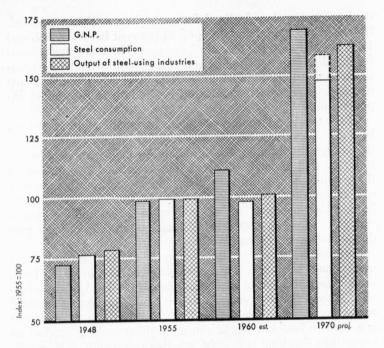

FIGURE 8. **New Factors in Steel Consumption.** There is no fixed relation between steel and the economy. Since 1929, steel consumption has been affected by the depression, World War II, the postwar shortages in 1947–50, and the Korean war in 1950–53. Surprisingly enough, however, *Fortune*'s index of steel consumption relative to G.N.P. was almost as high in 1955 (100) as it was in 1929 (103.5), despite the alleged shift from goods to services. But since 1955 steel consumption has dropped sharply relative to G.N.P.

The reasons for this latter change are shown in the chart above. Between 1955 and 1960, G.N.P. (lined bar) rose 12 percent in constant 1959 dollars. But output of the steel-using industries in the aggregate rose only 1 percent (crosshatched bar). Instead of rising, however, steel consumption (white bar) fell by 2 percent, indicating some net reduction in the use of steel per unit of production. In the preceding seven years, steel consumption had grown as fast as the output of the steel-using industries.

In the 1960s the economic environment will be more favorable to steel. On *Fortune*'s projections, output of steel-using industries will expand faster than the G.N.P. from here to 1970. How much

The basic cause of this change, of course, was the 1959 steel strike, though imports had started rising in 1958. While foreign competition will remain a problem for some time to come, the picture has been changing for the better this year. Imports were heavy during the first quarter, because of orders placed last year. But they have been declining ever since. In a few product lines, to be sure—e.g., barbed wire, concrete reinforcing bars, nails, and other "merchant products"—imports have clearly taken over a significant share of the market. For most product lines, however, foreign competition represents a potential more than an actual threat.

The 13 Per Cent Drop

This still leaves us with the problem of why steel *consumption* hasn't done any better; as we have seen, it has dropped 2 per cent since 1955. But meanwhile, G.N.P. was going up 12 per cent. Relative to G.N.P., therefore, steel consumption has fallen 13 per cent—a fact steel-company executives have tended to ignore in their frequent incantations of faith in their industry's growth prospects. This fall should, of course, be seen in perspective. Since 1929 steel consumption has been affected—one might say "distorted"—by depression, World War II, 1947–50 postwar shortages, and in 1950–53 by the Korean War. In a sense, therefore, 1955 was the first "normal" year since 1929. And it is significant that steel consumption was almost as high relative to G.N.P. in 1955 as in 1929. The ratio, that is to say, had slipped only 3.5 per cent in twenty-six years—a remarkable performance in view of all the talk about the supposed shift from goods to services.

Given this apparent long-term stability in the relation of consumption to G.N.P., there is all the more reason to ask why it has dropped so sharply since 1955, and whether the decline is likely

---

steel consumption expands, however, will depend on how steel firms meet the new competitive challenge. If they can prevent any further displacement, consumption could rise to an index of 158 by 1970. And if they can merely prevent any acceleration in the rate of displacement, consumption could rise to an index of 148. (Indexes of consumption and output of steel-using industries and steel inventory statistics from Alan Greenspan of Townsend-Greenspan & Co.)

to continue. To answer this question *Fortune* is using detailed analyses of steel consumption trends made for it by industrial economist Alan Greenspan of Townsend-Greenspan & Co. Fundamentally, this drop in steel consumption relative to G.N.P.—equivalent to a loss of 11 million tons—could have occurred for two broad reasons: (1) a relative decline in the output of steel-using industries—construction, autos, machinery, appliances, cans, etc.; or (2) displacement of steel in its regular markets, i.e., a reduction in the amount of steel used per car, per machine, per building, etc.

In the period at hand, as Greenspan's analysis makes clear, the first factor was the important one. Between 1955 and 1960 steel's chief customers expanded their production only 1 per cent despite the 12 per cent rise in G.N.P. As a result, over three-quarters of the decline in steel consumption relative to G.N.P. can be accounted for by the slowdown in the business of steel's traditional customers, and only 22 per cent is due to competitive displacement.

There would be small consolation for steel in this fact, of course, if it appeared that the steel-using industries were likely to continue losing ground indefinitely—if, for example, their decline since 1955 reflected a long-term deterioration in their role in the economy. Except perhaps for the railroads, whose use of steel has been declining for years, no such change has occurred. In part, the steel-using sector of the economy was hurt during the past five years by a few special circumstances that may have run their course by now. For example:

• Production of ordnance—tanks, guns, planes, etc.—declined sharply as a result of the growing reliance on missiles, satellites, and the like. The drop in ordnance production meant the loss of roughly 800,000 tons of steel consumption between 1955 and 1960. But steel consumption probably won't be cut any more, for output of conventional ordnance has gone about as low as it can go.

• Oil-well drilling activity also fell off substantially, because of a worldwide dislocation in oil markets. This drop meant the loss of 350,000 tons. While no recovery is likely in the near future, neither does it seem probable that drilling will drop much below the current level.

In the main, however, the decline in the importance of steel-using industries reflects the general slowdown in economic growth—2.3 per cent a year since 1955 vs. 4.3 per cent a year in the preceding eight years. Thus, business spending on new plant and equipment has been disappointingly sluggish, as have appliance sales, owing to the decline in home-building activity. Nor has the auto industry, despite a generally satisfactory performance this year, been able to match the record sales turned in in 1955, when a combination of radical changes in styling, very easy credit, and unusually aggressive sales tactics lifted sales well above the "normal" level of demand. The drop in car sales, which has meant the loss of several million tons of steel, is clearly reversible. Auto production will almost certainly expand during the 1960's, under the stimulus of rising replacement needs, a sharp growth in the car-owning population, and higher income. And an acceleration in over-all economic growth should mean a sharp acceleration in business investment.

The New Competition

More is involved in the decline in steel consumption, however, than just a cyclical slowdown in the major steel-using industries. As noted above, some 22 per cent of the over-all drop in consumption relative to G.N.P. has been due to a decline in the amount of steel used per unit of production in these industries. In actual tonnage, the displacement has been small. But from the long-run standpoint, *the significant fact is not that displacement hasn't been any larger, but that it has occurred at all.* Small as it is, the displacement of steel is symptomatic of a much larger fact: namely, that steel now faces real competition for the first time in its recent history. It is this new competition, rather than displacement per se, that is forcing such large revisions in steel-company strategy.

The bulk of the displacement that has occurred so far has been in construction, to the discomfiture of firms like Bethlehem and U.S. Steel, which are more heavily in structural steels than most of their competitors. Steel consumption by builders has expanded 3 per cent since 1955 against an 8 per cent rise in the volume of steel-using construction. For it is in construction that steel faces the broadest range of competitive materials. The most important of these is concrete—particularly prestressed concrete, which in just a few years has moved from an engineering novelty to a vitally important material in its own right. Prestressed concrete has already displaced some 500,000 tons of steel a year in bridge construction alone—particularly overpass bridges in highway construction.

And construction men are just beginning to use prestressed concrete for the erection of buildings. Thus, the Tishman Research Corp. (a subsidiary of Tishman Realty & Construction Co.) recently finished its first prestressed concrete structure, a 1,200-car parking garage for Abraham & Straus's Hempstead, New York, department store. Tishman Research general manager Joseph Newman is enormously enthusiastic about the cost savings of concrete, particularly from reductions in the on-site labor requirements; the Hempstead "Tierpark" went up at a cost of $1,200 per car, against about $1,700 for a conventional structure. The company has licensed some ninety-odd concrete firms to manufacture the component parts.

And concrete is by no means the only material replacing steel in construction. Copper and plastics (and to a much smaller extent, aluminum) have displaced about 600,000 tons of steel a year in the manufacture of standard pipe, used for plumbing and heating, water supply, etc. Aluminum has made some inroads in highway construction, most notably for guard rail, and it is also competing with steel for use in conduits, windows, roofing and siding, and electrical-transformer housing, among others.

"Displacement by Air"

In the long run, moreover, steel may be threatened less by displacement by other materials than by what Greenspan calls "displacement by air"—that is to say, engineering and design innovations that reduce the total weight of material, whatever material is used. Because of the relative slowness with which labor productivity has advanced in construction, architects and structural engineers are designing buildings that permit use of lighter materials or fewer structural members—in effect, substituting engineering for materials and for on-site labor. It is this that has led to the growing use of prestressed concrete, which involves a wholly new engineering concept as well as a new material. Engineering advances have also reduced the amount of steel used per unit in oil-well drilling; for example, oil-well crews can now use a single pipe to reach as many as five different levels, instead of drilling a separate hole for each level.

In the other steel-using industries the amount of steel per unit of production has held up since 1955, but competition from other materials and from "air" has begun to siphon off growth that steel might otherwise have enjoyed. In the auto market, for example, which is steel's second largest (22 per cent of total steel use, vs. 30 per cent in construction) steel sales have been hurt by engineering and design changes—e.g., "unitized construction" and the compact cars—which cut the amount of steel per car. The compacts use only about 2,700 pounds, on average, compared to 4,000 for conventional cars. Because the conventional cars are heavier than their 1955 counterparts, the amount of steel per car, taking the whole range of production, is still slightly above 1955 —i.e., 3,700 pounds this year compared to 3,650 pounds in 1955. But the long-term trend toward "more car per car"—one of the important stimulants to steel production—has been halted.

In the container market, which accounts for 9 per cent of all steel consumption, steel is feeling the competition of aluminum. Reynolds Metals has contracted with Minute Maid to supply it with 50 million aluminum frozen-juice cans this year, and Minute Maid is test-marketing an aluminum can that can be opened without a can opener, developed by Alcoa and United Shoe Machinery. In the aggregate, of course, the loss to aluminum so far has been less than the gains made by steel (tin) cans in other markets —e.g., soft drinks. But the threat is real; the aluminum companies are clearly planning an all-out assault on the container market. And most tin-plate producers feel that over the long run they face a far greater threat from polyethylene and other plastic containers than from aluminum.

Nibbled to Death?

Indeed, there is hardly a market for steel that has not suffered some inroads from competitive materials, or that doesn't face even greater competition in the future. Aluminum has largely replaced steel in the manufacture of truck and truck-trailer bodies, and it is beginning to compete with steel in the declining but still sizable railroad market; the Southern Railway has bought over 1,200 aluminum freight cars. Plastics are replacing steel in the manufacture of garbage pails, furniture (e.g., foam rubber instead of steel innerspring mattresses and cushions), and toys. The new "high performance" plastics, such as du Pont's Delrin and General Electric's Lexan, may supplant steel in a wide variety of uses— e.g., bearings, pumps, and conveyer belts. And manufacturers of nails, who have already lost nearly half their market to imports, face another serious threat from adhesives.

Although the inroads from competitive materials so far amount to only a modest proportion—perhaps 4 per cent—of steel's total market, on the estimate of Professor Robert Weidenhammer of the University of Pittsburgh, they affect a much larger proportion of steel's total profits. As U.S. Steel's Leslie Worthington points out, "Profit success or profit failure in business rests on a razor's edge." In some cases, the tonnages displaced have been high-priced and high-profit items—e.g., stainless-steel auto trim. More important, competition has put the steel price structure under pressure, thereby reducing profit margins. Taking everything together, it is abundantly clear, as the remarkably candid first report of the industry's Subcommittee on Competitive Materials points out, "that the total impact of competitive materials is neither small nor insignificant." Or as A. A. Archibald, vice president for engineering and plant of Jones & Laughlin Steel puts it, competition from other materials "may only be a nibbling," but "the question is, can you be nibbled to death?"

Unions and Prices

If they are to avoid being nibbled to death, steel companies will have to alter radically their price and wage policies, their sales and marketing techniques, and their management of research and development. Changes have begun in all three areas, and they are making steel a brand-new industry.

It's in the area of price-wage policy that the most radical changes are needed, for the policy the industry has followed since the end of World War II is, more than any other factor, responsible for the competitive bind in which it now finds itself. Steel companies opened the door to competition from other materials by increasing their prices 90 to 112 per cent since 1947—two and

one-half times as fast as concrete and two and one-half to three
and one-quarter times as fast as the average of all industrial
prices.[2] The margin would be narrower, of course, if 1940 were
used as the base; as steel companies like to point out, their prices
rose less than other prices under World War II price controls.
But steel prices also fell a lot less than other prices during the
great depression. Since 1929, in fact, steel prices have advanced
75 per cent faster than the average of all industrial prices.

Why did steel prices go up so much? One reason certainly is
constant union pressure for higher wages. Steel wages—i.e., total
employment costs per hour—have gone up by 7.8 per cent a
year—20 per cent faster than in the private economy as a whole,
and about three times as fast as steel labor productivity—i.e., output per man-hour. Unit labor costs—i.e., total employment costs
per ton—have consequently advanced by more than 5 per cent
a year, compounded. And, the steel industry has had to cope with
conflicting government policies as well as with a powerful union.
On the one hand, the federal government has used a variety of
methods, ranging from oral persuasion to outright seizure, to
force the steel companies to grant faster and more generous settle-
ments than might have been reached under freer bargaining.
And on the other hand, congressional committees, and at times
the White House itself, have been attacking the steel industry's
pricing policies since 1939.

It would be a mistake, however, to regard the steel industry as
just an innocent victim of a conspiracy between Big Labor and
Big Government. For to some degree the industry itself contributed to the wage-price spiral by its own strategy. This strategy
was to raise prices each time wages were increased, and in fact
to raise them *more* than the increase in unit labor costs. The fact
that price increases were preceded by above-average wage increases served to neutralize the political opposition to higher
steel prices. But the fact that the industry passed on each wage
increase with seeming impunity seriously weakened its ability

---

[2] The comparison varies according to how steel prices are measured. *Fortune*
used the Bureau of Labor Statistics Wholesale Price Index for all iron and steel
products, including ore, scrap, semi-finished products, etc., as well as finished
steel products. The BLS index of finished steel products alone has gone up
much faster—by 110 per cent since 1947, vs. 90 per cent for the broader index.

to resist the joint union-government pressure at the next go-around. As a result, wages and prices chased each other upward, and between 1947 and 1957 steel companies actually increased their prices 25 to 50 per cent faster than their unit labor costs (which in turn went up faster than materials).

Profits and Prices

This price strategy served to improve the industry's profit margins, and some improvement was badly needed in the early postwar years. As Professor Weidenhammer points out, steel firms were under enormous pressure from both their customers and the federal government to expand capacity, and they had to develop new sources of iron ore to replace the Mesabi range, whose deposits of high-grade ore were being rapidly depleted.[3] But they couldn't generate the necessary cash themselves; they entered the postwar period with depreciation far below replacement requirements and with a return on capital less than that of manufacturing firms as a whole. Nor could they raise new capital on advantageous terms. Because their return on invested capital was below average, steel stocks were selling at very low price-earnings ratios —in most cases, below book value. Sale of new stock was impossible, therefore, without dilution of the existing equity. And the memory of the depression years, when many steel companies had come dangerously close to defaulting on their debt, made most firms reluctant to borrow.

Faced with all this, the steel companies elected to improve their competitive position in the capital market at the risk of losing position in the market for materials. By raising prices more than unit labor costs (and by improving their production technology), they were able to improve their cash flow (net profit plus depreciation) as a percentage of sales from 9.5 per cent in 1947 to 10.9 per cent in 1957. More important, they raised their total return on invested capital from 16.8 per cent in 1947—13 per cent below the average for all manufacturing—to 20.1 per

---

[3] The life of the Mesabi deposits has since been extended by the development of techniques for using its large deposits of low-grade ore.

cent in 1957—17 per cent *above* the average for all manufacturing. And so the steel companies generated enough cash to finance the bulk of their enormous capital expenditures internally, and they forced a radical reappraisal of steel equities in the market place in 1954 and again in 1957–58. For all the decline this year, steel stocks are still selling close to their 1957 highs.

7 Cents a Pound

But this improvement in steel's profitability was bought at a considerable cost—i.e., a 50 to 60 per cent increase in the price of steel relative to other commodities. Such a differential price rise would normally spell danger for any industry, but for some time steelmen tended to underestimate its effects on their markets. In part, their reasoning was sensible. Until 1957, at least, steel prices appeared to be below true "market" prices, since certain types of steel were in chronically short supply. In raising some prices, therefore, the steel companies may have been making a needed adjustment. But many steelmen went far beyond this, and argued that in any case increasing steel prices would not—indeed, could not—affect their sales. Demand for steel, they said, was highly "inelastic," and besides, as Bethlehem Steel Chairman A. B. Homer told the Kefauver Committee in 1957: "The price of our steel is so low, about 7 cents a pound, that it accounts for a very small part of the cost incurred by our customers."

But in fact this kind of argument—repeated in one form or another by virtually every major-steel-company head—grossly underestimates the effect of steel prices on demand over the long run. As T. O. Yntema pointed out in his classic study of steel demand before the TNEC hearings in 1939, steel demand is inelastic only when steel is so cheap (as it was in 1939) that there are virtually no substitutes for steel. "If higher relative steel prices meant invasion of major steel markets by substitute products," Yntema wrote, "there would be imparted to the total demand for steel a degree of elasticity not now present." U.S. Steel's own Executive Vice President Richard F. Sentner once put the matter more bluntly. "Exorbitant prices," he said, "would only encourage our customers to engineer their own operations away from the use of steel."

"Just Another Myth"

This fact is now getting its due. Only three years ago U.S. Steel Chairman Roger Blough argued that "the so-called high price of steel is . . . just another myth, pure and simple," and that "the price of steel is amazingly low." But last January Blough himself announced his discovery that steel price increases had created "mounting competitive resistance." Indeed, Blough told a television audience, he had found that "in many cases our customers were buying foreign-made steel at prices considerably below American costs; and that in other cases they were finding it economical to turn to substitutes for steel—products like prestressed concrete, wood, plastics, glass, and aluminum and other metals produced right here in America."

New Look in Prices

It has become painfully clear, in short, that whatever the precise elasticity of steel demand may be, the steel industry cannot afford to keep on increasing its prices. Realization of this fact of life toughened the industry's attitude in wage negotiations last year; the new contract provides increases of 3.5 per cent per year, less than half the average annual increase since 1947. Moreover, U.S. Steel did not raise prices when the contract was signed last January and is unlikely to raise them when the first wage boost goes into effect this month. Steel prices, consequently, have been stable since the summer of 1958 and have even softened a bit this year. Bethlehem's Homer, to be sure, announced his intention to make a "careful appraisal" of the cost-price situation, and Jones & Laughlin Chairman Avery Adams, while conceding that stability of steel prices is a contribution to the control of inflation, thinks that "perhaps it is too much of a statesmanlike position for one industry to take." But no steel company can make a price increase stick unless U.S. Steel matches the advance—and U.S. Steel has no apparent intention of increasing prices in the current competitive environment.

"I don't see anything unique about December 1," says Executive Vice President Richard Sentner, who's responsible for the corporation's pricing. "We take cost increases all the time—in freight, materials, power—without raising prices. The fact that a wage increase takes place on December 1 doesn't mean it has to be taken care of on December 2." And Armco Steel, which led the 1958 price advance, now agrees that companies should absorb increases in wages or other costs until they can determine in practice how much can be offset through productivity gains. The policy of increasing wages and prices simultaneously, President Logan T. Johnston now says, "was not a sound approach to good pricing practice." Instead, Johnston believes the industry "should give our customers the benefit of the unknown. We owe it to them to try to maintain our profit margin through our own efforts rather than through automatic price increases."

And the industry is making a considerable effort to offset rising wages and freight costs. Research and development activities have been stepped up very sharply; employment of technical personnel by the Big Eight has jumped from 1,800 in 1954 to 3,200 this year and perhaps 4,000 next year. Steel firms are also in the middle of a large capital-expenditure program: outlays for the five years 1959 to 1963 will come to more than $5 billion; they are being directed largely toward modernization and cost reduction, especially through the ingot level, which accounts for 50 per cent or more of the cost of the average finished steel product. At the moment, of course, the capital-expenditure program is creating a dreadful cash squeeze for some companies, since the outlays are coming at a time when profit margins and profits have been cut. But the industry's capital outlays offer promise of a radical reduction in the steel breakeven point—already down to 40 per cent, on Professor Weidenhammer's estimate, and even below that on Greenspan's calculations.

Will Prices Be Cut?

One important reason for high costs is that steel companies were operating fairly close to capacity during most of the postwar period and so had to keep a lot of relatively obsolete capacity in use. By the time the current expenditure program is finished in late 1962 or early 1963, however, the steel companies will have retired most of their obsolete capacity. In addition, they will have made drastic reductions in the operating costs of their existing facilities, making them competitive with the most efficient plants now in use. For example, use of oxygen increases the productivity of an open-hearth furnace by 20 to 60 per cent, depending on the amount of oxygen used. (Indeed, industry has yet to find the point of diminishing returns from oxygen use.) A year or two ago, only 10 per cent of the industry's open-hearth capacity was equipped with oxygen roof jets. Now the proportion is up to 25 per cent, and by 1962–63, according to Air Products, no less than 70 per cent of open-hearth capacity (between 85 million and 90 million tons) will be so equipped. Besides the oxygen-equipped open hearths, new L-D oxygen furnaces with a capacity of some nine million tons will also be in operation, for the most part replacing obsolete open hearths at Jones & Laughlin and National Steel plants. Since the industry is not likely to operate at more than 75 to 85 per cent of capacity in the near future, most of the steelmaking capacity in use by 1962 or 1963 will be low-cost facilities incorporating the latest technology.

And so steel profit margins should be restored in the next several years. Indeed, it's even possible that with obsolete plants retired and the technology of existing plants brought up to date, the steel industry will be able to reduce some of its prices—e.g., for structural steel, tin plate, and other products facing direct competition from other materials. For oxygenation, while the most important, is by no means the only technological advance going on. Recent research into the chemistry of the blast furnace is producing substantial increases in blast-furnace yields, through beneficiating the ore burden to increase its iron content and increasing temperatures to reduce the necessary input of coke. Jones & Laughlin has been able to develop a mathematical model of its blast furnaces that permits experimentation with different combinations. A number of firms, among them National Steel, are building new, automated finishing facilities—e.g., the computer-controlled hot strip "mill of the future" that National Steel is building at its Great Lakes operation near Detroit. Better quality control may reduce the current heavy loss between the ingot and the finished steel product, thereby increasing the net yield per ingot ton by 8 per cent or more. And there is a real possibility that direct casting of steel will become economical in another five to ten years; this would be the most radical change in steelmaking technology since the introduction of the continuous rolling mill in the mid-1920's.

"Management-directed" Innovation

The technological advances in steelmaking are going hand in hand with a new marketing strategy—what Armco's Logan Johnston calls "the substitution of marketing and merchandizing for selling." In the first place, this new approach involves a substantial acceleration in the development of new products. In the past, product innovation all too often has been what one steel economist calls "customer-directed" rather than "management-directed." Innovations, that is to say, were made in response to changing needs of steel customers rather than as an active means of creating new markets or broadening old ones. When auto-company stylists, for example, decided to use flared fenders and tail-fins, they required steels that could take more drastic forming than the ones that were available. The steel companies obliged, but the impetus came from the auto companies.

Now, however, a good many steel companies are trying to increase demand for steel by creating new or improved types of steel—steel that will lower builders' and fabricators' costs, or increase the real value of their products. A good deal of effort, for example, is being devoted to the development of lighter steels. Both Bethlehem and U.S. Steel have started selling a new carbon structural steel that offers substantially greater strength per pound. This new steel permits a 4 to 6 per cent reduction in the weight of bridges and buildings at only a 1 per cent higher cost per ton; the net saving, therefore, works out to 3 to 5 per cent. Several companies—U.S. Steel, Jones & Laughlin, Pittsburgh Steel—have developed lighter piping that permits oil-drilling crews to go deeper with a given rig.

Perhaps the most impressive example of how steel can be improved—and the sharpest illustration of the industry's competitive counterattack—is the new, thin tin plate U.S. Steel has started selling under the name Ferrolite. Ferrolite is about 40 per cent thinner than conventional tin plate, and sells for 25 per cent less per "base box" (218 square feet of plate). Quite clearly, U.S. Steel's haste in introducing "skinny tin plate"—well ahead of schedule—reflected the growing threat of aluminum: Ferrolite reduces aluminum's weight advantage, which is one of the latter's main selling points (the other is less corrosion), and could afford savings to can manufacturers of as much as 15 per cent per can.

But U.S. Steel and Granite City Steel, which is introducing its own version next year, see the new product as an offensive weapon as well. They hope to create a number of new markets for steel—e.g., replacing cardboard cracker boxes, replacing aluminum in disposable cooking and baking tins, replacing glass bottles for soft drinks.

Besides trying to reduce the weight of their products, steelmen are also improving their finish and surface in an effort to reduce corrosion—perhaps the metal's greatest competitive weakness—improve steel's appearance, and reduce fabricators' production costs. Armco has developed an aluminized steel that combines the advantage of aluminum's resistance to corrosion with steel's greater strength; the new product is being used for making mufflers and tailpipes on several of the new cars. The company is also actively promoting a vinyl-coated steel, and it has hopes of developing an inexpensive technique to bond a thin coating of stainless steel to ordinary carbon sheet and plate. National Steel has developed a differential galvanized steel for auto production; this new sheet has a heavier coating of steel on one side, for the inside of the car body (for corrosion resistance), than on the other side, which is painted. Republic Steel has been quite successful with a plastic-coated steel pipe; the company hopes to be able to come up with a pipe that is coated on the inside as well as the outside. And Bethlehem has introduced a new enameling sheet, called Bethnamel, for use in appliances and architectural panels. The new steel requires only one instead of the customary two coats of enamel.

What is happening, it is clear, is that steel companies are rapidly upgrading their product mix, which enables their dollar sales to grow faster than tonnage shipments. They are beginning to think of steel less in tonnage terms and more in dollar terms, and to think of themselves somewhat more as producers of specialty products and somewhat less as producers of a basic commodity. In this regard Armco has led the way. "The specialty of today," says Logan Johnston, "is the commodity of tomorrow."

"Snowflakes" and Steel

Selling and promotion of techniques are changing, too. Here, the galvanizing force is U.S. Steel, for the corporation is now firmly committed to the heretical doctrine that a steel producer by its own activities can affect and change consumers' demand for steel. U.S. Steel first tried to influence consumer demand with its "Operation Snowflake," a national advertising campaign urging housewives to demand—and husbands to grant—a "white Christmas," i.e., to give consumer appliances as Christmas presents. Now U.S. Steel is actively promoting the sale of soft drinks in cans—a potential market for upwards of 850,000 tons of steel a year—by pushing the idea to bottlers, supplying them with advertising material, saturating each area in which the canned soft drinks are introduced with advertising, etc. The company has just started a nationwide promotion campaign in cooperation with large department stores, called "Rhapsody in Steel," in which the store windows are filled with steel products. And last year U.S. Steel engaged a firm of industrial designers, Peter Muller-Munk Associates, to explore steel's aesthetic and design potential. Muller-Munk came up with a number of new designs for steel office furniture, playground equipment, kitchen appliances and fixtures, among others, which U.S. Steel is making available to any interested manufacturers.

Many steel producers, to be sure, take a dim view of U.S. Steel's attempt to design products for the ultimate consumer. "I don't mean to criticize U.S. Steel," says one steel-company head, "but my own thought is that we're better off the way we are. We don't want to impose on our customers." But virtually all the steel companies are experimenting with new marketing techniques; they can't afford not to, for fear of losing position. For whether or not they think the total demand for steel can be increased by better selling, they all agree that promotion can drastically affect an individual company's share of that market. For example, Bethlehem has taken full-page ads in consumer magazines to promote steel innerspring mattresses and other products. Republic Steel, which sells 20 per cent of its output through independent warehouses, has spent $3 million since 1956 to train the warehouse sales forces through its so-called Order Makers Institutes. (The name reflects the industry's common complaint that warehouse salesmen "can *take* orders but can't make them.") And the entire industry is supporting the American Iron and Steel Institute's "Steelmark" program, which U.S. Steel originated. This is a national advertising campaign designed to persuade the public to discard its image of steel as an old-fashioned heavy, dirty metal

—a distinct disadvantage in competing with aluminum, which has capitalized on the American penchant for the new and up-to-date.

169 Million Tons

What, then, is the outlook for steel demand over the long term? As we have seen, the outlook depends on two factors: the rate of displacement of steel, and the trend of production in the steel-using industries, which in turn is related to the growth rate of the whole economy. As to displacement, it's important to note that steel's own competitive countermeasures cut both ways. The development of lighter steels, for example, could safeguard existing markets from encroachment and open up new markets; it also tends to increase the real value per ton of steel. But the reduction in steel weight also means a reduction in tons of steel consumed per unit of production; it contributes, in other words, to "displacement by air." Taking everything together, however, the vigorous response the industry is making to competition makes it seem likely that displacement will not accelerate beyond the relatively modest rate of the past five years. This in itself could be an enormous achievement for an industry as "mature" as steel. And it's even possible that the industry will be able to hold on to its present share of the total market for materials.

What that total market will be depends on the future of the steel-using industries, and this in turn is closely related to the rate of growth of the whole economy—a question on which there are sharp differences of judgment. In its studies last year of "the Markets of the 1960's," *Fortune* projected an acceleration in the growth of the economy to 4.2 per cent per year, which would bring G.N.P. to $759 billion by 1970. If this projection is correct, there will be a rapid rise in capital investment and in car sales, and the output of steel-using industries will rise from an index of 101 this year to 163 in 1970 (see Fig. 8, page 148.)

In this case, the future of steel is extremely bright, given either of the assumptions we have made about displacement. For if the steel industry were only to prevent any acceleration in the rate of displacement, steel consumption would go up from an index of 98 this year to 148 in 1970. And if steel were to prevent further displacement altogether, consumption would rise to an index of

158 in 1970. Hence steel *production* (assuming an export-import balance and some rise in inventories commensurate with the rise in output in the steel-using industries) would rise from this year's depressed level of 102 million tons to between 158 million and 169 million ingot tons by 1970. Steel dollar sales are likely to rise one-quarter to one-half per cent a year faster than ingot production, because of the upgrading in steel's product mix.

Steel, of course, may not do this well. The projections above are based in turn on projections of growth for the whole economy that are more optimistic than those being made by a good many other economists. A recent United Nations study, for example, making different assumptions about both displacement and economic growth, concludes that steel production in the U.S. will come to only 147,500,000 tons in 1972–75. Even that would be quite a bit of steel, however, in view of all the current pessimism. Someday, steel probably will become a "declining industry." It certainly isn't behaving like one now. And over the next ten years, on any estimate, steel has a good bit of growth ahead.

66

electronic computer may be the most important agent of change that business—or government or education—has ever known. Certainly no other technical innovation has changed so many human activities in so short a time.

Electronic computers have increased the businessman's ability to plan and control activities of all kinds, from simple machine operations to complex distribution systems. Thus, computers have enlarged human brain power as other man-made machines have enlarged muscle power. Surely this development is going to change radically the art and science of marketing management and business administration.

*The Boundless Age of the Computer**

by Gilbert Burck

"The electronic computer," says Ray Eppert, president of Burroughs Corp., "has a more beneficial potential for the human race than any other invention in history." This colossal judgment might seem merely the occupational extravagance of an ardent computer salesman, which Ray Eppert surely is. But the Burroughs chief weighed his words with care, and put the case for the computer no more extravagantly than many a Ph.D. with reservations in his mind and footnotes in his voice. More and more people with special competence in computer circles are coming to the same conclusion.

What, the computer more beneficial than the printing press or the wheel? More than the steam engine or the dynamo and elec-

* *Vol. 69, March 1964, pp. 101–110, 230–232.*

tric motor, to say nothing of atomic power? An impressive case can be made for putting the computer at the top of the list— giving the qualification that the latest great technical innovation often exerts the greatest impact because it feeds on previous achievements. The dynamo obviously never would have amounted to so much if a steam prime mover had not existed. The computer itself is classified as a product of the electrical manufacturing industry, and without that industry's tremendous advances it would have remained a challenging but impractical museum piece. A hundred and thirty years ago the functions of the modern computer were understood by a few people (see *Fortune,* March 1964, p. 112); but it remained for the vacuum tube to make the computer practicable, and for diodes and transistors to make it the prodigy it is today.

Certainly no other single item of capital goods has changed the basic terms of so many human activities in so short a time. Within a few years, as the engine of modern information technology, it has profoundly altered the techniques of science, has begun to make government efficient, and has provided a new basis for the strategies of national defense. Above all, it is radically changing business' production methods and the art and science of management. Although the machine is the bête noire of critics who fear it will accelerate unemployment and compound the worst problems of modern society, it seems destined to shine as a powerful instrument for making business more creative and efficient and hence for raising the nation's real income per person, for eliminating a vast amount of drudgery, and for increasing leisure. In short, for measurably expanding free man's range of choices.

One of the characteristics of the computer that make it unique among technical achievements is that it has forced men to think about what they are doing with clarity and precision. A man cannot instruct the computer to perform usefully until he has arduously thought through what he's up to in the first place, and where he wants to go from there. Even scientists, once they have wrestled with a computer's demands on knowledge and logic, are astonished to discover how much of their mental activity travels in ruts. The rethinking process gets more difficult as the computer gets better. Wherever the machine is used, it is improving enormously the quantity and quality of human cogitation; and it is rapidly becoming a kind of Universal Disciplinarian.

The Great Processor

Perhaps the best way to explain the machine is to compare it with man himself. In his long and unfinished struggle to master his physical environment, man progressed by processing knowledge. That is to say, instead of relying wholly on his favorite haruspex, or gut reader, he learned to gather and differentiate knowledge, and so to transform it into something useful. It is hardly more than a tautology to observe that practically all the wrong decisions over the centuries, from Darius' attack at Marathon to the birth of the Edsel, have been at bottom the result of insufficient or inadequately processed knowledge. On the other hand, the gods themselves have been on the side of mortals who knew enough not to bother them with everything—who could process knowledge well enough to relate cause and effect and count consequences with tolerable accuracy. Given adequate knowledge, man learned to rely more and more on deductive or analytical judgment, which proceeds from a body of facts, and less and less on guesses and intuitive judgment, which he necessarily uses when a lot of relevant facts are missing.

The electronic computer is basically a device for ingesting, judging, and otherwise processing or usefully modifying knowledge. Thus it enlarges brainpower even as other man-made machines enlarge muscle power. Like man, the computer expresses knowledge in terms of symbols; man's symbols are letters and numbers, and the machine's symbols are electromagnetic impulses that represent letters and numbers.[1] Although man must usually instruct or program the machine minutely, its chief present advantage is that it can manipulate symbols a million times faster

---

[1] There are two categories of computers: (1) the analogue, which measures and compares quantities in one operation and has no memory, and (2) the digital, which solves problems by counting precisely and sequentially and has a memory. The electric analogue computer is about fifty years old, enjoys a big and growing use in simulation and process control, and is "hybridized" with digital computers in some applications. But it accounts for a very small percentage of the market and its potentialities at present are not so catholic as those of the digital machine. Unless this article specifies otherwise, it means digital when it says computer.

than a man with pencil and paper, and can make calculations in a few minutes that might take man alone a century. Richard Hamming of Bell Telephone Laboratories has remarked that the difference between doing a calculation by hand and by computer is the difference between having one dollar and having a million. Sometimes the difference is infinite; only a computer can calculate swiftly enough to analyze the data from a satellite, or to enable man to control the flight of a missile.

But the computer adds more than lightning calculation and fact sorting to man's brainpower. Besides an arithmetic unit, it is equipped with a memory that holds its knowledge on call, a stored program device that follows a set of instructions by code, and control units through which it reads and executes instructions. Perhaps its most portentous faculty is what is called conditional transfer, or sometimes the branch or jump operation, which allows it to choose from alternatives. Without the transfer, the machine must run brutelike through all the alternatives in a given problem to hit the right one; with the transfer, it can *assess* and then *conclude.* In effect, the machine searches its memory and makes judgments and in general acts remarkably like a sentient being. That is how the computer can make selective payroll deductions, and beat the house at blackjack, and why it is indispensable in cybernation, or the process of automatic communication and control.

Most problems presented to computers are algorithmic or "well structured"—that is, problems leading inevitably to a conclusion, such as billing customers, calculating trajectories, or solving equations. But now computer men are trying to make the machine do more. As the lovely Lady Lovelace (see *Fortune,* March 1964, p. 113) once wrote, the computer can perform only what we know how to order it to perform. But since it embodies a conditional transfer, suppose we instruct it to learn from experience. Professor Herbert A. Simon of Carnegie Institute of Technology has in effect done just that. He has demonstrated to the satisfaction of a lot of people that he can instruct a computer to solve relatively "ill-structured" problems, which are the kind that infest all life, by using rules of thumb and by trial-and-error search. In the new jargon of computers, Simon has made the machine behave "heuristically" ("serving to discover") as well as algorithmically.

Thus Simon and the other dedicated computer men are writing of machines "which do not merely substitute brute force for human cunning. Increasingly they imitate—and in some cases improve upon—human cunning." Some talk of the immortal brain, or a computer whose external memory store can be expanded indefinitely, to include the wisdom of the ages. This computer would be a paragon of intelligence, able to relate all its stored knowledge accurately, to reason without being corrupted by emotion, to discover new relationships between old things, to solve more of the world's problems than anyone solved before, even to create works of art. Man would be superior to this machine god, the joke goes, only because he presumably could still pull the plug or throw the switch.

Such extrapolations, so uncomfortably reminiscent of the androids of science fiction, have aroused a storm of opposition, and revived in intellectual circles hoary textbook issues like free will vs. determinism and vitalism vs. mechanism. At one extreme are people like the late Norbert Wiener, a pioneer in computers, who originated the word cybernetics and who solemnly warned that computers could be improved to the point where they would get out of man's control. At the other are embattled skeptics who denounce the notion that machines can ever really simulate human beings. In between is a group taking various potshots at abuses of the computer, real and imaginary, and at the "dire threat" it presents to employment and the social order.

A Game for Mental Gear Shifters

The "acceptance" of the electronic computer, appropriately enough, has been extraordinary, if not unique. Unlike some other great innovations, which have needed anywhere from fifty to one hundred years to assume their role in the scheme of things, it has taken a very big role in a few years, and is headed for a vastly bigger one. A dozen years ago there were fewer than two score machines in the land; today there are about 16,000 installations; including accessory devices, they are probably worth around 4 billion. Most other great inventions have flourished mainly within single industries; this ecumenically versatile one is already indispensable in most important human activities. Several thousand distinct applications have been catalogued, and the list is out of date before it leaves the presses. Never before, surely, has a single device generated in so short a time so many technical papers, pamphlets, articles, and books; merely to scan the daily flow of new and important information about the computer, to say nothing of the bales of quasi-information about it, is beyond the capacity of anything but the computer itself. Yet only a small minority of technical experts wholly understand the machine; the vast majority of enlightened laymen know it mainly as a kind of mysterious twelve-foot refrigerator with blinking lights and whirring tapes. The gulf of incomprehension between the experts and laymen is doubtless far greater than the gulf between Christopher Columbus and the savage Indians who knelt to worship him on San Salvador.

And never before, probably, has a single innovation generated such a technically sophisticated, talented, competitive, expansion-minded, well-heeled manufacturing business. Staffed by thousands of men with advanced degrees, confidently risking billions on research and development, jubilantly peddling machines that embody sensational advances and yet are almost obsolete by the time they hit the market, the computer industry is a union of science and business that makes the auto and appliance industries in their great old days seem like a bunch of kids playing mumblety-peg. The game today is surely one for men who know how to shift mental gears swiftly. If anything is changing faster than computerized business, it is the business of making computers. About 60 cents of every dollar spent on computer hardware now goes for the central processor, and the rest for "peripheral" equipment like input-output devices, files, and communications. But in a decade, according to the Diebold Group, management advisers, peripheral equipment will account for 75 or 80 cents of the hardware dollar. At the same time, the "software" or programing business seems to be growing even faster than the hardware industry; some predict that in seven years software volume will equal hardware volume.

The industry is dominated and in a way protected by International Business Machines, which a dozen years ago in a remarkably skillful shift changed itself from the world's biggest punched-card office-machine company into the biggest electronic-computer company, and one that is always preparing a "sensational" new line. But I.B.M.'s competitors, which include such names as

Sperry Rand's Univac Division, R.C.A., G.E., Burroughs, Minne-apolis-Honeywell, N.C.R., and Control Data, are heavily armed with brains, ambition, and money. Their assault on fortress I.B.M. is gathering way as one of the most arresting showdowns of business history.

To Business, on a Platter

The benefits that the computer has conferred on government and science are tolerably familiar, and may be covered briefly. For government the machine has done something that nothing else has ever done before, at least on a big scale: it has vastly improved the productivity of bureaucracy. In 1951, for instance, the Census Bureau bought a Univac I. By 1960, fortified with several more, the bureau needed only half as many people to do twice the work that 4,500 had done in 1950. The federal govern-ment, including the Defense Department and the AEC, now uses some 1,250 electronic computers, against 730 as recently as 1961, and expects to be using 1,500 or more within two years. However, the computer's contribution to government efficiency doesn't get into the national productivity figures because statistics assume that government output per man-hour remains constant.

To science and technology the computer has of course been a colossal and unprecedented boon. Chemistry, weather forecasts, physics, education, missile design and operation—these are only a few fields in which the machine is responsible for totally new techniques and achievements. Before Bell Laboratories' scientists possessed computers, they spent months building laboratory pilot plants of transmission systems; now they simulate systems by constructing models on paper and running the figures through a computer, and they come up with the ideal system in a matter of days. About 10 percent of the laboratories' experiments are performed on the computer, but in time, Richard Hamming estimates, perhaps 90 percent of them will be.

The combination of World War II and the computer put the military into business in more ways than one. War itself, these days, is only a highly unfriendly kind of business. Of the 800 or more computers operated by the Defense Department, the Air Force employs more than 400. The largest group of these—about 125—manages the Air Force's worldwide inventory, which is worth no less than $12 billion. Computers helped the Air Force Logistics Command to reduce its head count to 146,000 from 212,000 in 1956; and one of the most advanced inventory controls anywhere is its Automatic Resupply Logistic System, which balances inventories by automatically sending out shipping notices whenever the stock of an item anywhere descends to a given level.

Clemenceau, who remarked that war is too important to be left to generals, would be agreeably amazed by the Air Force's SAGE (semi-automatic ground environment), set up in 1957 to protect the U.S. from a surprise air attack. Using strategically located computers to interpret information gathered by radar, SAGE automatically identifies and categorizes as friend or foe every craft in the air above the U.S. and Canada, supplies details of its speed, specifications, location, and physical environment. If necessary, it alerts Air Force planes, assigns targets, or dispatches intercepting missiles. Thus SAGE simulates a large business system with strategically located division offices, all bound together by an information-and-control network. This network, in effect, not only keeps the home office instantaneously aware of regional and system fluctuations in sales, costs, inventories, and profits, but takes the necessary steps to correct imbalances.

Machines Need Managers

Such military demonstrations of computer ability, together with the research and development done to produce scientific and military systems, have enormously accelerated the business world's "acceptance" of the computer. In 1954, when experts were estimating optimistically that as many as fifty companies would eventually use computers, General Electric's new Louisville appliance plant took delivery on the first data processor used by a private company, a Sperry Rand Univac. Today the vast bulk of American computers operate in the plants and offices of several thousand companies. Last year alone, U.S. business absorbed more than 4,000, worth nearly $2 billion including peripheral equipment; and the accompanying software cost perhaps another $2 billion. Although a few industry specialists think that business installations will remain on a plateau for a few years while these companies absorb what they've got, others see a steadily rising volume. In any event, all predict that delivered value of business computers will rise sharply in a few years, and even double or triple by the early 1970's.

By no means have all installations to date been unqualified blessings. In a study of more than 300 installations in twenty-seven major manufacturing companies more than a year ago, McKinsey & Co., the management consultant, found that eighteen of the companies weren't earning enough on the computers to cover their investment, and apparently U.S. business as a whole was making little if anything on them. Overselling was not the basic problem, though doubtless there was some. The main reason for the trouble seems to be that management, particularly top management, did not give enough study and thought to the potential of computers.

The success stories help explain the failures, and why there are steadily fewer failures. Almost invariably the companies that made the machines pay off put computer operation decisions in the hands of senior managers. These men did not look upon the machine as a gift package that needed only to be plugged in, but subjected themselves to its rigorous discipline. They analyzed their businesses and kept looking for new ways to use the computer even when they were employing the machines profitably on routine jobs. They were also willing to reorient their operating routines and their company organizations, if necessary, to exploit the computer. They are the kinds of managers, many are convinced, who will be running U.S. business tomorrow. "The time when executives could fool around with the machine is gone," says one computer-company officer. "Either they make the computer an indispensable part of their business, or they become a dispensable part of business."

This somewhat dogmatic conclusion on the whole seems justified. The machine is developing far more capabilities than anyone dreamed of a few years ago, and no business organization can afford to bypass them summarily. The indefatigably resourceful manufacturers are developing new "peripheral" equipment, making more tractable machines, finding countless new uses for them, introducing models with startling new powers, and reducing unit costs of using them. And many large users of the machines have taken the initiative and developed applications so original that they regard them as proprietary, and refuse to talk about them.

Most of the profitable operations are still confined to such "routine" jobs as fulfilling payrolls, making out accounts payable and receivable, and processing insurance data, but even these applications are growing vastly more refined. Thousands of insurance policyholders pay their premiums annually, semi-annually, quarterly, monthly; some die, some marry. When billing them, an insurance company's machine has to update information about them. Until recently the data was punched into cards, and the machine had to shuffle through the cards seriatim until it found the right ones. Now random-access storage devices enable the machine to snatch policy records and extract the information it needs in the twinkling of an eye.

Much more portentous, however, are several sophisticated developments still in their infancy but promising to change business methods radically. One is the information feedback principle, which some regard as one of the world's most important concepts because it governs everything done by individuals, groups, and machines in the process of adjusting to one another. A familiar mechanical example of the principle at work is the common thermostat, where temperature and furnace continually interact to keep heat at a predetermined level.

Life with the Feedback Principle

Owing in large part to the efforts of Professor Jay Forrester of M.I.T., the feedback principle is being combined with the computer to create an important management tool. The computer's great role here is to eliminate delays in communication; in an automated oil refinery, for example, hundreds of measuring devices lead to the machine. The computer, having been given thousands of instructions on how to react to the readings of the measuring devices, *instantaneously* applies heat or pressure or otherwise adjusts the controls. Because it keeps on reacting and making adjustments instantaneously, it never has to make large adjustments.

And so with inventories, which are a prime problem for both corporations and the economy. To show how difficult it is to keep stocks in line with demand, computer people like to play an inventory game. In its simple form, several people participate. One represents a retailer, two represent distributors, and a fourth the factory warehouse manager. Others represent customers and the factory. When goods are bought by the customers, a chain of events is begun that ends in the factory the equivalent of five weeks later. The game quickly fouls up. Owing to the long lead time, retailers, distributors, and warehouse managers misjudge their needs because they don't know what happens until some time after it has happened. They find themselves with either insufficient or excessive inventories. Thus a tiny disturbance at the sales end results in a big dislocation at the factory. In real life the inevitable adjustment proves very expensive. Ill-adjusted inventories, for individual companies, result in high costs or worse; for the economy as a whole, excessive inventories usually result in recession, which in its majestic impartiality hits companies that have managed to keep their inventories in line—though not nearly so hard as those that haven't.

Owing in part to computers, significantly, modernized inventory management has already had a stabilizing effect on the economy. The national ratio of inventory to stocks has not changed much over the years, but many businesses, notably auto dealers, must carry larger stocks to afford wider ranges of choice; in other words, better inventory control has enabled manufacturers to offer better service without increasing costs and risks. So although relatively few companies are yet using advanced inventory systems, restraint in inventory buildup is one of the strongest supports of the economy's current salubrity. What might happen when all big companies use computers to control inventories is an exhilarating speculation.

Another portentous development is simulation. Note that the inventory game, by simulating a real inventory system, allows the players to study its faults and correct them with computers. In much the same way, simulation is being applied to management problems. Professor Forrester, using one minute of computer time, has simulated the operation of an entire business over a period of 400 weeks. In real life, a description of a company's operations is fed into the computer, which produces several alternatives for decisions about financial, manpower, product-flow, and other operating factors. From these alternatives, management merely has to choose the best ones. In planning new service stations, for example, some oil companies estimate profitability by simulating two or three years of operation at proposed sites, and so eliminate most if not all guesswork in their planning.

Ken Powell, I.B.M.'s manager of educational research, says that every application of a computer is a simulation; properly understood, it provides unique insights into business. Companies are catching on. What often happens, says Powell, is that a businessman starts with a payroll job whose purpose is merely to get the checks to his employees. He begins to see how the computer can be used to analyze distribution and manufacturing, and then how it can do routine inventory work. Next it dawns on him that in programing the computer to do certain jobs, he must in effect set up models of parts of his business. In the end he finds himself making experimental models of his company's activities. From these he can make decisions about them that he could have made no other way; instead of relying on guesses and intuition, he now can go ahead on logical deductions from facts.

Finally, there are new methods of scheduling work such as Program Evaluation and Review Technique (PERT) and the Critical Path Method (CPM), which were discussed at length in *Fortune* in April 1962 ("Helping the Executive to Make Up His Mind"). Suffice to say here that these time- and money-saving systems are proving highly "popular" and that without computers they would be impossible; moreover, they, like some of the other techniques we have discussed, use the machines heuristically.

Such are some of the commercial avenues down which computers are leading. As yet, these avenues have not joined in the construction of the "total" system about which some computer men descanted so persuasively a few years ago. A total system, as the name suggests, would be one in which all a company's inputs and outputs are automatically coordinated. Orders would result in the appropriate allocations of labor and materials, and inventories would be appropriately adjusted. Payments and bills would be mailed. Markets would be gauged, and managers would have only to read the tape and make key decisions. Perhaps the nearest thing to a total system is SAGE; but business is much more complex than cold war, and it may be a while before the business equivalent of SAGE is working.

Meantime, there is plenty to be done in making use of existing techniques and systems. John Diebold, whose group has advised many firms on automation, insists that most companies have yet to realize what is happening to the handling of information in a business. "In some companies," he says, "this will mean a change in methods; in others, a change in the whole core of the business."

The "General Problem Solver"

Since the machine can guide and fortify and even make some decisions, what will it do to the men who now make the decisions? The computerized executive world twenty years from now is a special interest of Herbert Simon, who was a political scientist specializing in administrative behavior when the computer was a cloud on the horizon. Simon takes the viewpoint that executive decision making is analogous to the behavior of the computer. He therefore divides it into (1) solving programed or well-structured problems; and (2) solving non-specifically programed or ill-structured problems. Examples of the former: clerical and other routine jobs such as ordering office supplies, pricing orders by catalogue, and working out payroll deductions—plus a long list of somewhat less repetitive jobs such as balancing assembly lines, determining the product mix for an oil refinery, planning manufacturing and employment schedules, and even choosing trust portfolio investments. Examples of non-specifically programed problem solving: consequential decisions for which there is no exact precedent, such as a general's decision to attack, or a company manager's to mount a sales campaign.

Mathematical techniques and the electronic computer have already revolutionized the whole business of routine programed decision making. Now they are pushing into many middle-management decision areas, such as those in manufacturing and warehousing. Before long, Simon says, they will make most of a company's programed decisions, just as they will control manufacturing operations. But as big a revolution, he predicts, will occur when heuristic techniques enable the computer to make more non-specifically programed decisions, which are the kind on which the experienced manager exercises his judgment and intuition. A good example of decision making or problem solving on the heuristic borderline is the prevailing practice of assigning computers instead of engineers to modify the designs of standard electric motors according to the customers' specifications. When the order comes in, the computer searches through its memory, finds the right design, and modifies the design to fit the need.

In more complex decision making, such as deciding on company strategy, ill-structured problems must be broken down into goals or subgoals, and means must be related to ends. Simon, together with his associates Allen Newell and J. C. Shaw, in projects sponsored by Rand Corp. and Carnegie Tech, has done a lot of work in analyzing complex problem solving and in instructing a computer to perform accordingly. The chef-d'oeuvre of the three men is what they call a General Problem Solver, or a set of instructions that frees the computer from the rigidities of ordinary programs. This GPS, they claim, enables the machine to behave adaptively, to reason in terms of means and ends, to solve problems by first solving subproblems, and to "adjust aspiration to the attainable." Using the GPS principle, Geoffrey P. E. Clarkson of M.I.T. has successfully simulated a trust-investment officer (*Portfolio Selection: A Simulation of Trust Investment*, Prentice-Hall).

"Centralized Decentralization"

Regardless of what happens in heuristics, computer men predict, jobs at the middle management level will become more specialized, specific, and highly programed; they will also become fewer. On the other hand, managers at the top levels, freed of the need for analyzing details, will more than ever require the faculties of innovation, creativeness, and vision. The computer, precisely because it will make all relevant information instantly available to top management, will mean more centralization; the phrase in computer circles is "centralized decentralization." Owing to teleprocessing, or the integration of all corporate outposts with the central office (as in SAGE), centralization will be a simple matter. All information will be "on line" or sent directly into a computer as soon as it is born; the whole operation will be "real time"—that is, data will be processed and fed back into the machine to control each "situation" as it develops.

Such developments, many argue, will tend to humanize rather than dehumanize business. The company man, the Organization Man, will still exist, but only to the extent that he does or ever did exist. The kind of large-scale organization that the machine will encourage should encourage personal initiative. At the average worker's level the machine, because it continually reports back on a job, is already improving his sense of personal participation. "Constant monitoring," says William Norris, founder and president of Control Data Corp., which uses one of its own management systems, "makes employees feel part of the team effort, because their performance is judged without bias. We've found that people consequently upgrade their own performance."

At the middle management level, Simon argues, much time is now taken up with pacesetting, work pushing, and expediting. As decision making becomes automated and rationalized, these functions are likely to become less important. The manager will deal with well-structured problems and won't have to spend so much time persuading, prodding, rewarding, and cajoling "unpredictable and sometimes recalcitrant people." Some managerial types, he admits, get a lot of satisfaction out of manipulating personal relationships; but he believes the diminution in general frustration, for middle managers as a group, will more than offset the other loss.

Heuristically programed computers, Simon predicts, will be a long time surpassing men on jobs where they exercise their senses and muscles as well as their brains—i.e., running a bulldozer over rough ground, examining a piece of tissue in medical diagnosis, face-to-face service jobs, and so on. "Man has an advantage in rough environment," he explains. "Who would be easier to automate—the theoretical physicist or the experimental? The theoretical. The experimental physicist still has to cope with outside environment, whereas the theoretical one deals with concepts, ideas, and other inputs that have been highly processed."

Relative costs, in the last analysis, will decide who does the job; if a decision-making computer comes to $10,000 a month, it obviously would cost more than three middle managers. As yet, computers put to heuristic problem solving do not have anything remotely like the advantage over man that they boast in arithmetic and scientific computing. But the unit costs of using a computer are declining steadily.

"Changes Have Got to Be Made"

The realization that the computer may be able to do a lot a man can do has accelerated the uproar about unemployment, in certain quarters, to panic proportions. Fevered by vague premonitions about the long-range consequences of the computer, many social pundits are discharging pneumatic predictions about how the machine will plow up the whole order. The consensus of a high-level symposium at last November's convention of the American Federation of Information Processing Societies seemed to be that the computer would be a large factor in making relatively full employment hard to achieve.

Most pessimistic of the lot was W. H. Ferry, vice president of the Fund for the Republic, director of its Study of the Economic Order, and a man given to looking into the future farther than the human eye can see. It is Ferry's oft-stated thesis that the U.S. is caught on a horn of plenty, and that economic theories adequate to the old industrial revolution are no longer good enough. Since the individualism of the eighteenth and nineteenth centuries and "old theories of private property" are casualties of technology, Ferry argues, the complexity of the scientific-industrial state calls for more and more national planning. "These machines are ingenious but not necessarily important," said Ferry at the computer symposium. "Our sociopolitical thinking is still back in agrarian days. Changes have got to be made."

This kind of thinking, like King Lear's threats to do such things as "What they are, yet I know not, but they shall be the terrors of the earth," gets considerably ahead of the facts in the short run, and woefully distorts the possibilities over the long run. Social change is nothing new. In the main, social progress, as it is measured today, is a result of rising productivity. If output per person remains constant or declines, all that governmental power can do is to distribute poverty more evenly. Rising productivity, because it changes the relative value of jobs, produces most if not all significant social changes, such as those described in *Fortune*'s articles on changing markets and classes. (See Part I, pp. 3–70.) The critical question, obviously enough, is whether the computer will help accelerate the present rate of productivity growth so explosively that the economy will be unable to absorb people as fast as they are displaced.

Despite spectacular individual examples of the computer's ability to displace people, it seems to have had little effect on the nation's aggregate productivity—so far. Although productivity in the private economy has grown at about 3.5 percent annually for three years now, against an average of 2.5 percent in the seven previous years, similar spurts have occurred in the precomputer past. And what is often disregarded is that the economy is showing a gratifying ability to create jobs. It is true that U.S. manufacturing employment hardly increased at all in the past four years, while manufacturing output rose 18 percent; but in the same years other employment, despite a brace of rolling recessions, expanded enough to elevate total employment from about 65,600,000 to about 68,800,000. In 1963 alone, when rising productivity in effect subtracted about two million jobs from the economy, nonfarm wage and salary employment increased by more than 1,500,000. In other words, the economy in effect created a total of more than 3,500,000 jobs, and practically all were provided by private enterprise. *Fortune's* Roundup estimates that if G.N.P. rises to $650 billion (in late 1963 prices) by the middle of 1965, unemployment will be approaching "normal" levels, and the economy may absorb nearly all the employables. The unemployables, particularly the unskilled, will of course remain the problem.

The doomsday prophets ignore this. The moment of truth, they keep insisting, is still to come, and it will come all of a sudden. Their arguments run like this:

1. Computer applications have not yet affected national employment figures partly because their ability to displace people has been temporarily offset by more jobs in computer manufacturing and in new installations. Much heavy initial expense is charged to current account, which tends to hide the rate at which productivity improves. But soon the development phase will be over.

2. What intensifies the grim outlook is that the computer's great impact will come at a bad time. The labor force, owing to the wartime baby boom, is increasing at a net rate of around a million a year, and by the end of the decade will increase by nearly two million a year. Owing to computerized automation and cybernation, the number of blue-collar jobs is likely to increase little if at all; and one has only to look at the computer's successful routine applications to see what it may do to white-collar employment.

3. The computer indirectly spurs productivity. Not only does it make existing machines more productive, but it stimulates the purchase of newer and still more efficient machines, thus compounding its threat to employment.

Millions of New Jobs

These points are apposite and worth attention, and therein lies their potency in debate. But they are only one side of the story. Computers are not made out of thin air, and emphatically they do not operate unattended. The computer industry, including the infant "software" business of processing information for the computer, is employing more and more people. Paul Armer, of Rand Corp., estimates that it will create a million new jobs in the next five years. Some say that programing alone will employ 500,000 by 1970.

The key factors are payoff and total investment. Just as the importance of any machine to the economy may be roughly gauged by the amount of capital invested in it, so its disemployment effect may be roughly gauged by the net return on that capital. Last year, as already noted, U.S. government and industry bought or leased computers and accessory devices worth almost $2 billion, and in five years may be spending two or three times as much. These outlays are great, but they are a small part of the roughly $80 billion that industry and government will be investing in the private economy this year; five years from now they will still be a relatively small part of the money government and industry will be investing then.

Assume that computer users will eventually save a staggering 50 percent annually on the capital value of their equipment, a margin the average user won't remotely approach for a long time. Five years hence, on annual hardware shipments valued at some $4 billion, they would earn some $2 billion, which could be equated with perhaps 200,000 fewer jobs. Or to be safe, double the number. But remember that in 1963 alone the economy in effect created a total of more than 3,500,000 jobs.

Such reckoning, it is true, takes no account of the fact that the computer pervades so many activities and makes so much other capital equipment more productive. But the disemployment effect of all other plant and equipment, some of it automated and computerized, may also be measured roughly by its payoff. An uncontrollable upward surge in unemployment would necessarily be accompanied by a huge increase in payoff, and the expectation of the payoff would be generating a colossal boom in capital spending. The steel industry is a case in point. It has far more than enough capacity, but it is spending huge sums on oxygen converters and automatic mills because it believes they will pay off handsomely. If all industry were anticipating similar payoffs, U.S. capital investment today probably would be vastly greater than it is.

The Timely Replenishment

What is too often forgotten is that machines immemorially have not merely replaced men, but freed them to do other things, and so enlarged consumers' range of choices. The cause and effect relationship between displacement by the machine and the creation of new jobs is hard to trace, but it has always been there. It still is there. The computer, too, will indirectly help create new jobs. A computer-controlled oil refinery employs fewer people than a conventional refinery, but it helps bring costs and prices down; and a steady reduction in the real price of petroleum products helps increase the demand for them and so generates thousands of jobs in their distribution and sale. An automated plastics plant creates jobs for managers, engineers, salesmen, manufacturers, retailers. Sometimes, moreover, productivity increases are "hidden" in the form of a product's improved quality and utility. Thanks in part to computers in factories and offices, today's automobile is a much better car than previous models costing the same; thanks to computer-guided inventory controls, the consumer has a wider range of choice in cars than he has ever had before.

An excellent case could be made for the proposition that if the computer did not exist, it would have to be invented. Only a few years ago a good many economists were wondering whether U.S. productivity could keep on rising as it rose in the early postwar years, and some were skeptical when in 1959 *Fortune* projected an average annual increase of about 3 percent for the 1960's. Their skepticism was hardly whimsical. Ever since the original industrial revolution, the per capita growth rate of nations has been the result not of a single development but of a series of developments. As one innovation began to exhaust its power to multiply human effort, another came along. In many U.S. industries, such as agriculture, mining, and some manufacturing, there were portents of such exhaustion. In others featherbedding was (and still is) rife. The big question was not job displacement, but what would provide a new lift to the per capita growth rate. The answer to the question appears to be the computer. It will doubtless go down in history not as the scourge that blew unemployment through the roof, but as the technological triumph that enabled the American economy to maintain and gradually increase the secular growth rate on which its greatness depends.

part III

INSTITUTIONS

The discount house, like other major innovations in retailing, has challenged traditional methods of distribution and "shaken up" the whole system of moving goods, from manufacturers to consumers. During its brief history, the discount house has forced retailers of every description—department stores, specialty shops, supermarkets, variety stores—to reappraise and frequently alter merchandising policies and operating procedures. At the same time, these changes at the retail level are forcing many manufacturers of consumer goods to reexamine channels of distribution.

*The Revolutionists of Retailing**

In a mood of reflection some months ago, Professor Malcolm McNair of Harvard Business School, the dean of U.S. authorities on retailing, nominated the six greatest merchants in U.S. history. The six men are Frank W. Woolworth; John Wanamaker; J. C. Penney; General

by

Charles E. Silberman

Robert E. Wood, who in the 1920's and 1930's converted Sears, Roebuck from a mail-order house into the world's largest retailer; Michael Cullen, the "inventor" of the food supermarket; and a diffident young man of forty-one named Eugene Ferkauf.

The name, which means "sell" in German, is only dimly known even in retailing circles. But Ferkauf's influence has been explosive. He is the founder and controlling stockholder of E. J. Korvette, the nation's largest "discount house." Korvette started operations in 1948, selling luggage and appliances at less than

* Vol. 65, April 1962, pp. 99–102, 254–265.

list price in an upstairs loft on New York's East Forty-sixth Street (*Fortune*, November, 1956). Today Korvette sells a full line of department-store merchandise, from sheets to shirts to furniture, at prices 10 to 30 per cent below the prevailing level, in seventeen department stores in New York, New Jersey, Connecticut, and Pennsylvania. The company has opened four stores since August, and plans seven to ten more over the next two years; in May, 1962 it opened a store at Fifth Avenue and Forty-seventh Street in New York, two blocks down from Saks Fifth Avenue, in the building formerly occupied by W. & J. Sloane, the hundred-year-old furniture store.

Ferkauf rates a place on Professor McNair's list of great merchants not because of the fortune he has accumulated, although that is considerable. Ferkauf's prestige is due to the chain reaction he helped set off. Only a few years ago, the discount house was a familiar but marginal figure on the retail scene, limited, for the most part, to the appliance trade in the downtown sections of a few large cities. Ferkauf saw that the same low-margin, low-service, high-turnover technique that had sold appliances could sell every other kind of merchandise as well.

Korvette opened its first department store in Westbury, Long Island, a heavily populated suburb of New York, in 1954. Since then, in the suburbs of every large metropolitan area—New York, Boston, Philadelphia, Detroit, Chicago, Houston, Los Angeles—in almost every medium-sized city, e.g., Springfield, Massachusetts; Nashville, Tennessee; Akron, Ohio; and in small towns like Canton, Mississippi; Kokomo, Indiana; and Yakima, Washington, huge new discount stores of 70,000 to 200,000 square feet have sprung up, and more are on the way. Most of them are being built by firms as new to retailing as Korvette and bearing such unfamiliar (and frequently unlikely) names as Two Guys from Harrison, Gem, GEX, Zayre's, Spartan, Fed-Mart, Unimart, Bargain City, Bargain Town USA. But a growing number of discount houses are being put up by some of the oldest and most respected names in retailing—firms like F. W. Woolworth, S. S. Kresge, Grand Union, Jewel Tea, Food Fair, Allied Stores, City Stores, L. S. Ayres, Dayton Co., which have either acquired going discount chains or have set up their own discount-house subsidiaries.

The discount house, says Lester F. Davis, general manager of Woolworth's new Woolco Department Stores division, which is building eighteen discount houses in the next eighteen months, "is now at the stage that supermarkets were at twenty-five years ago." Whether or not they achieve the same market penetration, it is clear that discount houses have already made a lasting imprint on U.S. retailing. "The discount house," says one retailing consultant, "is producing the greatest deflation of stuffed shirts ever to hit American business."

Retailers of every description—department stores, five-and-dimes, specialty shops, supermarkets—are being forced to examine, and frequently to change, their store hours, prices, accounting techniques, inventory selection, and merchandising policies. The changes at the retail level, in turn, are forcing manufacturers of consumer goods to take a fresh look at their distribution policies.

The discount house is itself a response to the explosive growth of suburbs and to the enormous shift in the distribution of income during the last two decades—forces that are reshaping every aspect of American society and of the U.S. economy. In the process, some profound changes are taking place throughout the entire system by which goods are distributed from manufacturers to ultimate consumers. Since the discount house is unquestionably the most important single factor in the current upheaval, this article will analyze the phenomenal growth of discounting in recent years and speculate on its future course. The next article will examine the different strategies being employed by the new discount-house chains in their fight for supremacy—a fight being waged against the old-line retail organizations and against one another. The third article in this section will analyze the strategies that the department stores, supermarkets, and other conventional retailers are employing to meet, or to escape, discount-house competition.

The Great Cornucopia

Just how many discount houses there are in the U.S., and what sales volume they do, are matters of some uncertainty. Trade sources put the number of full-line discount houses at between 1,500 and 2,400, and estimate their 1961 sales volume at $4 billion to $4.5 billion. The figures are at best rough estimates, though they undoubtedly indicate the right order of magnitude. There are no government statistics on discount-store sales; the Census Bureau and Federal Reserve Board statisticians responsible for retail-trade data have not yet recognized the discount house as an independent phenomenon. (The government's Standard Industrial Classification contains no category for discount houses.) One reason the trade sources differ so widely on the number of stores is that it's sometimes hard to determine who is and who is not a discounter; the popularity of discounting has led a good many conventional retailers to try to use the "discount" label. ("It's like shopping at a discount store when you buy a car at Duckler Pontiac," Milwaukee radio audiences are being told these days.)

The fact is, however, that the new full-line discount department stores (which are the ones that are causing all the furor) are as recognizable—and virtually as indistinguishable one from another —as Howard Johnson restaurants. The typical discount house is a cavernous, free-standing, one-story building with plenty of parking space, located on a well-traveled suburban street or highway. The roof beams are usually exposed, as are the fluorescent fixtures, and the general decor is, to use a polite term, spare. To be sure, a considerable number of discounters are trying to upgrade the appearances of their new stores—to make them, as they stoutly insist, "as attractive as a regular department store." They have a long way to go; any shopper, put down in the middle of the most upgraded discount store, would know he wasn't in Marshall Field's.

The overwhelming impression is of an enormous cornucopia: the unadorned shelves, pipe racks, and other fixtures are filled to overflowing with goods of every description—men's, women's, and children's apparel; sheets, towels, curtains, and other home furnishings; drugs and cosmetics, toys, records, appliances, hardware, auto accessories—and, in a substantial number of discount houses, food. The customers serve themselves, loading their merchandise into wire supermarket carts. Loudspeakers blare away at frequent intervals, offering "fifteen-minute specials," the signal for bargain hunters to stampede to one department or another. Transactions are generally cash-and-carry, though most discount stores offer home delivery for a charge, and a growing number are offering credit—also for a charge. Needless to say, merchandise is not gift-wrapped.

Most discounters assiduously cultivate what retailing consultant Perry Meyers calls a "family fair" atmosphere. Women shop in slacks or shorts and bring the children and their husbands along. Newer stores frequently have a small nursery equipped with TV sets, tables and benches, crayons, and baby-sitters. In one enormous new discount house in Long Island's Levittown, the baby-sitter's principal function is to make change so that the small fry can play the pinball machines.

Frugal decor and almost total absence of sales service are what enable discounters to operate at considerably lower costs than most conventional retailers. According to estimates by Fairchild Publications, construction costs of discount houses run from $5 to $10 per square foot, compared to a typical range of $14 to $18 per square foot for department stores, and the discounters' fixtures average $1.50 to $3 per square foot as against $5 to $8 per square foot for department stores. And the discounters' payroll costs average only 6 to 7 per cent of sales, compared to an average 18.25 per cent for department stores.

Just how much of this saving in costs is passed on to the consumer in lower prices is a matter of heated debate. Discounters claim to sell 10 to 30 per cent below the prices prevailing in conventional stores; conventional retailers argue that price comparisons are misleading, since in their view discount houses carry inferior merchandise. But in a considerable number of departments—e.g., small and large appliances, tires and auto accessories, cameras, books, records, toys, sporting goods, drugs and cosmetics —advertised brands constitute the principal stock in trade, and the merchandise consequently is the same in both groups of stores. In these departments, which account for one-third or more of discount-store nonfood volume, the discounters' prices unquestionably are lower on average, although the differential is beginning to narrow now that department stores and other retailers find it necessary to meet discount-house competition. Discount-house food prices also tend to be somewhat lower than prices in conventional supermarkets, especially for canned and packaged foods. For one thing, a good many discount houses run their entire food department as a "loss leader" operation, in order to generate traffic for the rest of the store. But discounters' food-department costs are lower, too, by 3 to 5 per cent, and so prices

are usually lower even where the food department is run at a
profit by a lessee, which is frequently a large supermarket chain.
The food departments that Kroger runs for Gem International
in St. Louis, for example, undersell Kroger's own supermarkets in
that area.

However, when it comes to soft goods (men's, women's, and
children's apparel, sheets, curtains, etc.) and to furniture, price
comparisons are more difficult. Branded merchandise accounts
for only a small proportion of sales of these items, and discounters generally have been unable to gain access to the major
branded lines—e.g., Arrow shirts. To the casual eye, the quality
of the apparel found in the average discount house is not so high
as that found in the better department stores. But the discount
houses aren't competing against the better department stores;
they are competing against the department store basement or
budget shops and against the popular-priced apparel and variety
chains and the so-called "junior department stores." To be sure,
the merchandise varies widely from store to store, and some alleged discount houses—like some conventional stores—are in
reality "schlock" operations offering manufacturers' "seconds"
at inflated prices. But discount chains like Korvette, Interstate,
Gem, Zayre's, and Spartan, and most, if not all, of the independents carry largely first-line merchandise, and their soft-goods
prices do run 10 to 25 per cent under the prices in conventional
stores or basements that cater to the same market. All told, the
discounters operate on gross margins of 18 to 25 per cent (calculated as a percentage of selling price, not cost of merchandise),
compared to 36.4 per cent for department stores, 38.5 per cent
for specialty stores, and 37.2 per cent for variety chains.

The Battle in the Suburbs

Like all revolutions, the one wrought by discount houses cannot be measured by statistics alone. Their impact is considerably
greater than the sales figures of $4 billion to $4.5 billion out of
total U.S. retail sales of $220 billion suggests. For one thing, the
discounters' competition is being felt principally by two types of
conventional stores: apparel, home-goods, and general-merchandise stores, which are the ones most people think of when they
talk about retailing, and grocery stores.

Food sales through discount houses account for 4 per cent of the $50-billion total retail food sales; their impact on supermarket profits is considerably greater, since so many discount houses use food as a loss leader. And discounters now account for 6 to 8 per cent of sales in the $50-billion apparel, home-goods, general merchandise market. Discount-house sales are already considerably larger than total sales by variety (five-and-dime) chains or by mail-order firms, and they are roughly one-quarter as large as total department-store sales.

Moreover, discount houses are heavily concentrated in the suburbs of major metropolitan areas. It is therefore the suburban branches of department stores and variety and apparel chains—and even more, the independent specialty shops in large suburban shopping centers—that are feeling most sharply the heat of discount-house competition. And the heat hurts; the downtown department stores and the downtown branches of the large chains had been suffering from shrinking volume and profits for a decade or more before the discount-house competition began, because their customers were moving to the suburbs. They had come to rely on suburban branches to supply most of the sales growth and the profits. But no sooner had the department stores made their move to the suburbs than they began to meet discount-house competition.

Now the competition is really getting keen. Of the eight large discount houses in Milwaukee, for example, seven opened last year, and another four are planned for this year. Twenty large discount stores opened in Los Angeles in 1961, doubling the number of major units; in the suburb of Covina alone—a community of 100,000 families—there are eight discount stores averaging 100,000 square feet each. Twelve discount department stores opened in Detroit last year, and another eleven are planned for this year. In Springfield, Massachusetts, where the number of discounters jumped from one to ten in just two years, the discount stores now account for perhaps 20 to 25 per cent of total sales in the apparel, home-goods, general-merchandise market. All told, according to estimates by Fairchild Publications, some 400 new full-line discount department stores were built last year, totaling 28 million square feet, and 500 more stores will be built this year, totaling 40 million square feet. (Discount houses may account for one-quarter or even one-third of total store construction in the apparel, home-goods, general-merchandise category.) For example, Korvette is opening seven new stores this year ranging in size from 145,000 to 250,000 square feet. Spartan is opening twenty-eight new stores, Interstate twenty, Zayre's twenty, Gem International twelve. By the end of this year, discount-house sales might well be up some 50 per cent from last year, and be running at a $6-billion to $7-billion annual rate.

The New Millionaires

This dizzy pace of expansion is possible in large part because the discounters—in sharp contrast to the cautious bureaucrats who run most old-line retailing organizations—are entrepreneurs who delight in taking risks and in playing the long shots. So far, at least, the long shots have paid off well; the discount business has spawned a number of millionaires besides Gene Ferkauf of Korvette. For example, Ollie Cohen and Murray Candib, the soft-spoken partners who started King's Department Stores in an empty motorcycle plant in Springfield, Massachusetts, in 1949, have parlayed initial investments of $30,000 each into stock now worth $8 million each.

Their high rate of return on invested capital also enables the discount chains to finance a considerable rate of expansion out of earnings alone. Last year, for example, Korvette earned 18.5 per cent on net worth, after taxes. Indeed, Sol Cantor, president of Interstate Department Stores, insists that "if you can't earn at least 20 per cent on capital, you don't belong in the discount business." By comparison, Federated Department Stores—the largest, and by general consensus the best-managed department-store chain in the U.S.—earned 12.9 per cent on capital in 1960, and department stores as a group earned 7.2 per cent. (Variety chains earned even less.) To be sure, the discount firms tend to be under-capitalized, with much higher debt in relation to capital than department stores. But their profitability is impressive nonetheless.

Glamour in Wall Street

Discount firms, moreover, are able to open new stores with surprisingly small cash outlays. For one thing, they almost invariably rent their stores, and they have had little difficulty finding real-

estate operators who are willing and able to finance the construction. (Shopping-center promoters, in fact, are now eagerly seeking discount-house tenants, because of the traffic they attract;
indeed, in one West Coast shopping center, which includes a
branch of a large department store, several national chains made
their leases conditional on the presence of a large discount store
as well.) A good many discount stores rent even their fixtures.
And a substantial proportion of discount firms, especially among
the independents and smaller chains, do not directly operate their
merchandise departments. Instead, they lease most or all of the
departments to other entrepreneurs, many of whom run departments for a number of different discount houses and chains.

The discount-store owner who leases out his departments has
no inventory expense and only a small payroll; he is primarily a
contractor who provides a number of central staff services, e.g.,
advertising and promotion, and exercises a certain amount of
supervision and control, the amount varying from firm to firm.
Gem International, Consumers Mart of America, Towers Marts,
Floyd Bennett Stores, among others, all lease most or all of their
operating departments; Woolworth plans to lease many of the
soft-goods and hard-goods departments in its new Woolco discount stores, and City Stores (an old department-store chain) is
planning to lease a large number of departments in the new discount store it is opening in downtown Boston. But even the discount firms that operate most departments directly, e.g., Korvette,
Interstate, Zayre's, Spartan, have little difficulty financing their
inventory requirements. They turn over their stocks so rapidly—
seven times a year for Korvette, compared to a department-store
average of less than four—that they sometimes are able to sell
most of their opening stock before the merchandise has to be
paid for.

The discounters' profitability and rate of growth have given
them ready access to the capital markets; discount-department-
store operators have replaced electronics and space companies as
Wall Street's most glamorous stock issues. Last year, for example,
Korvette enjoyed the largest percentage gain of any stock listed
on the New York Stock Exchange; it rose 309 per cent, from
31½ to 128⅞ before splitting three for one. (In 1960, Korvette
had sold as low as 14¾.) At recent prices the market is valuing
Korvette at nearly $200 million—more than the giant Allied
Stores, third-largest conventional department-store chain, whose

sales are nearly quadruple Korvette's. On the Big Board, also, Interstate Department Stores last year went from 17⅛ to 52¼ and Spartans Industries from 27 to 51½; Vornado (operating Two Guys from Harrison), which was listed on the N.Y.S.E. this January, had shot up from 12⅜ to 45 on the American Stock Exchange. The popularity of discount-house stock has made it relatively easy for discounters and operators of leased departments in discount stores to sell stock to the public; a dozen firms "went public" last year, and a number of others are in registration now.

Catering to the New Masses

To understand why the discount house is having such an impact on retailing it is necessary to understand why it has been able to gain such broad and rapid acceptance from the consuming public. For one thing, most of the new suburbs have been "understored," notwithstanding all the shopping-center construction of recent years; except for supermarkets, store building just didn't keep pace with population growth. The discounters have been filling the vacuum; with no previous background in retailing, they had no investments to protect, hence were able to go wherever the customers were.

More important, the discounters recognized that the suburbs were changing character as well as growing—specifically, that they were becoming the home of the blue-collar as well as the white-collar class. Department stores have always catered to the low and low-middle income groups through their basement stores, which account for 10 to 20 per cent of store sales and a much larger proportion of profits. During the flush years of the early postwar period, however, store managers became infatuated with the explosive growth of the middle-income group and the consequent possibilities for "trading up." When they built their suburban branches, therefore, the department stores usually left their basements behind; they failed to see that their basement customers were moving to the suburbs, too. As a result, they left unsatisfied a substantial demand for low-priced staples and semi-staples—children's clothing, sheets, towels, women's lingerie, men's sport shirts, etc. These are precisely the soft-goods lines with which the discounters have had the greatest success.

But the discount house appeals to more than just the bottom income group. In a study of Springfield, Massachusetts, for example, Perry Meyers discovered that, while the discounters' greatest appeal was to the $5,000-a-year group, nearly everybody in the area did *some* shopping at the discount stores. Among middle- and upper-income families, the discounters have gained their best acceptance in children's clothing and domestics (towels, sheets, etc.), and in housewares, small appliances, and toys. The middle and upper-income groups are least inclined to shop at discount houses for fashion merchandise—i.e., dresses, coats, and suits—but their inclination is growing.

In view of the trend of rising income and the general emphasis on "trading up," this broad acceptance of the discount house may seem an anomaly. Actually, it is deeply rooted in the sociology of the consumer market. There was a time, not too long ago, when a worker's spending pattern was rigidly circumscribed by the traditions of working-class culture and by the relative paucity of goods and services available to the blue-collar family. When incomes rose suddenly, as they did during World War I, the extra went for silk shirts or beer.

No longer; the prosperity of the last two decades has shattered, once and for all, the old differences between the blue-collar and white-collar styles of life. The great emphasis on trading up during the 1940's and 1950's, and the impression of uniformity that resulted, simply reflected the fact that the workers were shedding their old working-class spending patterns in favor of the habits of the middle-class. "The man in the Ivy League suit," as *Fortune* put it three years ago ("The New Masses," May, 1959), "may be a millionaire or a skilled machinist, and so may the man at the wheel of the sports car and the man on the beach in Miami. To the spectator, this may look like a new uniformity; to the machinist, it involves a new diversity."

Now, as a result, the consumer market has entered a new and wholly different phase, in which "trading down" is as important as "trading up." For most Americans, the 1950's produced an explosive widening of choice, as mass markets developed for a long list of goods and services that formerly were the prerogatives of the well-to-do. *Nouveaux riches* always become prudent and discriminating in time, and so the new masses are becoming more discriminating about the way they spend their rising incomes. Far from being sated with goods and services, as critics like John Kenneth Galbraith have suggested, Americans are finding it difficult to accommodate all their desires even within their rising incomes, and so they stint where stinting is possible. Consumers who want a new car, a boat, a trip to Paris, and a college education for their children are likely to go out of their way to save 10 to 20 per cent on their children's underwear.

"Fireworks and Location"

But price is not the only reason consumers patronize the discount house; strange as the notion may seem to devotees of Marshall Field's or Neiman-Marcus, a good many Americans actually enjoy shopping in discount houses. "The discount store's growth," says architect-industrial designer William Snaith of Raymond Loewy/William Snaith Inc., "is not so much due to its prices as to its fireworks and location. The discount store has brought a large, exciting store into decentralized shopping areas." Indeed, in the Meyers survey, price was fairly far down the list of reasons people gave for patronizing the discount stores. Convenient location, good parking, self-service, and the opportunity to browse without being browbeaten by a clerk were mentioned more frequently, though price, of course, was always mentioned.

Discount houses also capitalize on the fact that most suburbanites are unwilling to travel very far to shop and are reluctant to spend much time shopping. To the suburban wife who has to attend a P.T.A. meeting, chauffeur the children to the Boy Scouts, and hold down a part-time job to meet the payments on the house or boat, shopping has become a chore to be finished as quickly as possible, not a recreation for a leisurely afternoon. The discount houses offer the convenience of location of the neighborhood store, together with the range of merchandise previously available in the suburbs only in the large regional shopping center. They offer more convenient hours: discount stores are open every night and frequently on Sundays as well. (In a number of states, e.g., Missouri, authorities have recently started to enforce old "blue laws"; in a number of other cities and states local merchant associations have been pressing for enactment of new legislation.) And they offer self-service, which speeds shopping and which has been accepted as a matter of course by a younger generation brought up to buy food in supermarkets and to carry laundry to a Laundromat. Self-service makes it possible for discounters to lengthen hours without a commensurate increase in costs; conventional retailers have resisted night and Sunday hours in part because owners and managers don't want to work at those times, in part because the longer hours would raise costs substantially.

Their informal atmosphere enables the discount stores to attract considerable numbers of male shoppers, especially blue-collar workers who feel out of place in the more sedate department-store atmosphere. This adds to store volume, for men are notoriously susceptible impulse buyers. (The discount stores have found auto-supply, sporting-goods, and hardware departments to be excellent means of generating more male traffic, besides being profitable operations in their own right.) Here, too, the discount stores are capitalizing on a more general trend—toward more male participation in the shopping process. It didn't used to occur to men to take an interest in shopping; they were too absorbed in their jobs, and besides, with a six-day week, they didn't have time to shop. Today men naturally become interested in shopping, for consumption has become too important to be left exclusively to the women.

Jayne Mansfield and 9-Cent Coffee

But the discounters are not only providing convenient locations and hours; they are flamboyant and unorthodox merchants. Unlike the old hard-goods discounters, the new discounters strongly believe in advertising, and they draw large crowds with razzle-dazzle promotions. This winter, in each of its stores, Consumers Mart of America featured a drawing for a thirteen-day trip to Acapulco. And when it opened its 132,000-square-foot store in Phoenix, Arizona, last November, for example, C.M.A. arranged for personal appearances by Jayne Mansfield and George Raft. More to the point, perhaps, it offered coffee at 9 cents a pound, eggs at 29 cents a dozen, Coke at 9 cents a carton. (Employees of the company are currently involved in a test case of a newly amended California law barring loss-leader sales below cost where the quantity per customer is limited.)

"Traffic" is important to most discounters because they depend on impulse buying rather than personal selling to move their merchandise. "If you bring enough people into the right kind of store," says C.M.A. President J. A. Keilly, "they'll buy everything." For self-service, as the discounters (and the supermarket operators before them) have demonstrated, is not simply a means of cutting labor costs; it also tends to increase sales by bringing the merchandise out where the customer can see it and feel it. More often than not in the conventional store, the salesclerk is simply an obstacle between the customer and the merchandise.

There is, however, one group of discounters who rely less on traffic and more on customer loyalty to build up sales volume. These are the so-called "closed-door discount stores," which admit only "members," who pay a $2 or $3 initiation fee (and in some instances, a $1 annual renewal fee) for the privilege of shopping. The stores make quite a ritual of the membership; to be admitted, shoppers must show their membership cards to a guard at the door; and again with each purchase. (There are an estimated five million card-carrying shoppers, and perhaps eighty closed-door stores, in the U.S.) The closed door and the ritual are designed to create an ingroup psychology that will lead customers to buy everything they need in "their" store, instead of shopping around from discount house to discount house. The experiment has had mixed results. Some firms, e.g., Gem International, have been quite successful; but in the past year a number of closed-door firms have opened their doors.

The discounter's greatest advantage—his faster turnover of inventory—comes from a radically different approach to merchandizing. The department-store operation too often resembles the proverbial old-maid librarian, who cherishes her books but resents letting them out; as Perry Meyers puts it, the department store tends to treat each piece of merchandise as if it were a precious jewel. The discounter, on the other hand, sees the store not as a place to display merchandise but simply as the channel through which the goods move as rapidly as possible from manufacturer to customer.

"Thick on the Best"

More important, the discounter—consciously or not—recognizes the most fundamental law of distribution: that whatever the line, a very small number of items will account for the great bulk of sales. (See "The Economy's Dark Continent," page 294.) "Instead of the traditional department-store motto of 'Thick on the best, thin on the rest,'" says Sol Cantor of Interstate Department

Stores, "the discount operator says 'Thick on the best, to hell with the rest.'" Cantor finds that his discount stores can cut 50 to 60 per cent out of what his department stores consider a conventional assortment. To take another example, Macy's New York carries 129 separate styles of men's white dress shirts, ranging in price from $1.99 to $14.09; Korvette carries thirty-five styles ranging from $1.49 to $6.99. Macy's carries nineteen sizes of flat and twenty-two sizes of fitted sheets ranging from $1.49 a sheet to $69.50 for a set consisting of one sheet and two pillowcases; Korvette carries six sizes of flat and four sizes of fitted sheets, ranging in price from $1.29 to $3.69.

How To Lose a Sale

The discounters thus have reversed the retailing trend of the last fifteen years, which saw an enormous proliferation of types of merchandise and of models, colors, styles, etc., in every branch of retailing. The discounter's policy grew out of his mode of operation. Self-service means that, by and large, a store can sell only what it can display; conversely, the discounter can afford to display only those items that will sell. But small quantities of an item tend to be lost in the vast jumble of goods; hence the discounter needs a lot of whatever he does stock. Merchandise consultant Fred M. Glass suggests as a general rule of thumb that discounters should buy only quantities large enough to cover at least a five-foot display.

It is a mistake, however, to assume that the discount house merely concentrates on the "hot" items. On the contrary, by narrowing the choice to a few items offered in depth, the discounter *creates* fast-moving items. One of the oldest rules of retail selling —a rule the department stores and supermarkets have tended to forget—is that the sale is lost if the customer is given more than three or four choices.

The discounter's "thick on the best, to hell with the rest" not only speeds his inventory turns but leads to economies at the manufacturing level as well. When he analyzed incoming orders, for example, Charles C. Bassine, chairman of Spartans Industries, a large manufacturer of low-priced apparel, discovered that discount stores typically bought five to ten times as much of a given item as conventional retailers of the same size. That is to say, a fifty-dozen order from a conventional store would be spread over five to ten styles, while the same size order from a discounter would cover just one or two styles. Bassine was so struck by the economies in handling the discounters' orders that he commissioned engineering studies of what would happen if Spartans were to ship its entire output to discounters; the studies suggested enormous potential reductions in the cost of packaging, paper work, warehousing, and selling, as well as in manufacturing itself. The indicated cost reductions, Bassine says, were "frightening, they were so large." As a result, Spartans began building its own chain of discount stores in November, 1960; the firm expects to have fifty stores in operation by the end of this year, doing a retail volume in excess of $175 million.

"The Only Crap Game"

There are limits, of course, to discount-house expansion. The discount store will never fully replace the department store or specialty shop or supermarket; the U.S. consumer market is too huge and varied and complex for any form of retailing ever to predominate. And so discount chains cannot go on indefinitely building stores at the current pace. Indeed, current expansion programs are bound to lead to oversaturation in some cities, and to stiffening competition in every city.

This new competition will force a lot of changes on the discount industry. Until recently, as Interstate's Sol Cantor puts it, most discounters had been operating "the only crap game in town." Under these conditions, it seemed as though discounters could do no wrong; almost any kind of merchandise seemed to sell in almost any kind of environment. It won't any more. As the new stores now on the drawing boards open their doors, and as old-line retailers begin to fight back, discounters will have to find some means of distinguishing themselves from their competitors if they are to continue to attract customers.

The search is already on. A good many discounters are trying to improve the appearance of the new stores they build; a small expenditure on paint, for example, can make a big difference in the "feel" of a store. Some stores are using food as a "loss leader"; some stores are venturing into fashion merchandise, in order to

broaden their appeal; others are adding new service departments
—e.g., gas stations, barber-shops, dry-cleaning establishments,
and even, in one Long Island discount store, a mutual-fund sales
booth. There are, in short, a great many different strategies that
the discount chains and the independents are following.

In the fight for supremacy that's shaping up, quite a few of the
discounters will find the going rough. But it is too early to call
the shake-out now, as a number of pessimists are doing. Even
Barron's weekly, which knocked discount stocks out of bed this
winter with a bearish article, had grudgingly to admit that "to
date, earnings of the discount-house specialists give little indication of an approaching shake-out." Nor is there yet any indication
of serious overbuilding. To be sure, in Springfield, Massachusetts,
where the number of discount houses jumped from one to ten in
just two years, Towers Marts found the going so rough that it
sold its two stores to Bradlee's, the discount-house division of the
Stop & Shop supermarket chain. But what made this deal possible
was that Bradlee's was anxious to expand in Springfield. If the
Springfield experience proves anything, therefore, it is not that
the city is overstored with discounters, but that intense competition will enable the stronger firms to take over the weaker ones.[1]

There will be plenty of business for the strong firms to feed on.
Discount stores as a group are likely to continue expanding their
share of the market for some time to come. By 1965 the discounters may well have captured 20 per cent of an expanded
apparel, home-goods, general-merchandise market, which would
means sales of about $12 billion—more than three times last year's
nonfood volume. And by 1970, in the opinion of Perry Meyers,
discount-store sales, excluding food, could very well exceed $20
billion. This would represent 30 per cent of the market, which is
as large a share as department stores now enjoy. The 1960's
clearly will be an interesting decade for U.S. retailers—and
consumers.

---

[1] The few discount stores that have gone into bankruptcy so far have been
obvious cases of total mismanagement. One firm, for example, had liabilities
exceeding its total sales—i.e., it had literally sold its entire inventory for less
than cost. "We just marked the merchandise down until it moved," the
proprietor explained.

Now that discount houses have gained a significant place in retailing, they face a fundamental question about the strategy that should be pursued for future growth. Discounters themselves disagree on what the most appropriate course of action should be, but the decisions they make will determine the future role of discounting and will influence the fortunes of other types of retailers and the marketing strategies of consumer goods' manufacturers as well.

The Discounters Choose Their Weapons*

When E. J. Korvette recently announced plans to open a store on Fifth Avenue at Forty-seventh Street in the heart of New York City's luxury shopping district, one outraged Fifth Avenue merchant called the move "degrading." Curiously enough, a number of Korvette's discount-house competitors also disapproved, though for different reasons. Fifth Avenue, in their view, is no place for a discount house. "Discounters," says Sol Cantor, president of Interstate Department Stores, "will be successful only if they stick to honest discounting."

by

Charles E. Silberman

At the bottom of the debate over Korvette's move is the fundamental question of what strategy discount stores should pursue, now that they have gained a significant place on the retail scene. Should they, as Cantor seems to think, continue to cater predominantly to the blue-collar class and the less affluent members of the white-collar class—in which case their greatest asset is the drab, cluttered atmosphere that proclaims their devotion to "low

* Vol. 65, May 1962, pp. 118–120, 186–188.

overhead"? Or should they go after the patronage of the growing middle and upper-income group of managers, professional and technical workers—in which case they need more highly styled merchandise and something approaching the decor of the conventional department store against which to display it? If they choose the latter course, can they continue to sell at prices 10 to 30 per cent below those in conventional stores?

Nor are these the only issues animating the discount-house industry. Discounters disagree on the proper mix of "soft goods" and "hard goods"; on the proper breakdown of soft goods between staple, "semi-fashion," and "fashion" merchandise; on whether to operate their own food departments (and nonfood departments for that matter) or to lease such operations to supermarket chain stores or to independent specialists; on whether and how to advertise; on how large stores should be; on promotional techniques—in short, on virtually every aspect of merchandising policy. The debate over discounters' strategy is the subject of this article.

The answers that the industry evolves will affect more than the discounters' own future. They will influence the fortunes and the strategies of department stores, supermarket and variety chains, specialty shops—indeed, virtually every type of retail outlet—and of manufacturers of consumer goods as well. (The discounters' choices will also affect the fortunes of a good many individual investors who have purchased discount-house stocks.) For the enormous proliferation of discount stores in the past several years is one of the most convulsive revolutions in the history of U.S. retailing. There are between 1,500 and 2,400 full-line discount department stores in the U.S., and their total 1961 volume was $4 billion to $4.5 billion. Some 400 new stores were built last year, and another 500 or so are being added this year; by the year end, therefore, discount-store sales could be running at an annual rate of $6 billion to $7 billion, and by 1970 the discounters may have captured a larger share of the market than department stores now have.

It is their sheer success that is now forcing the discounters to rethink their strategy. The great population shift to the suburbs and the old-line retailers' infatuation with trading up created a large vacuum, and it sometimes seemed that discounters had to do little more than put up a sign and install shopping carts. No longer; department stores, variety and apparel chains, and super-markets are beginning to fight back. (Their strategies will be analyzed in the following article.) This, plus the enormous pro-liferation of new discount stores, means that the discounters for the first time are running up against the cutting edge of com-petition.

To some degree, discount firms' strategies are following the particular path along which each particular firm developed. Some of the most familiar discount department stores (e.g., Masters and Two Guys from Harrison in the East, and Fedco, Fed-Mart, White Front on the West Coast) started out as discounters of appliances and other branded hard goods, and they still show their origins; hard goods form the mainstay of their business. An-other group, by contrast, started out in the apparel business (usually in smaller cities) and apparel and other soft goods still account for the bulk—up to 70 per cent—of their sales. Some of these firms (e.g., Zayre's, Shoppers Fair, now national chains) were launched under reasonably auspicious circumstances by old-line apparel chains. Others (e.g., King's, Arlan's, Ann-Hope) had extremely humble origins in New England in empty textile mills and factories, which were fitted with pipe racks and unpainted plywood tables. And still a third group of national chains (e.g., Gem International, C.M.A.) began on a big scale as full-line dis-count department stores, organized by promoters who had no retail experience but who recognized discounting as a great in-vestment opportunity. Not surprisingly, discount firms with this sort of background lease most or all of their merchandise depart-ments to outside firms and place roughly equal emphasis on hard goods and soft goods.

Eugene Ferkauf of E. J. Korvette, however, is a daring inno-vator who has departed far from his original pattern of operation. His first store was a 1,000-square-foot loft on a side street in mid-town New York, where he sold luggage and small appliances.[1] In November, 1954, he opened the nation's first full-line discount department store in Westbury, Long Island. (Ferkauf's initial

---

[1] Ferkauf picked the name Korvette because he happened to like the sound (though obviously not the spelling) of the small British warship. The "E" stood for Eugene, the "J" for Joseph Zwillenberg, a high-school buddy who is now treasurer.

$4,000 investment is now worth $50 million in Korvette stock.)
Korvette always attracted a lot of well-heeled bargain hunters
looking for books, cameras, records, hi-fi sets, appliances, sheets
and towels, and housewares, but these customers disdained the
usual run of discount-house apparel. Like most discount houses,
Korvette was able to sell soft goods only to members of the blue-
collar class. But Ferkauf and his colleagues think that *everybody*
loves a bargain. "The customer who wants to save money," Merchandising Vice President Jack Schwadron argues, "is not necessarily the customer who has to save money." Schwadron and
Ferkauf now think they can pull in affluent customers for clothing
who *want* to save money.

To this end Korvette has designed a broad strategy. For its new
Fifth Avenue store, which one company officer calls "a palace,"
Korvette has hired a well-known fashion designer, Charles James,
to create an exclusive line of dresses and suits selling for $50 to
$200, and in all its department stores the emphasis is now on such
things as men's suits, women's dresses, coats, bathing suits, mil-
linery, etc. Korvette's new suburban stores—seven this year, ranging from 145,000 to 250,000 square feet—represent a completely
new look in discount houses. The two-story Huntington, Long
Island, store, for example, has wood-paneled walls in the men's
department, antique mirrors and gold carpeting in the women's
department, and attractive decor throughout; it is as attractive as
almost any conventional department store in the area. The emphasis is still on self-service ("You'll know you're not in Lord &
Taylor's, darling," a Korvette publicist told a *Fortune* researcher)
but salesclerks are available for customers who want assistance
and are willing to wait.

The Old "Mill-Store" Look

There are many in the industry who think Korvette is making
a big mistake, that the upgrading will destroy Korvette's discount-
house image and its discount-house cost structure and so put it
in a no-man's-land between the "legitimate" discount house and
the conventional department store. "We want self-service as close
to 100 per cent as possible," says Martin Chase, founder of Ann-
Hope Factory Outlet, one of the pioneer soft-goods discounters.
He is against selling men's suits in a discount house because the

sales help and fitting that are needed "add to the cost of the suit and destroy the value you're trying to give in the first place."

Others who say Ferkauf is getting off the track contend that while Korvette may gain upper-income customers, it will lose its more numerous blue-collar clientele. Lower-income people need the old "mill-store" look to reassure them that they're getting a bargain. "There's no sales weapon greater than the masses of merchandise on the tables and racks of the discount store," says Bernie Elfman, vice president of American Discount Stores.

But Ferkauf and Schwadron think they have a better weapon, i.e., their own merchandising skill. They are confident that they can attract the new white-collar clientele without losing the old blue-collar customers, and that the higher costs of the new stores will thereby be offset by higher volume. They insist on calling the firm a "promotional department store" chain—but they also intend to keep the discount-house reputation for bargains. Adding more expensive fashion merchandise has enabled Korvette to improve its gross margin without raising prices on its older lines. The company does not work on any basic percentage markup; to Ferkauf, any article is "worth what you can get for it," and he can get more for fashion merchandise, while still staying 15 to 20 per cent below the usual department-store price.

Nor has Korvette abandoned its basic discount-house "thick on the best, to hell with the rest" approach to merchandising, though its assortments necessarily have broadened somewhat. Thus, Schwadron eschews any desire for style leadership. "We want the hot designs that are in the market already," he says.[2] And the company prides itself on its young, lean, penny-pinching management group. The company offices still remain in the shabby loft building in which Ferkauf opened his first store. Ferkauf, who runs the company as chairman of the executive committee, puts in a ten-to-twelve-hour day six days a week, visiting at least one store every day. He doesn't bother with a private secretary (the switchboard operator handles his messages), nor does he have his own office; he shares the desk of whichever officer he happens to be dealing with at the moment.

---

[2] Charles James was hired to design clothes for the Fifth Avenue store because "big-name" dress manufacturers still refuse to sell to Korvette. If the James styles go over well, Korvette probably will design more of its own merchandise, à la Sears, Roebuck.

In any event, the new strategy seems to be paying off handsomely. In the first half of Korvette's 1961-62 fiscal year, the company increased its earnings 79 per cent on a 24 per cent sales rise. And for the twelve months ending January 28 (Korvette's fiscal year ends July 31) the company netted $5,760,000—better than 2.8 per cent on sales of $203 million.

Between a Quonset Hut and Marshall Field's

For all the catcalling, Ferkauf's innovations are being closely studied, and widely imitated. Although firms like Interstate, Zayre, Spartan, King's are still emphasizing staple and "semistyle" merchandise, e.g., work pants, wash slacks, housedresses, men's sport jackets at $15, etc., they are also dabbling in style items, e.g., fur-trimmed sweaters; and they are assiduously trying to make their new stores more attractive. "What we're looking for," one discounter explains, "is a compromise between a Quonset hut and Marshall Field's." The compromise may be much closer to the Quonset hut than to Marshall Field's, but the upgrading is unmistakable. Even Atlantic Mills, which aims entirely at the bottom income group (it sells boys' polo shirts at 41 cents, a three-piece "Danish Den suite" for $34.88), is now putting up one-story air-conditioned store buildings. By contrast, its Providence, Rhode Island, store—opened less than four years ago—is on the second story of a shabby warehouse in a shipyard.

Some firms have gone a good deal further in Korvette's direction. Gem International, for example, which admits only dues-paying members drawn largely from civil service and the employee rolls of large corporations, finds that its white-collar clientele is quite willing to buy better merchandise. Thus, its new Boston stores are able to sell women's fur-trimmed coats at $118 ("comparable value" $169 in Boston department stores) and shoes for $18. Gem Chairman Wolfson agrees that higher-priced merchandise needs more attractive surroundings, and Gem's new Boston stores have a department-store look, with carpeted floors, dropped ceilings, plastered walls (instead of the usual metal or cinder block), and fancy fixtures. In Washington, D.C., Towers Marts International found that it was aiming below the economic and taste level of the community. This spring, therefore—after only seven months of operation—Towers revamped its four Washington stores. It is now planning to install shoe boutiques and specialty shops for women's apparel, and it is changing the store name from Towers Discount City to Towers International—"to lend an international flavor to the new fashion look," says a company spokesman.

Ringing the Cities

The controversy over "upgrading" that Korvette has generated is only one of a number of strategic issues over which discounters differ, as has been pointed out. There are violent differences of opinion over how large new stores should be and where they should be put. "Anything less than 150,000 square feet in a fair-sized population area," says Chase of Ann-Hope, "would not serve the public adequately"—which is to say that anything smaller cannot have the number of departments and the array of merchandise that is needed to generate a really large sales volume. Most national chains, however, have preferred to build smaller stores of 70,000 to 125,000 square feet, and the old-line retailers who are going into discounting—e.g., Woolworth, Kresge, Dayton's, L. S. Ayre's—are doing the same. They feel that when competition intensifies at the end of the current store-building binge, discounters will find the trading area from which they draw sharply reduced and circumscribed, and that smaller stores will be better able to maintain their profitability than the Goliaths. (The "draw" of the average supermarket in the Los Angeles area, for instance, has dropped from a three-mile radius to one mile in the last five years.) "There are going to be a lot of expensive white elephants," warns Sol Dobin, president of Bargain Town USA.

In picking locations for new stores, most of the large chains are following a strategy of market saturation, in which they ring a major metropolitan area with a number of stores. Korvette has put all its stores so far in the great megalopolis that stretches from Philadelphia to Hartford, Connecticut, though it is now planning to enter the Chicago and Washington, D.C. markets. Interstate has five stores in Chicago and is expanding to seven; Spartan is building six stores around Detroit. This enables the chains to advertise at a relatively low cost per store; it also helps them overcome the handicaps of their newness and relative anonymity. But some discounters are taking a different tack. King's, for example, puts only one store in each city. Saturation, in the opinion of its chairman, Ollie Cohen, simply means smaller sales per individual store.

The one strategy on which the discounters do seem agreed is to expand at breakneck speed, in order to pre-empt the best locations before the old-line retailers—or other discount chains—get there. Once they have staked out the prime locations and are enjoying a large sales volume—so they reason—they'll be able to build the necessary management organization and create the needed internal controls. Indeed, Sol Cantor of Interstate argues that size is a prerequisite for a first-rate management organization since top-notch talent is expensive. "You've got to get big if you're going to stay on top of the best talent," he argues: "You can be hurt in this business if you don't have size."

"Ready To Be Plucked"

In the competitive brouhaha that's shaping up, however, survival will depend on more than size. A large and vocal group of retailers believes that one whole category of discount stores will succumb in the next several years: namely, those that lease all their major departments to outside concessionaires. "These fellows are ready to be plucked," says T. E. Cummings, president of Food Giant Markets (a California supermarket chain that recently went into discounting).

The reasoning is that stores which lease sacrifice control and maneuverability. Stores that operate their own departments can retain tighter control over the quality of the merchandise, the methods of display, and relations with customers. "A store is as good as its weakest department," says Sol Dobin of Bargain Town USA. "You can do a hundred good things for a customer—but just louse him up once and the whole store is no good." Then, too, stores that operate their own departments have much greater flexibility over the allocation of space during the year; for example, they can squeeze their men's apparel departments and expand their women's departments before Mother's Day, and then reverse the allocation for Father's Day.

Most important, however, the discounter who operates his own departments can take a far more flexible position on prices: when circumstances require it, he can run a whole department at a loss indefinitely. In the fully leased store, on the other hand, goods must be priced so as to return a profit to every department, since each is run by an independent company.

Self-operation is particularly important in food, since the whole point of a discount-house food department, in some discounters' view, is to attract customers into the store several times a week. "If the food operator in a discount house is to serve his purpose," one discounter argues, "he *cannot* make a profit."

But in the usual babel of voices that is heard on every big or little point about the business, Harold Gottfried, vice president of Virginia Dare (Atlantic Mills), can be heard saying that customer traffic into a food department may not raise sales of non-food items at all. Says he, women who are shopping for food don't want to linger, they want to rush home and get the food into the refrigerator. Interstate concedes that food is a useful lure but prefers to lease the department to supermarket operators anyway. (The company operates most of its own nonfood departments.) It sets a nominal rental; that way, Interstate Vice President Barry Golden thinks, the lessee can undersell local supermarkets by at least 5 per cent and still make a profit.

Developing "a Means of Distribution"

The most obvious attraction to leasing is that it enables an undercapitalized discounter to expand rapidly on other people's capital. "Our first objective," Samuel J. Rosenstein, board chairman of Towers Marts International, says, "was to develop a means of distribution." Towers' sales were $9 million in fiscal 1960, $20 million in fiscal 1961, and $38 million in the seven months ending last December 31, during which time it opened fourteen new stores. Rosenstein expects to open another twenty-two stores this year, which would bring the total to forty-five. He readily concedes that the firm could not have expanded at anything like this rate had it been necessary to finance its own inventories. The exponents of 100 per cent leasing feel, moreover, that they have developed a number of techniques to give them close control of their lessees' operations. Gem International, for example, has thirty or sixty-day cancellation clauses in all of its licensing agreements, so that it can get rid of an inefficient or uncooperative lessee with virtually no difficulty. The company can force a lessee to meet a competitor's price on an individual item, and Gem's central merchandising staff coordinates and controls merchandising policy.

Some old-line retailers like Woolworth and City Stores that are now going into discounting will lease most or all of their major departments. Obviously they aren't doing it because they are strapped for cash. Rather, they feel that leasing makes up for their own lack of the specialized mass-merchandising skills needed for success in the competitive discount fields. They have experienced merchandising men—but their experience may be more of a hindrance than a help. For discounting is a distinctive form of merchandising, and merchants brought up in conventional retailing frequently have a hard time unlearning their old habits and attitudes.

Retailers who lease out their departments, moreover, can now draw upon any of a number of specialists in operating leased departments for discount houses; some of these new specialists are substantial firms in their own right. The largest, in all probability, is Grayson-Robinson, which operates a chain of 229 conventional women's apparel stores, five discount camera stores, and the 241-store Beck Shoe chain. Grayson-Robinson began operating leased departments in discount stores a year or so ago to counteract the sales and profit decline in its conventional stores; it now operates women's and children's departments in fifty-six discount stores, photographic departments in twenty-seven, and shoe departments in twelve. The leased departments are now generating sales at a rate of $40 million a year, and Grayson-Robinson President Stanley Roth expects to be up to $100 million in another year; the firm is now in the black. Rockower Brothers, which just won the men's and boys' clothing concession in the new Woolco stores, used to operate a chain of twenty-one conventional men's clothing stores with a volume of $1,500,000 a year. When the proprietors tried to sell out for $75,000 in 1956, they could find no takers. Instead, they went into discounting. Sales are now running $15 million a year, and at recent stock prices the firm was valued at $13 million.

Such successes as these have attracted the attention not only of Wall Street investors but also of the discount-store operators themselves, who now feel they are missing something by leasing. Because discount stores with leased departments have to split their profits two ways, they generally operate on a much narrower margin than discount stores that operate their own departments —e.g., 1.4 per cent on sales for Gem vs. 2.8 per cent for Korvette and 2.6 per cent for King's. As they feel surer of their merchandising ability, there is a strong incentive for the lessor firms to try to take over direct operation of major departments—by acquisition of the firms to which they have been leasing. Floyd Bennett Stores, a small New York chain of leased discount department stores, recently acquired half a dozen firms operating housewares, hardware, paint, and garden-furniture departments. Towers is setting up a new corporation to acquire the stock of its Canadian concessionaires; Towers and the lessee firms will each own 35 to 40 per cent of the new company, with the remaining shares to be sold to the public.

"Who'd Come To Look?"

Another major issue on which discounters disagree is how to advertise—or whether to advertise at all. Most firms rely rather heavily on flamboyant advertising in which "low discount prices" are featured in bold type. Some discounters, however, have come to question whether the tactic doesn't ultimately become self-defeating because customers become inured to the price appeal. Thus Leonard's, a four-unit California chain, has dropped the word "discount" from its advertising. "We're trying to establish a well-respected organization," merchandise manager Jerry Moss explains. And Sol Dobin of Bargain Town USA, which spent only $45,000 on advertising last year, thinks that advertising just draws "lookers" rather than paying customers. "Who'd come here just to look?" he asks of his out-of-the-way Brooklyn store. "When a woman walks in, she's 90 per cent sold," he adds. "She's come to buy."

For much the same reason a number of discounters opppose the use of "loss leaders." Cohen of King's Department Stores, for example, thinks that loss leaders and frequent sales undercut its principal sales weapon, i.e., a reputation for day-in, day-out low prices; its advertising motto is "Every day is sale day at King's." And some discounters have abandoned the usual technique of marking goods with two prices: i.e., the "discount price" and the "comparative value." For one thing, Abraham Jacobson, vice president of Virginia Dare (Atlantic Mills), explains, customers might find the item elsewhere for less than the "comparative value," and so lose faith in the discounter's integrity. And women may exaggerate the saving if no comparative price is shown. For example, a woman might think that a $4.74 dress (which sells in conventional stores for $5.99 to $6.99) was really worth $10. "At *such* savings," Jacobson explains, "she wouldn't be thrifty unless she did buy the dress."

Like everyone else in retailing, in short, discounters are trying to probe the psyche of the U.S. consumer. It is obviously too early to judge which of the competing strategies will be successful. Indeed, if the history of retailing is any indication, any of the various strategies will work for some firms—and all will fail for others. What counts, in short, is less the specific strategy a firm adopts than the vigor and effectiveness with which it uses that strategy—which is to say, the degree to which it satisfies the desires of one or another group of consumers. For in the last analysis, the consumer is king.

The managers of many old-line department stores slept through the great convulsion in buying habits brought about by the automobile, the post-war flight to the suburbs, and the rise of the discount house. As a result, department store profits per dollar of sales dropped by nearly half in 15 years. But department stores are waking up. Some are opening their own discount stores but keeping them separate in name and location from their quality stores. Others have been successful in mixing self-service and discount operations under the same roof with their high-fashion departments. In addition, merchandising policies and operating procedures have been revised to meet the acute situation created by discount houses.

The Department Stores Are Waking Up*

by

Charles E. Silberman

There was a note of pride, almost of challenge, in the rotund old gentleman's voice as he read from his company's annual report for fiscal 1961. "In the light of relatively poor economic conditions during the first half of the year and of discount-house development," he reported, "two achievements, particularly, stand out. Our sales volume, even without that of new facilities, grew more rapidly than consumer income; our profits increased at a greater rate than sales."

The speaker was Fred Lazarus Jr., board chairman of Federated Department Stores, the largest department-store chain in the U.S. (It is, as its name indicates, a federation of twelve department-

* Vol. 66, July 1962, pp. 143–147, 246–252.

store groups with fifty-eight stores in all, among them Abraham & Straus and Bloomingdale's in New York, Filene's in Boston, Foley's in Houston, Shillito's in Cincinnati, and the Boston Store in Milwaukee.) Lazarus' pride was understandable: in the year ending February 3, Federated increased its sales by 9 per cent, to $856 million, and its net income by 11.7 per cent, to $36,800,000 —a return of 4.3 per cent on sales and 14.1 per cent on invested capital. Since 1947, Federated has increased its sales 2.8 times, its net profit 3.5 times, and earnings per share 2.5 times. "Much has been said about the changing patterns of retailing in the past few years," Lazarus concluded. "We believe we have learned how to meet more intense competition, whatever the source."

But not many of the old-line department stores could echo Lazarus' confidence. With $14.6 billion of sales last year, department stores make up the largest single segment of the $49-billion G-A-F (for general mechandise, apparel, and furniture and appliances) market. But since 1947 their total earnings as a percentage of sales have dropped by nearly half, from 4.2 per cent to 2.3 per cent, and return on investment has declined at least as much. Some of the largest chains, such as Allied Stores and May Department Stores (No.'s 2 and 3 after Federated), reached their profit peak right after World War II and have been unable to do as well since. Allied's earnings per share in 1961 were 47 per cent below 1946 (although its sales were 96 per cent higher. Smaller department stores have fared even more poorly, and a considerable number had to close their doors—e.g., R. H. White in Boston, McCreery, Oppenheim-Collins, Hearn's, Namm-Loeser, and Jay Thorpe in New York, William Taylor in Cleveland, and Boggs & Buhl, Frank & Seder, and Rosenbaum in Pittsburgh.

What has knocked some of them out and brought others to an awareness of an acute situation is the explosive rise of the discount store. Fully 70 per cent of the department stores surveyed by the National Retail Merchants Association last January reported that competition from discount houses was affecting their volume. And the full weight of discount-house competition is still to be felt. According to Audits & Surveys Co., discount sales last year came to $4.4 billion. Expansion is so rapid that they could be running at an annual rate of $6 billion to $7 billion by the end of 1962. And by 1970, according to some projections, discount-house sales could come to $20 billion, or 30 per cent of the G-A-F market. This is as large a share as department stores now enjoy.

Small wonder, therefore, that a number of students of distribution (including quite a few producers of consumer goods) have begun to ask whether the department store has passed its prime. "There is a more or less definite cycle in American distribution," Professor Malcolm McNair of Harvard Business School has told the industry. "The wheel always revolves, sometimes slowly, sometimes more rapidly . . . Sooner or later," he warned, "marketing institutions seem to arrive at the point of vulnerability." When they do, "they must either innovate and evolve, or drop into positions of secondary importance."

The department store is clearly at the "point of vulnerability." How much of their market share department stores can hold on to in the face of discount-house competition will depend, in the last analysis, on the vigor and creativity with which they defend themselves against the discounters' varied strategies. The big news is that some department-store executives are taking their heads out of the sand.

Not all of them, to be sure; some store managers still prefer rhetoric to action. Last January, for example, Alfred C. Thompson, a Richmond, Virginia, department-store executive who was then president of the N.R.M.A., threatened reprisals against manufacturers who sell to discount houses. Retailers, Thompson warned, "are becoming Madame Defarges, creating a list of makers' names for future use." (Thompson apparently forgot the unhappy end to which Madame Defarge herself came.)

But a sizable number of department stores have decided that self-improvement is a more potent weapon than talk. Federated has demonstrated that a department store *can* continue to grow and prosper in the face of discount-house competition. And so across the country department-store managers are revamping their price lists, their selection of merchandise, their methods of display, the size, character, and location of their branch stores—indeed, every aspect of their merchandising policy—in an effort to meet and beat the new competition. These strategies form the subject of this article.

"More Than a Business"

The department store has a good deal riding for it. For all its troubles, it is still the great middle-class merchandising institution. The large department store, as its advocates never tire of

pointing out, is "more than just a business"; it is a community institution. In most communities, department stores have prestige
and a reputation for reliability that can be potent weapons in
the struggle with newer competitors. And they have a good deal
of financial strength.

But they have also been laboring under a number of disabilities.
For one thing, their dependence on downtown has been a grave
handicap in adjusting to the great postwar dispersal of population
from city to suburb. The city and the department store grew up
together. If the well-being of the department store depended on
that of the city, department-store owners and managers could be
forgiven for occasionally thinking that the reverse was also true.
For downtown was, in good measure, the product of the department store; its radical notion of selling everything under one roof
in a convenient, centrally located spot revolutionized retail trade
at the end of the nineteenth and the beginning of the twentieth
century and gave birth to the downtown shopping district. Most
of the major stores operating today were built in the two decades
before World War I—Macy's and Marshall Field in 1902, John
Wanamaker in 1910, Jordan Marsh in 1911—when cities were
building mass transit systems to speed the flow of people from
the outskirts to downtown.

In the postwar period, however, the population movement has
been the other way, and most downtown shopping districts have
suffered an erosion in trade. The department stores have found
themselves saddled with excess capacity; their old buildings are
uneconomically large and expensive to operate. Their managements have had to grapple with the difficult decision of whether
to abandon the old investment or pour good money after bad in
an effort to salvage it. They have built suburban branches, to be
sure (though many firms were late in starting), but generally
branch profits have not been enough to offset the decline in earnings downtown. And in their branches they made another kind of
mistake: they became infatuated with the "trading up" phenomenon. As a result, they did not take their "basement stores" and
"budget departments" to the suburbs. Thus they left a vacuum in
the market, which the discounters have been quick to fill.

Their inability to break with the past has handicapped the
department stores in another way. They have traditionally been
dedicated to great breadth of stock—i.e., many different styles
and brands in every department. In the beginning this was sound

merchandising policy; the department store's reputation for "carrying everything" was the magnet that attracted people from all over the city. But the stores have tended to take this policy beyond the point of diminishing returns. When one large department store, for example, installed a new inventory-control system that significantly reduced the number of times it would be out of stock on particular items, it found that its sales did not increase as a result—a sure sign that it had been carrying wider selections than customers really needed or wanted. The problem has been compounded in recent years by the enormous proliferation of shapes, styles, colors, and patterns coming out of the factories. As a result, department stores have steadily increased their inventory investment per dollar of sales. Since 1947 their turnover rates have declined 23 per cent—a major reason for the profit erosion.

Department stores have also been hampered by out-moded methods of management—in particular, their practice of offering the same package of services with every item and marking everything up by the same percentage, regardless of the costs incurred or the elasticity of consumer demand. "Retailing," as Theodore Schlesinger, president of Allied Stores, puts it, "has been captive to the percentage markup." Department-store executives forgot that markup is only a means to an end—that what counts is return on investment, which is a product of turnover as well as markup. Instead, the "game" has been to maximize gross margin. Buyers' bonuses, for example, are frequently geared to the gross margins they realize on the goods they sell, not to their dollar return on investment. The simplest way to achieve the required margin is to mark everything up by the same percentage—and to avoid high-volume items that carry a low initial markup. The department stores thus created a price umbrella under which the discounters were quick to swarm.

Cracking the Expense Nut

In the last analysis, however, the department store's greatest competitive disadvantage is the fact that it is a relatively high-cost method of distribution. "The crucial thing," says retailing consultant Perry Meyers, "is your expense nut"—and the department-store nut is large and hard to crack. Some of the expenses simply reflect the operation of Parkinson's Law. But the stores have been hampered in dealing with their costs by an obsolete accounting system, the so-called Retail Method of Accounting. In the Retail Method, all costs—sales personnel, warehousing, delivery, credit, theft, etc.—as well as initial markups and ultimate profit are calculated as percentages of sales. Because of the tremendous variety of merchandise, items are lumped together by departments; departmental averages of costs, not the actual costs, are used to determine what initial markup to apply and to calculate how much profit is returned by a given item. The technique has a very appealing logic, but it sometimes tends to obscure rather than illuminate the real cost situation. If, for example, the operating costs of an appliance department average 25 per cent, the Retail Method suggests to a buyer that the costs of selling a $500 refrigerator are 25 per cent of $500, or $125, while the costs of selling a $250 model are only $62.50, or half as much. In fact, of course, the costs of selling either model may be the same. If he had an accounting system that revealed the true costs—and if he were seeking to maximize return on investment—the buyer might use a lower markup on the more expensive model in order to sell more.

Despite their great authority, buyers as a rule have no responsibility for any costs other than those of the merchandise itself, and those involved directly in selling it. Quite frequently, therefore, buyers generate unnecessary expenses. In one classic case, a buyer bought $100,000 worth of English bikes, and ordered a second $100,000 worth when these were sold, because the bikes carried a larger than usual markup. But a subsequent audit (using the new technique called Merchandise Management Accounting) found that the store had actually lost money on the first shipment because of unduly heavy costs of handling and assembling—costs of which the buyer wasn't even aware. They were incurred, after all, in the warehouse, which was someone else's responsibility.

The Awakening of a Stuffed Shirt

The department stores are now trying hard to correct their past mistakes. They are moving in a variety of directions to meet and beat their new (and old) competition. Two broad strategies have emerged: first, moving in two directions simultaneously—i.e., upgrading the conventional department store but at the same time opening up a separate discount-house organization to meet discount competition; and second, introducing what Federated's Lazarus calls "flexibility"—i.e., operating self-service and discount departments and high-fashion departments under the same roof.

The first strategy is being tried by two midwestern department stores—L. S. Ayres of Indianapolis and the Dayton Co. of Minneapolis. Instead of trying to meet the discounters' competition in their traditional department stores, they are building their own chains of discount houses from the ground up, while at the same time "trading up" their old-line stores. "The retail revolution of today," President Donald Dayton says, "will end with two successful operations at opposite ends of the spectrum, the quality, fashion-right store at one end, the discounter at the other—and trouble for the merchants in between." David Williams, merchandising vice president of L. S. Ayres, agrees that "the store in the middle can't survive."

Both firms decided to start discount chains, not only in self-defense, but because they were convinced, as Lyman S. Ayres, board chairman of L. S. Ayres, puts it, that "there was a large untapped reserve of revenue in the town and that the department store was not the way to go after it."

Ayres has already opened two discount houses—one last October, a second in March—and it has plans for three more. The new stores are called "Ayr-Way," and they are obviously designed to exploit the parent company's reputation for quality. (With sales of $61 million, Ayres is the leading store in Indiana.) The buying is being handled by the L. S. Ayres basement-store buyers, and the decor and layout are a good deal more attractive than in the run-of-the-mill discount house. Dayton, by contrast, is not anxious to have its discount operation identified with its regular department stores. The firm is calling the new discount chain "Target" and has set up a completely separate organization to handle the buying and merchandising.

Meanwhile, to get clear of that fatal middle ground, Lyman Ayres has been assiduously cultivating "the Ayres look" throughout each of his conventional department stores, and the merchandising effort is being directed toward the middle and upper price lines. A few departments have been converted to self-service, but the firm makes no effort to meet all discounters' prices. "We don't want to muddy up the Ayres image," David Williams explains; in his view, the Ayres customers want service and are willing to pay for it.

Dayton's is even more determined in its trading up; Donald Dayton refuses to install self-service anywhere in his department stores. "Check-out," he says, "doesn't belong in a quality store." The company is backing up its faith in "the fashion-right, dominant downtown store" by building a new 400,000-square-foot branch in downtown St. Paul as well as a 200,000-square-foot suburban branch.

Federated Is Flexible

Some of the leading department-store merchants, however, think that the department store *can* appeal both to the discount-house customer and to its traditional clientele, and that Ayres' and Dayton's either/or strategy is misguided. "There is a tendency," Federated's Fred Lazarus Jr. says with some acerbity, "to divide up retail trade into separate categories—discounters, department stores, variety stores, etc. Our story is that we started seven years ago to put into effect our own philosophy, and that is flexibility in all our stores. This is the key to meeting competition."

Flexibility, in Lazarus' view, extends to service, pricing, merchandise selection, type of store—virtually every aspect of retailing. For example, Lazarus does not agree with Donald Dayton's insistence on providing the same high level of service throughout the store. Federated varies the service according to the department and the kind of merchandise in it. "If your wife wants to buy you underwear," says Walter Rothschild Jr., executive vice president of Abraham & Straus, Federated's largest outlet in the New York area, "she doesn't want someone to explain the glories of pima cotton nestling against your bottom. All she wants is to see what's available quickly and easily, pay for it, and get out—whether she's buying the underwear at Kresge's, A. & S., or Brooks Brothers." And so Federated stores generally offer the merchandise "bare bones" in some departments, with the full range of traditional department-store service in others.

Flexibility in service in turn permits flexibility in pricing. Federated meets the discounters' price on comparable items, e.g., appliances, toys, records, drugs. More often than not, the stores have discovered that they could make more money discounting than selling at list, and they have recaptured substantial volume in merchandise lines such as cameras and radios that they had once virtually abandoned to the discounters. But Federated's stores meet competitive prices even if it means operating a whole department at a loss. "This is a business of averaging," one executive explains. Because of its wider range of merchandise departments and price lines, a department store is in a better position than a discount house to get a profitable over-all mix even with substantial loss leaders.

The mix is profitable, moreover, because of Federated's mastery of "the art of merchandising," i.e., the ability to present attractive merchandise in an appealing way. "It's more important to be right than to be cheap," says Executive Vice President Paul Sticht. "What counts is buying the most wanted merchandise." In some departments, of course—drugs, records, appliances, for example—the "most wanted merchandise" consists of advertised brands that the discounters also carry. But the main thrust of Federated's strategy is to escape discount-house competition wherever possible by carrying more distinctive merchandise—i.e., shifting as many items as possible from the staple to the fashion category. In housewares, for example, the emphasis increasingly is on highly styled casseroles and earthenware cooking utensils rather than on aluminum pots and pans. The buyer's job, Sticht argues, is not just to comb the market for what's available, but to work with manufacturers in creating new styles. The objective is to create the kind of store to which women will come not just to buy a specific item, but "to see what they're showing."

This, of course, has long been the aim of all department stores. But what makes Federated distinctive is that it stresses narrow assortments, whereas most of its old-line competitors go in for great breadth. R. H. Macy, especially in its New York store, prides itself on offering every style, shape, and color a customer might conceivably want. A recent Macy advertisement for men's shoes showed an array of 144 separate styles.

Federated's theory is that too much breadth simply bewilders the customer; and that the store's responsibility as a merchant is to simplify the problem of choice. Excessive breadth also means a lower return on inventory investment. "It's just not economically sound to be all things to all people," a Federated executive argues. The idea is to make every item in an assortment count for something and represent a real alternative choice.

This doesn't mean that Federated shares the discounter's "thick on the best, to hell with the rest" merchandising approach. Nor does it try to be as narrow as Sears, Roebuck, which, in retired Board Chairman Charles Kellstadt's formulation, "always offers the customers at least two choices, but rarely more than three." (Sears offers most merchandise in three grades: "good," "better," "best.") Federated officials argue that their stores require broader assortments than the typical Sears store, because they are aiming at a much larger segment of the market. Even so, they keep the Sears assortments in mind as a target of sorts. "The better we do our job," Sticht says, "the closer we come to Sears' three choices."

Social Climbing at Bloomingdale's

If Federated thinks it sees a good special market, it will concentrate on it. The chain's conversion of Bloomingdale's into one of New York City's top-quality stores is one of the great retailing success stories of the postwar era. Fifteen years ago Bloomingdale's was a nondescript promotional department store with a poor location—at the fringe of a residential district rather than in the heart of downtown. But the residential district happened to be the upper East Side, one of the wealthiest residential neighborhoods in the U.S.—and the store also bordered an area slated for a lot of new office construction.

The Bloomingdale management set out, therefore, to exploit its location and convert it into a store that would appeal to East Side residents, as well as to middle-income office workers. The conversion required a ruthless selectivity in pruning old lines and adding new ones. Merchandisers sought to raise the level of taste throughout the store. They had to make the change subtly so that the old customers wouldn't be scared away before lots of new ones could be attracted. "The trick," says Sticht, "was to do it so slowly no customer ever realized we were taking a walk away from her." The trick was turned: since 1946, Bloomingdale's has been able to expand sales in its main store by 40 per cent, and it is virtually immune to discount-house competition.

Few department-store organizations have been as fortunate; for most of them, the problem of what to do about the attrition downtown must remain their central concern. Only a few firms, moreover, are in a position to pull up stakes entirely and move the whole business to the suburbs, as Broadway-Hale, a California department-store chain, is doing. (Broadway-Hale has announced plans to close its downtown San Francisco store when the lease expires next June, and the firm may not renew the lease on its downtown Los Angeles store, which expires in three years.)

In most cases, therefore, the merchants have pinned their hopes to a revival of downtown itself, and they are in the vanguard of pressures for new highways, new traffic-control devices, new municipal parking lots, and, above all, urban renewal. But there is an air of wistful unreality attached to almost all this talk and effort. On occasion, the measures actually backfire; in New Haven, for example, Shartenberg's, an eighty-year-old department store, went out of business in part at least because the city's elaborate redevelopment of downtown diverted traffic away from the store. More generally, the department-store managers, like the urban planners with whom they work, have failed to face up to the seriousness of the racial problem that lies at the heart of the city's difficulties. (See "The City and the Negro," *Fortune*, March, 1962.) As the economist for one large chain puts it, "Most managers don't recognize the full extent of the changing character of downtown."

It is to the suburbs, therefore, that the department stores must look for most of their growth. Here, too, Federated is showing "flexibility." The one major mistake the chain has made in the postwar period was to allow Bloomingdale's success to blind it to the different requirements of the suburban market, and so to leave the "budget" or "basement" shops out of its branches. As a result, a large and lucrative market has been going to the discounters by default.

The mistake is being rectified now. A fourth level, for example, is being added to Federated's two-year-old Shillito branch outside Cincinnati, to house a complete "basement store." Elsewhere, Federated is building separate, free-standing "basement" stores of 50,000 to 125,000 square feet. The strategy enables Federated to penetrate suburban markets that can't support full-fledged branches and counteract the discounters' usual advantage of convenient location.

"The Consumer's Purchasing Agent"

In trying to expand their suburban sales, however, department stores are coming up against competition not only from discount houses but also from the colossus of retailing, Sears, Roebuck.

With sales of $4.3 billion—about $1 billion from catalogues, the rest from retail stores—Sears last year accounted for 8.8 per cent of total sales in the G-A-F group.

Sears' growth—sales have quadrupled over the postwar period —stems in good measure from the fact that General Robert E. Wood, who ran Sears for twenty-six years, was the only pre-World War II merchant of consequence in the U.S. who understood the implications of the automobile for retail trade. As Wood himself put it, "Sears made every mistake in the book of retailing except one—it catered to automobile traffic."

But Sears' success also reflects its unique approach to distribution. Virtually all department-store men see themselves as "purchasing agents for the consumer," whose job is to select from what is already available in the market those items they think consumers are most likely to want. They see their responsibility beginning, therefore, when they take legal title to the goods they buy. They consider the delivered cost of the merchandise as their starting point, adding their markup to it—and making little attempt to influence the design of their merchandise, its packaging, production techniques, etc. Indeed, department-store executives repeatedly argue that they are powerless to reduce the cost of distribution because the Robinson-Patman Act forbids them from getting price concessions from manufacturers—as if beating manufacturers down in price were the only means of cutting the cost of distribution.

Sears goes at it from a different angle. It decides on the assortment of goods it wants and the prices for which they should sell, and works backward from there, organizing and supervising the entire process from the purchase of raw materials through the manufacture of the goods and their transportation to the stores. It specifies the design, materials, production standards, packaging, etc., for some 60 to 65 per cent of the goods it sells. (About 30 per cent or a little less are produced in Sears-owned or affiliated factories; 30 to 35 per cent are made by independent factories operating under Sears' specifications.)

Critics argue that the Sears approach is adaptable only to staple merchandise, but Sears uses its "specifications cost" technique for women's apparel, home furnishings, and other so-called fashion merchandise as well as for its traditional hard-goods lines. Even in lines in which style and fashion play the greatest role, Merchandising Vice President George Struthers contends, the great bulk of sales comes from "classics" whose styles change rather slowly, in more or less predictable ways, and whose production therefore can be scheduled in advance. "There is no more risk in a well-planned fashion assortment," says Struthers, "than in any other type of merchandise." The Sears technique, Kellstadt claims, "takes out of the cost of distribution all those things that do not increase the intrinsic value of the goods." Although Sears operates at a much higher gross margin than most discounters do, its prices are generally as low or lower—and for many items its quality may be higher. As a result, Sears has weathered discount competition extremely well.

Now Sears is taking aim at the department store as well as the discount house. It is increasing the emphasis on soft goods and fashion in its existing stores, and it is also building new stores that have the size of a conventional department-store branch, if not precisely the same assortment of merchandise. For example, Sears' store in the new Oak Brook, Illinois, shopping center outside Chicago runs to 273,000 square feet, only a little smaller than the Marshall Field branch in the same center.

Sears is moving in several other directions as well. It is experimenting with a chain of Super Value "drugstores"—drugstore being a euphemism for a small store that is free to carry any item that will sell rapidly, but that has no obligation to carry the conventional assortment of a regular Sears store. (The hottest item in the first drugstore to be opened was women's bras.) More important, perhaps, Sears is trying to carve out as big a position in the area of consumer services as it has in consumer goods. It is beginning to provide complete auto servicing, more and more extensive home modernization and repair services, and rental of all sorts of equipment.

Broadening the Sales Base

Sears' diversification into new merchandise lines is being widely imitated. For example, J. C. Penney, the largest apparel and soft-goods chain in the U.S., is building much larger stores and moving into hard goods—furniture, home furnishings, small and large appliances, cosmetics and drugs, sporting goods, hardware, and tires and auto accessories. "We think our acceptance in soft lines can be used as a wedge," says President William Batten, "provided we meet competitive factors." To broaden its sales base even more, Penney recently acquired a small mail-order house, General Merchandise Co. of Milwaukee, and will gradually install catalogue sales desks in its stores, thus enabling them to sell a broad range of merchandise whose volume doesn't justify in-store stocks.

The variety chains have also found that change is the price of survival; the five-and-dimes have been harder hit by suburban-ization and by the rise of the discount house than any other type of retail outlet. S. S. Kresge, for example, has suffered a 59 per cent decline in earnings since 1948, and S. H. Kress's earnings are off 79 per cent. To reverse the trend, a number of chains have been trying to turn their five-and-dimes into junior department stores. J. J. Newberry recently opened a 158,000-square-foot store in Fort Lauderdale, Florida, which carries furniture, carpeting, and virtually every other kind of department-store merchandise. Other chains are opening their own discount houses. Kresge, for example, is building eighteen large K-Mart discount houses this year and another thirty or so next year, and it is converting a number of small five-and-dimes to discount operation, cutting their range of stock by 80 per cent. And, by and large, the chains are tending to close their unprofitable downtown stores as the leases expire. As a result of the new strategy, most chains have been able to raise the proportion of suburban sales to about 50 per cent and in some cases even higher.

"Who Is Going To Be Shaken Out?"

What is happening, clearly, is that stores everywhere are get-ting larger and the lines of demarcation between types of stores are getting more and more blurred. Supermarkets are becoming general-merchandise stores; mail-order firms are operating dis-count houses and conventional department stores; apparel and variety chains are turning into junior and even full-fledged depart-ment stores. Indeed, it sometimes seems that *every* retailer is trying to become a department store. The result will certainly lead to more intense competition throughout retailing, and it is likely to create serious problems for smaller stores. (A trend toward larger stores has been going on for some time; since 1948 average sales per store, in dollars of 1961 purchasing power, have risen nearly 50 per cent.)

Generally speaking, department stores that have been able to establish a clear-cut character for themselves will continue to do well. Those that haven't will find the going even rougher in this decade than in the last. The showdown, however, may not occur for another three to four years, after the current wave of discount-house construction. "A shakeout appears to be inevitable," Professor McNair told the N.R.M.A. last winter. "But who," he asked, "is going to be shaken out?" No one yet knows; the answer will form an exciting chapter in the history of U.S. retailing.

As cars become more complex, there are more parts that can go wrong and have to be replaced. There are some 15,000 different parts in an automobile today, and nobody-knows-how-many in all the models produced by all the car manufacturers. On the comparatively rare occasions when a part fails, the motorist demands fast and efficient service. Whether it is a fuel pump for a 1960 Chevrolet or a bearing for a 1953 Dodge, the motorist expects the part to be almost instantly available. The distribution system required to provide the fast, efficient service demanded by motorists is a vast, complex network that functions exceedingly well.

*Anyway, It Works**

The Distribution System
for Automotive Replacement Parts

The hardest part of the $7-billion automotive aftermarket to get in focus is the distribution system. The distributors' problem is to have replacement parts immediately available in every corner of the United States—and not to go broke in the process. The way it is done baffles outsiders.

by

Freeman Lincoln

The first fact to grasp is that there are actually two distribution systems: one was set up by the car manufacturers, and consists principally of their dealers' "sales and service" organizations; the other, and by far the larger, is an "independent" distribution system—a diverse network ranging from warehouse operators to

* *Vol. 65, March 1962, pp. 84, 85; 223, 224; 226; 228.*

local jobbers—which channels the products of parts makers from factory to service or retail outlets. Complicating matters is the fact that the two systems crisscross at certain points. Any car dealer who needs a part in a hurry is likely to get it from the independent system, rather than from his manufacturer. And General Motors has always been a major user of both distribution systems.

The elements of the independent distribution system can be visualized on an "organization chart" that indicates the route followed by parts from factory to consumer. At least, the route is followed by *some* parts.

At the top of the chart would be the more than 1,000 manufacturers of all sizes that supply the market. Just below them would be the so-called warehouse distributors, or "W.D.'s" These are not parts manufacturers, but independent businessmen that maintain warehouse facilities for the manufacturers whose lines they carry. A big W.D. will carry an inventory of 40,000 to 50,000 items, worth more than $1 million, and will supply parts within twenty-four hours to any one of hundreds of customers within a radius of several hundred miles.

Just below the W.D.'s on the chart there will be some 15,000 jobbers. A big jobber may have sales of several million dollars and a dozen or more branches. But not all jobbers are big; many of them operate hole-in-the-wall shops of the kind ordinarily found near any Automobile Row.

At the base of the independent distribution chart would be a variety of retailers—mostly garages, service stations, and repair shops. In most instances these retailers get their supplies from jobbers and the jobbers get their supplies from warehouse distributors.

This sounds orderly enough, so far, and so does the pricing system—which usually works something like this: The car manufacturer publishes lists of "suggested" prices for replacement parts at each level of the distribution system. The W.D. buys an item at a 55 to 60 per cent discount from the suggested retail price— e.g., he pays 40 to 45 cents for an item that retails for $1. He sells it to the jobber for the same price that he pays. He reports this transaction to the manufacturer, who pays him a redistribution "compensation" that ranges from 15 to 20 per cent of his purchase price (e.g., he gets from 6 to 9 cents). The repair man, in turn, gets the product from the jobber for 30 to 40 per cent off list (e.g., for 60 to 70 cents), and sells it to the car owner at list.

If the distribution system always worked this way, everything would be nice and neat. But it works in many other ways, too. For instance, a manufacturer often distributes some of his products via non-automotive channels. He may use oil or tire distribution channels in order to reach gasoline service stations. Or he may bypass wholesalers altogether, and sell directly to such mass retailers as the mail-order houses and the chains of automotive specialty repair shops, like Midas, Rayco, etc.

But even when the manufacturer uses automotive channels, he does not always go down the same road. The manufacturer, for instance, does not sell only to the W.D. As often as not he sells directly to the jobber. The W.D. does not always act as a pure redistributor by selling only to jobbers. More often he operates his own jobbing stores, too, thereby competing directly with his own customers.

The jobbers also refuse to stay in place. Frequently, a manufacturer who is unable to get space on a W.D.'s shelves will get a jobber to handle his problem, i.e., to sell to other jobbers, and will give him the same redistribution compensations he pays the W.D. Since the distributor jobber also sells to retailers, he is, of course, in direct competition with his jobber customers.

Actually, the distributor jobber offers pretty tough competition all around. Because he does not always have the big inventories and expenses of a W.D., the redistribution compensation gives him a big advantage over warehousers in competing for redistribution business. With a wider margin, he also can afford to sell to a retailer cheaper than a competing jobber can. (If he is not too ethical, he may claim the redistributor's compensation from the manufacturer on goods he actually sells to a retailer.)

How N.A.P.A. Does It

As the foregoing might suggest, most of the aftermarket's distribution system is quite loosely coordinated. Within the system, however, there is one group that is very well put together. This is the National Automotive Parts Association, or N.A.P.A. It is the only organization in the U.S. today that offers an automotive jobber a *single* source of supply for virtually everything he needs to be in the parts business. (Most jobbers customarily use four or five warehouses or redistributors as their source of supply.)

N.A.P.A. grew out of a 1925 meeting of engine-parts distributors who wanted to establish a system of making any replacement part for any car make and vintage available overnight at any point in the U.S. The members of N.A.P.A. today are twenty-two noncompeting warehouse owners. They are financially independent of each other, but work together as a team in setting certain standards and offering certain uniform parts and services to their jobbers. Between them they blanket the U.S. with forty-five warehouses, each of which carries an inventory valued at more than $1 million and stocks from 40,000 to 60,000 different kinds and sizes of parts.

The biggest distributor on the West Coast, for instance, is Colyear Motor Sales Co. of Los Angeles, which operates nine N.A.P.A. warehouses with total sales of about $40 million. In about the same sales class is Boozer Test Co., of Indianapolis, an N.A.P.A. member that has ten warehouses in the Midwest and Southwest. But the biggest N.A.P.A. company of all—indeed, the biggest independent parts distributor in the world—is the Genuine Parts Co. of Atlanta.

Genuine Parts has thirteen warehouses in major cities stretching north from New Orleans to Boston, and west to Denver; the largest of these, in Memphis, has annual revenues of about $14 million. The total 1961 sales volume of Genuine Parts Co. was $80,500,000, on which it earned about $3 million. Total assets at year end were over $25 million. The late Carlyle Fraser, founder of the company and its largest stockholder, made Genuine Parts stock available to the public in 1948 at $11 per share. In mid-February the stock was listed at about $84 bid—after the company had declared a 100 per cent stock dividend.

In addition to the warehouses, G. P. runs 110 jobbing stores, most of them in its thirteen warehouse cities. The company also owns two parts-rebuilding plants, which account for some 11 per cent of all sales. President Wilton Looney explained the growth of the rebuilding business: "A rebuilt four-barrel carburetor will cost a car owner about $15 instead of $60 if he has an old one to turn in. It is the original housing that is expensive, and that can be used again."

Most of the N.A.P.A. product lines carry the association's private-brand names but are manufactured for it by well-known companies. Martin-Senour paints, for example, are made by Sherwin-Williams. Soundmaster mufflers and tail pipes are made by Walker Manufacturing Co. Modac is the name under which Gates Rubber supplies N.A.P.A. members with fan belts and radiator hose. Some of the N.A.P.A. lines are manufactured for its members and for nobody else. Echlin makes ignition parts exclusively for N.A.P.A. Still other products are supplied to N.A.P.A. by the Balkamp Co., which is owned jointly by association members. Balkamp gathers together, and packages under the Balkamp and B.K. brand names, some 7,000 miscellaneous parts and supplies that an automotive jobber could duplicate only by ordering from about 300 different sources.

N.A.P.A. supplies some 3,000 automotive jobbers—these are not members but customers—and for these it provides what is sometimes called a "cradle-to-grave" service. Says Looney of Genuine Parts (which does business with 1,400 N.A.P.A. jobbers in thirty-one states): "If you are an N.A.P.A. jobber, we try to give you any assistance that will help you become the top jobber in your town. If you are just getting into business, we'll give you recommendations on what part of town to locate your store, on floor layouts and similar matters. We'll ship you at cost such equipment as bins, billing machines, stationery. We'll set up your book-keeping and inventory systems, and if your place looks shabby, we'll send a man to clean it up."

Perhaps the single most important service rendered by the N.A.P.A. warehouses to their jobber customers is protection against inventory obsolescence. This is done by classifying each jobber in an *A*, *B*, *C*, or *D* category, based on a study of vehicle registrations in his natural trading area. The *D* jobber, for example, operates in the smallest town, and so will stock only the fastest-moving parts numbers. At the other extreme, the *A* jobber operates in the large metropolitan areas, and therefore carries everything in the N.A.P.A. classification book except a few items that are always supplied directly from the warehouse. All parts numbers are closely watched by N.A.P.A. specialists to determine the trend of their sales activity, and twice each year an N.A.P.A. classification committee brings the system up to date. If sales of a *D* item, for example, should slow down so that it is reclassified as a *B* item, then all *C* and *D* jobbers can return their stocks of this item to the N.A.P.A. warehouse for credit, without handling charges. All together, N.A.P.A. credited its jobbers with $10 million in returned parts in 1961. With inventories that are always up to date, N.A.P.A. jobbers remain in good financial health, and heavily prejudiced in favor of N.A.P.A.

The N.A.P.A. system has still another advantage. Because he orders daily from his warehouse, the jobber does not have to maintain a big inventory, which means that his investment is small and his turnover rapid. N.A.P.A. claims that the average annual return on investment of its jobbers is better than one-third.

The System Is Growing Up

The success of the N.A.P.A. system has spawned at least two new emulators (and competitors). The largest of these is Gulf & Western Industries Inc., a publicly owned corporation that, from a small beginning in 1957, has grown almost geometrically, so that its sales are now running at an annual rate of over $57 million. G. & W. was put together by Charles G. Bluhdorn, a young, Austrian-born investor who had earlier made a lot of money trading in coffee. Bluhdorn's study of the automotive aftermarket convinced him that it was depression-resistant and destined for plenty of growth, and also that it could be made to show greater profits if it were ever exposed to the methods of modern management. As key man in his operation, Bluhdorn selected Thomas E. Plant, formerly general sales manager of G.M.'s United Motors Service, and regarded as one of the more knowledgeable executives in the aftermarket.

When he came to G. & W. in 1960, Plant correctly guessed that many wholesalers would be delighted to trade their own companies for stock in a public corporation like Gulf & Western— i.e., for something readily convertible into cash. Since then G. & W. has acquired seventeen wholesale parts companies with 119 branches. Both Plant and Bluhdorn say that acquisitions will continue until Gulf & Western has a nationwide distribution system.

Another company, competing with G. & W. in an effort to build a nationwide distributing organization, is Chanslor & Lyon of San Francisco, one of the largest and oldest automotive distributors in the U.S. (it was founded in 1904). C. & L. was acquired at the beginning of 1960 by Elias Pinto and Elias Lasry, two natives of Casablanca (both now are U.S. citizens). Pinto, who is the new chairman of C. & L., was formerly an exporter of textiles and commodities. Lasry still controls a large parts distributing company in North Africa.

Since the acquisition of C. & L., Pinto and Lasry have bought, and absorbed into C. & L., three more parts distributors, so that they now have twenty warehouses. A Texas acquisition, completed early this year, will give them a 1962 sales volume of over $20 million. C. & L., Gulf & Western, and a few others like them suggest that the automotive aftermarket may get to be pretty well organized one of these days.

part IV

PROCESSES

The old-time, loud-laughing, back-slapping salesman is being replaced by a new kind of man doing a new kind of job. The new salesman knows more about customers' needs, has more prestige and commands more technical assistance. He no longer merely drums a particular product but helps tailor merchandise to the needs of customers, aids in promotions, provides service, assures delivery and proper use of products. This article traces the changes in selling in a number of leading firms, including General Electric, du Pont, and National Cash Register.

The Salesman Isn't Dead
—He's Different*

There is no more abused figure in American life than the salesman. One group of critics scorns him for certain qualities that another group sneers at him for losing. To many novelists, playwrights, sociologists, college students, and many others, he is aggressively forcing on people goods that they don't want. He is the drummer, with a dubious set of social values—Willy Loman in the Arthur Miller play. The second group of critics, which includes the Secretary of Commerce and many business executives all over the U.S., charges the salesman with lacking good, old-fashioned, hard-hitting salesmanship. He was spoiled by the postwar days when competition was easy. If only he would get up off his duff, and get out and *sell*, the goods would move and business would be in fine shape.

by Carl Rieser

* Vol. 66, November 1962, pp. 124–127, 248–259.

Both sets of critics are swatting at a target that doesn't matter much any more. The plain fact is that, as one Boston sales executive recently said, "The old drummer type of salesman has gone by the board." Nor are his talents especially needed in today's economy. To be sure, there are plenty of aggressive, hard-hitting salesmen still around, and there will always be a place for their brand of selling. But this kind of man is no longer the archetype.

From bits and pieces of evidence in all sectors of U.S. business, it is now possible to discern the emergence of a new dominant type, a man with a softer touch and greater breadth, a new kind of man to do a new—much more significant—kind of job. Whereas the old-time salesman devoted himself primarily to pushing a product, or a line of products, the new-era salesman is involved with the whole distribution pipeline, beginning with the tailoring of products to the customer's desire and extending through their promotion and advertising to final delivery to the ultimate consumer.

The salesman has been cast in his new role by "the marketing concept," a term that originated at General Electric around 1950 and has gained wide currency recently. It means essentially that companies are orienting their organization and effort toward the market, toward the ever-changing needs of the customer, and the ever-shifting calculations of their own production costs and opportunities. The emphasis is less concentrated on the isolated point-of-sale; it is spread forward, into the buyer's operations, and backward into the seller's operations. The profound consequences of this trend have been suggested by Orm Henning, marketing manager of industrial products at Texas Instruments:

"One should remind oneself that selling is only part of marketing—particularly in the scientific-industrial world. Marketing is communicating back to your factory your individual customer's needs and particular problems. When you realize and practice this, you open an entirely new vista in the area of sales. You cannot afford to sell a product, a static product—not in our business."

And what's true today in the electronics business—and many others—is going to be true of more and more businesses tomorrow.

The great change in selling affects practically all industries and all kinds of goods, whether they are what the marketing profession calls "pull-through" or "push-through" products. Pull-through refers generally to mass-produced consumer items, where a sort of siphon is already working. Pull-through products and services are presold by the manufacturer to the final consumer by mass advertising and promotion, which in effect creates a demand that almost literally pulls the goods through the distribution pipeline. Push-through products are wholly new consumer goods for which the siphon has not yet begun to work or, more commonly, they are industrial materials and equipment. Since the latter are usually highly technical in nature, they must be explained to the buyer and they require more personal selling so as to generate in the buyer the idea that he needs the product.

The distinction between pull-through and push-through is becoming less important. The retailer now stocks Kleenex tissues, for example, because he is persuaded that Kimberly-Clark Corp. will maintain public recognition of the brand and will see to it that thousands of boxes are siphoned rapidly and profitably right through his warehouse and off his store shelves. The job of the Kimberly-Clark salesman is to service the account so that the buyer will keep buying. He expedites and consolidates the shipments, keeps track of the retailer's inventory, sees that the goods get the greatest display and promotion possible, keeps himself available in case of any trouble or emergency. The job of the man who sells computers is much the same. The computer is one element in a whole system of mechanical devices and programing techniques, which is sold on the basis of what the customer is persuaded it can do for him.

The salesman's responsibility becomes greater as technology advances and producers offer products of ever mounting complexity. "We are tending toward the marketing of systems and services," says James Jewell, marketing vice president of Westinghouse. "The customers want to buy greater production—not equipment. We take the full responsibility for engineering and installing, and we are moving further into servicing."

This orientation toward the customer's needs is pointed up in a recent book that has received wide attention in the trade— *Innovation in Marketing*, by Theodore Levitt, a management consultant and a member of the faculty of Harvard Business School. Levitt, who speaks for a new generation of believers in "the marketing concept," states flatly that "a strictly sales-oriented approach to doing business can be suicidal. The difference between selling and marketing is more than semantic. Selling focuses on the needs of the seller, marketing on the needs of the buyer. Selling is preoccupied with the seller's need to convert his product or service into cash; marketing with the idea of satisfying the needs of the customer by means of the product or service and by the whole cluster of customer-getting value satisfactions associated with creating, delivering, and finally consuming it."

In this quotation Levitt seems to be oversimplifying the contrast between selling and marketing. Any implication that "the marketing concept" isn't motivated by the seller's desire for profits is, of course, mistaken. While his motives remain the same, the seller now sees marketing as a more elaborate link between production and consumption, a link that has to be carefully constructed and maintained.

Two situations may illustrate the change. In the past, a factory would overproduce the market and unload on the sales force the responsibility for unloading the goods on the customers. In the other situation, the salesmen kept their volume up by selling those products in their line that were easiest to sell—even those that were the least profitable. The incidence of both these cases tends to be diminished by the new trend with its more delicate alignment of markets and production, and its careful analysis of product profitability. The salesman is less often stuck with the necessity of a fast, hard sell. But he is steadily pressed to make the sales where the profit lies. Altogether, the marketing concept has played a vital role in developing the enormous velocity in the flow of goods, a phenomenon that will be described in the next article as the "short-order economy."

The Mirror of the Markets

There is little doubt that the impact of "the marketing concept" has reduced the stature of the sales manager in scores of companies. He has lost his former autonomy and now reports to the marketing vice president rather than directly to the president. He has less say over such vital matters as pricing and credit policies. The sales force must fit its work into an over-all corporation marketing policy. Furthermore, over the decade, the autonomy of the sales manager has been further trimmed in many companies by the creation of the job of product manager, who has both line and staff authority for a given product or group of products and coordinates production with advertising, research, and field selling.

The marketing concept has had very decided and significant structural effects on sales forces. This can be seen very clearly at General Electric, father of the marketing concept. G.E.'s salesmen used to be essentially product specialists, each selling only the line of a specific manufacturing department, even though it went into a variety of markets. It took time for G.E. to orient its sales force toward markets rather than products, but this process finally began seven years ago in the company's electrical-apparatus business. Instead of specializing in one product, e.g., cord sets, fan motors, push buttons, the salesman began selling a whole group of products to a particular market—for example, the air-conditioning industry. Early this year more than a dozen separate departments selling G.E.'s biggest single customer, the government, were reorganized into one defense sales force. In other words, instead of being product-oriented, the sales organizations have become "mirrors" of the markets G.E. serves.

Recently, Westinghouse reorganized its entire 13,600-man field sales organization along somewhat similar lines, in accord with what the company calls the "province concept." The company wants to be represented wherever possible by a "Mr. Westinghouse" rather than by a confusing bevy of different salesmen from various production divisions. (Significantly, in reorganizing, Westinghouse also seized the opportunity to put more salesmen in jobs where they actually meet customers and eliminated virtually an entire "staff" layer of some 104 sales managers who never called on customers.)

The same kind of reorganization has gone on in scores of companies in such diverse fields as motor trucks and optical equipment. At American Optical Co., for example, salesmen who used to be product specialists now sell a line that includes every piece of furniture and equipment for the doctor's office, from lenses to tables.

Thus the kind of man needed for this new kind of sales job has to be a generalist. The trend is away from the "sales engineer," the technically trained salesman, of a few years ago. His successor is a man capable of absorbing stacks of information churned out by the marketing department, and of applying it to his customers' problems. He goes forth armed with a tremendous amount of data on his customers' needs, their products, their corporate organizations, and their supply and delivery schedules.

He is also a man with more executive ability than the salesman of yesterday. A Boston sales manager describes the new salesman as simply "businessmen who travel." One Milwaukee executive notes that increasingly the new salesman is being given the authority and stature to make important decisions in the field without having to go back to corporate headquarters for an O.K. General Foods has adopted a new title of prestige for its senior salesmen, each of whom lives with one food-chain customer and attends to its needs. They are called "account executives" and they command the services of junior salesmen, who do the routine housekeeping chores of servicing the customers' stores.

In the new order of things there is obviously still a need for hard-selling, aggressive salesmen to open up new accounts, to introduce new and untried products, to sell the wares of new companies that have no national reputation. Since the service-oriented sales staff has turned away from this kind of pioneering effort, the door has been opened to a new kind of specialist, typified by a New York firm called the George N. Kahn Co. This company provides a crew of highly aggressive young salesmen who open up new territories for companies that don't want to retrain their own sales force for such sporadically necessary missions. (Kahn is not a manufacturer's representative; it works on a flat-fee basis rather than a commission and, after pioneering the sale of a product, expects that the manufacturer will take it back for handling by his own sales staff.) There is now some thought in the top management of a number of companies that the way to deal with this basic problem is to set up special sections of sales staffs with the specific function of going after new business. Thus what has been commonly thought of as the primary function of all salesmen is now becoming the specialty of a few.

The Service Troops

The new salesman has a tremendous advantage over his predecessors. Not only does he have access to much more information about his customers, but he is also backed up by formidable technical and other kinds of assistance. For example, in reshaping its inorganic-chemical sales recently, FMC Corp. (formerly Food Machinery & Chemical Corp.) has beefed up the number of its technical people directly behind the salesmen by some 20 per cent. The present ratio: one technical man to every four salesmen. The great pioneer in this development was du Pont, which years ago saw the close connection between selling and customer service. Today, at Chestnut Run, ouside Wilmington, du Pont has an impressive $20-million, campus-like complex of laboratories and workshops, employing 1,700 scientists, technicians, and others devoted to providing sales literature, solving technical problems, providing all kinds of services for customers or potential buyers of du Pont products, and otherwise aiding the sales effort. Companies selling all kinds of goods have developed similar assistance, though, naturally, the more complex the technology, the more elaborate the technical backup.

The development of sophisticated electronic data-processing systems is revolutionizing inventory handling, ordering, warehousing, and other physical aspects of marketing. This, in turn, relieves the salesman of a great deal of detail that used to absorb valuable hours of his time—writing up orders and reports, checking whether goods are available and how soon they can be delivered, and performing other niggling drudgery.

At the same time, the computer also introduces an element of impersonality in the relations between a seller and a buyer. Much of today's ordering of goods and materials, from packaged foods to industrial chemicals, is done, as it were, by a computer, which tells the buyer when to reorder; the transaction is handled routinely and a salesman never enters into it. This disencumbering of the salesman releases him to function on a new level of performance, to use his time more creatively. At Allis-Chalmers, which has just set up a department of marketing, an executive says, "Now our salespeople won't get bogged down in a lot of detail that goes hand in hand with selling, like the preparation of presentations, charts, convention exhibits, and whatnot. We'll do all the work, including the training of salesmen, in cooperation with company divisions."

"You Lose One of the Big Babies . . ."

The rise of the new salesman is the result of changes in the marketplace that have drastically altered the relationship of buyer to seller. One of the most significant developments has been the growing importance of the big customer. In almost every line of business, fewer and bigger customers are responsible for an increasingly large part of any given company's sales. Twenty-five years ago, when independent grocers were an important factor in food retailing, food processors did the bulk of their business with thousands upon thousands of chains and stores. Today, with the concentration of business in the hands of a relatively few big chains, some 300 buying offices throughout the U.S. account for 80 per cent of all food bought at wholesale. Preoccupation with the "key customer" affects every industry, from steel to office supplies. Sighs an officer of the Acme Chemical Co. in Milwaukee, "You lose one of the big babies and you're in trouble."

This whole trend is building up momentum as smaller buyers band together to increase their purchasing power and efficiency by buying cooperatively. It affects suppliers of school equipment, for example, because schools are consolidating on a county basis. Independent hardware stores and even hospitals are doing it.

How this has affected the food business has been fully explored in a new book with a provocative title, *The Vanishing Salesman,* by E. B. Weiss, a New York marketing specialist in the consumer-goods field. Actually, Weiss does not believe that the salesman is vanishing; his point is that the shift to the service-oriented sales function has so greatly altered the nature of personal selling that companies are faced with entirely new conditions in the hiring, training, and organization of salesmen. Weiss also notes that as retail food chains have become bigger and bigger, and their purchases have reached stupendous volume, the position of the individual buyer, once regarded as the salesman's opposite number, has greatly diminished. The buyer in a food chain used to be an important figure; he made the decisions on what the chain was going to buy. Now his power has been usurped by buying committees. The buyer has become merely a technician who interviews the salesmen from the food processor and passes on his findings to his superiors. Says Weiss: "Members of the buying committee tend not to be buying specialists. Moreover, they make decisions covering the entire range of merchandise inventoried by the organization. Since they tend to be at executive levels considerably higher than that of the buyer who appears before them, they are more apt to depend on their own judgment than that of the buyer. And, by the same token, the buyer is not apt to put up much of a battle. . . . In buying-committee sessions, it is presumably the majority that rules. But since it is traditional in large organizations for so many committee members to vote with the head of the table, the majority rule prevails more in theory than in fact."

So the man that the seller must get to is the man at the head of the table. And this is true not only in the food field. Throughout U.S. industry, key buying power has steadily risen up through the corporate structure to higher echelons of authority. In industrial selling, an increasing number of purchasing decisions tend to involve bigger and bigger outlays of capital. In large part this is the result of the rise of what is now commonly called *systems selling*. Instead of buying components from many suppliers, a company often buys a whole integrated system, be it a system for heating and air conditioning, protecting a plant from theft and fire, automating a production line, or handling materials. As technology becomes more complex, users, intent on eliminating technical headaches, are ever more anxious to buy such systems, while suppliers, intent on greater profit, are ever more anxious to design and sell a whole package. Naturally, the final approval for such an expenditure or commitment moves up the line, from the plant superintendent or manager, to the corporate controller or treasurer, perhaps all the way to the president or board chairman.

"The President's Project"

Not only has this created the need for salesmen with sufficient stature to talk to the customer's top management, but it has also drawn top executives more directly into the selling act. In company after company, higher officials now make a very determined effort to get out in the field and call on the big customers, and even to do considerable pioneer work with potential customers. This kind of thing, of course, is not new. Many companies were built by star salesmen at the top, a very good example being the late Thomas J. Watson Sr. at I.B.M. ("What my father used to do when people began to talk about the great complexity of the products," says Tom Watson Jr., the present head of the company, "would be to sweep his hand and say, 'It's all so simple. All it does is add, subtract, and multiply!' ") And in industries where enormous capital investment is required, such as the utility business, intimate and continued contact between seller and buyer at a high level has always been important. But now personal selling by top executives is becoming much more common. Raytheon, for example, has divided up its list of big customers among managers and officers of the company, and assigned each the responsibility of keeping in touch with a few accounts, with a view to bolstering the salesman's efforts.

General Foods was one of the pioneers in this. When Charles Mortimer was president of the company, he started "The President's Project," a series of meetings with customers all over the country. "In the beginning the meetings started out 100 per cent social," explains Wayne Marks, now president of the company. "They were strictly for pleasure—and we invited more than one customer to a meeting. But we found that nothing *happened*. Except that we got acquainted. We didn't find out what to improve in our business operation. So the format was quickly changed."

Now Marks's office sets up his customer-visiting schedule at least a month in advance. The customer is requested to have all his key people at the meeting, and several weeks before the encounter, G.F. sends along a "questionnaire" to elicit comments on G.F.'s performance and suggestions for items to discuss. In the past eighteen months Marks, accompanied by a team of executives and salesmen, has visited fifty-four customers throughout the U.S.

Marks has found the customers "avid" for this kind of contact. Not only does G.F. come out of these encounters (some of them lasting for five or six hours over dinner and drinks) with a fuller idea of what it should be doing—but the customers learn a great deal about their own organizations that they weren't aware of. Says Marks: "Many a meeting, at the end the boss man will say, 'Why don't *we* go out and find out what's happening in our own stores?' At the end of a recent meeting the top man told me, 'I've been frank with you and told you what I don't like about your operations. Would you be willing to report back to us on what you think of us?' "

The "Sellingest" Firm

Personal selling is now a company-wide endeavor, and the contact with the customer takes place at many levels in an organized, formal way. The best illustration of how this has changed fundamentally the relations between buyer and seller is offered by

National Cash Register, long known as perhaps the "sellingest" firm in the country. N.C.R.'s founder, the late John H. Patterson, has been called the father of many of the standard techniques of modern selling. He established the first formal training courses for salesmen, the first yearly sales quotas, the first guaranteed sales territories for salesmen, the first annual sales convention. Patterson's earlier sales methods were comparatively crude; cash registers were sold to storekeepers by appealing to their fear that dishonest clerks were pocketing money out of the till. But over the years the company refined its appeals, and forty years ago, when it began selling accounting machines, it even evolved a primitive kind of systems selling. But its big leap came about five years ago when the company introduced, somewhat belatedly as compared with the competition, its first electronic computer.

N.C.R. had to set up a whole new sales force for the computer, and in doing so it made a profound discovery: it was not easy to make a salesman of accounting machinery into a computer salesman. Says one N.C.R. senior salesman: "It was the death of salesmen like Willy Loman. At N.C.R. a few were left behind. They couldn't make the switch. It wasn't that they were too old—some were in their forties. But men's intellectual capabilities get set at various ages, and some *were* too old at that age." The company also found that it had to alter its time-honored compensation system. Normally, the N.C.R. salesman collects an advance that is charged against the commission he makes on his sales. Says marketing director Harry Keesecker, "Computer selling is still incentive selling, but due to the kind of product—sometimes the long time between sales—we have to compensate the salesmen by salary plus commission."

At the same time N.C.R. set up an elaborate organization to give the salesmen technical support. This now includes 325 mathematicians and technical people; the number has doubled in size in the past twelve months. They develop manuals and presentations, help the customer define his problems, train his computer operators for him, set up his E.D.P. system, and produce the programing for it. The support organization also trains the computer salesman, a departure for N.C.R., which years ago built its whole sales-training program around the use of experienced salesmen, borrowed from the field, as instructors. (The total computer sales and support staff numbers about 500 people, as against 2,100 in accounting machines, but the company is supplementing the small computer force by training as many of the accounting-machine men as possible to sell both kinds of equipment.)

The Willy Lomans Are No Longer Feasible

The difference between the old and new eras at N.C.R.—and in salesmanship in general—is dramatically illustrated by the story of how the company landed a rather sensational contract for the sale of a computer to the Dime Savings Bank of Brooklyn, New York, the country's second-largest mutual savings bank. The bank and the company had long-standing ties dating back to 1929, when the Dime bought its first N.C.R. posting machines for the tellers' windows. In subsequent decades the bank bought other N.C.R. equipment. In those years the chief link between the two was an N.C.R. salesman, Anthony de Florio, now district manager of sales for accounting and computer systems, and Karl Stad, who is now vice president of methods and systems at the Dime. The relationship was a cordial one, and N.C.R., which is mainly known for its experience in retailing and banking, was solidly in with the Dime.

In the late 1950's, however, there was a sudden change in the old easygoing ways. The bank decided, in 1957, that it was time to think about tying its entire bookkeeping operations into a computer to keep up with its bounding growth, and Stad was told to set up a task force to study the entire field and to recommend the "ideal" system. De Florio observes, "This was the beginning of group selling. The salesman had to understand the problems and systems of the customer. The staff at the bank had to define what was required. And we at N.C.R. had to be sure that the bank wasn't running away from us in know-how." (To N.C.R., as to many another company, the growing sophistication of the buyer has become an important factor to reckon with.) N.C.R. also had to reckon with competition; every other computer manufacturer came in for the kill at Dime. For the next two years Stad and his team studied the field and enlarged their expertise. By 1959 they had winnowed the choice down to four systems, including N.C.R.'s, and asked the competitors for feasibility studies. (Says de Florio: "By the time you get to feasibility studies, the Willy Lomans are no longer feasible.")

Now the contacts between the company and the bank multiplied. N.C.R. sent teams of technical people from Dayton headquarters to confer with Stad—they submitted a technical proposal two inches thick—and Stad went out to Dayton to talk to N.C.R.'s research people. He was put up at N.C.R.'s plush Moraine Farm, the estate of a former board chairman, which the company now uses to entertain groups of customers and potential customers. (Like du Pont and other companies, N.C.R. uses its factories and laboratories as a sales showcase.) By the end of 1959, Stad decided that N.C.R.'s 304 computer, then just being delivered to the first purchasers, was the one for the Dime.

Thereupon the Dime's board of trustees decided that Stad's decision ought to be second-guessed by an independent consultant in the electronic data-processing field. This, of course, opened up the whole matter again, and brought the competitors back in. Fortunately for N.C.R., the consultant confirmed the decision, and the affair between the bank and the company again resumed, in a deliberate and measured way. The Dime's board selected a committee of three trustees to study the proposal. They went out to Dayton—staying at an even more posh N.C.R. guest house, the old home of Orville Wright—and they talked with everyone from technicians to N.C.R.'s president, R. S. Oelman, and its then board chairman, S. C. Allyn. On the way back in the plane, the trustees decided to sign with N.C.R. It was an $800,000 decision, and it was a key one not only to the bank but to N.C.R., which closed some other bank contracts on the strength of Dime's decision.

N.C.R. was in the middle of a training program for the Dime's employees when, early in 1960, a crisis arose. N.C.R.'s technicians reached the chilling conclusion that the 304 computer would not have the capacity to do what the Dime eventually would require —i.e., a direct linkage from the posting machines at the tellers' windows to the computer without the intermediate use of tabulating equipment. The next model in the design stage, the 315 random-access computer, would do the job—but not the 304. De Florio had to come clean with the bank. "I called up Karl and said, 'Let's have lunch at the Brooklyn Club,' " recalls de Florio, still wincing at the ensuing conversation. De Florio offered to tear up the contract for the 304. The Dime's board accepted the proposal, and the whole computer question was back in the soup again.

Rival manufacturers had another chance to make presentations, and N.C.R. had to start all over again selling its 315 model, then two years from delivery. De Florio kept pounding on one main point: the bank already was using N.C.R. machines at its windows, and any company that finally got the computer contract would have to tie in to N.C.R.'s equipment. In the end the argument prevailed; Stad recommended the 315 computer on the grounds that it would be "just as good" as other computers—though no better—and that N.C.R. had "window experience." Along with the computer, the bank also agreed to use other N.C.R. equipment in its integrated system, so the total package came to $2 million. Says de Florio, looking back on the whole transaction, "In this kind of selling you can't see everything you buy. A lot has to be bought on faith. Therefore a company likes to work with big companies. Come hell or high water, they have to deliver."

One of N.C.R.'s brightest and most successful young computer salesmen recently expanded this doctrine. "A salesman is important," he remarked, "because the policy makers today come from a previous generation of doing business. They don't have the technical equipment necessary to make a decision about a computer that requires technical sophistication. So the salesman has to take the language of the computer man and turn it into language his customer understands. I used to think that those decisions would be made on a scientific basis—but it's a gross act of faith." The salesman's job, he said, is "to create an environment in which an act of faith can take place."

The "Foot Soldiers" Need Upgrading

There is doubtless still plenty of faith in sales transactions. But as the Dime Savings Bank affair shows, there is a great deal more. And this is the fact that salesmen do not seem to realize when they talk about their jobs. They are still trained to have a kind of emotionalism about their craft, and they carry with them a heavy load of outworn notions about their role. They view selling as both warfare and love, hostility and benevolence. They see themselves as "the men on the firing line," and "the foot soldiers of democracy." The combative nature of selling is stressed in almost every book on the subject, as in one of the most famous and widely sold of all books on selling, *Open the Mind and Close the Sale*, by John M. Wilson, who recently retired as N.C.R.'s sales manager. Wilson speaks of the "tension in every buyer-seller relationship," of the "challenge" in each encounter, of the need for "handling" the customer—though, of course, "in the way he wants to be handled."

This lag in the recognition of what has happened to selling is harmful, because the sales profession is still held in low esteem by the public. Just how low was indicated recently in a survey by *Sales Management* magazine of college students and their attitude toward selling. Selling ranked a very poor fourth, after teaching, law, and medicine, as a choice for a career. Only 6 per cent of the students favored it. (Of seventy-one students whose fathers are in sales, only *five* wanted to go into selling.)

The students did not particularly object to the working conditions in selling; relatively few said they were put off by too much traveling, for example. Nor did many feel that the financial reward was inadequate. The chief objections to a selling career (some even denied that selling *is* a career) were these: "I don't want to force people to buy things they don't need." "Job security is poor." "I'm not extrovert enough." "Selling has no prestige."

One student unwittingly put his finger on the ironic predicament business faces. He remarked that selling simply does not require "a college education or intelligence." The main feature of the new kind of personal selling, of course, is that it does require men who are able and intelligent; the new salesmen, quite obviously, must be recruited from among the better college graduates. But how are they going to be recruited if the better college graduates think selling is beneath them? The experience of Scott Paper illustrates the difficulties business has in luring these men into selling. The company prides itself on the fact that 95 per cent of its sales staff are college graduates. Each year, to keep the staff replenished, it interviews some 2,000 students, invites about 100 of these men to visit its Philadelphia headquarters, makes offers to about seventy-five—and lands thirty-five or forty of them.

The trouble is that business has signally failed to get across the idea that there has been a tremendous change in selling. (The *Sales Management* poll shows that this generation of students has not grasped one of the simplest and most fundamental changes— i.e., that by and large salesmen are no longer paid on commission but are salaried.) Business has a massive educational job to do. Perhaps as a start it might throw away a lot of the old inspirational literature on selling and let the facts of the new situation do the inspiring.

The capacity of electronic computers is greatest in precisely those areas where the human mind is most limited—the accurate handling of vast amounts of data in a short time according to prescribed formulas. Today there is no doubt that electronic techniques offer important opportunities to improve the distribution of goods. The following article describes the changes that occurred in several companies when they switched from traditional distribution methods to new computer-controlled systems.

*The Short-Order Economy**

On the outskirts of Pittsburgh, in an old warehouse that once housed transformers, switchgear, and hundreds of other products made by Westinghouse Electric Corp., sits a little machine with a fabulous memory. It is an I.B.M. 1401 computer hooked up to a random-access

by Carl Rieser

memory bank that holds some 20 million bits of information. To the observer, the bank is merely a stack of flat disks about the size of long-playing phonograph records. At one side of the stack, working up and down on a spindle, is a long stylus that flicks in and out among the disks faster than the eye can follow. That little machine is busier than a couple of hundred salesmen, order clerks, stenographers, traffic men, and switchboard operators.

It knows more about the territory—indeed, about scores of territories—than the oldest salesman. It has more information about sales than the smartest sales manager. It remembers far more

* *Vol. 66, August 1962, pp. 90–95, 140–148.*

accurately than the stock clerks where the nuts and bolts can be found in any warehouse. It is a wondrous combination of traveling salesman, mathematical genius, and the Sears, Roebuck catalogue. With affectionate pride, the people who work with it call it their "monster." It is revolutionizing distribution at the producers' level, just as the discount merchants discussed earlier have revolutionized retailing. The distribution of goods has finally begun to get the full benefit of the accumulated technology of the Western world, which for two centuries has been miraculously transforming the production of goods.

What the monster is doing to old Westinghouse is awe-inspiring. It knows all the pertinent facts about some 15,000 customers who buy Westinghouse industrial products directly from the company, including about 500 distributors who in turn supply many thousands of smaller customers. The computer knows each major customer's address, what normal trade discounts he is entitled to. The memory bank stores data about some 60,000 finished industrial products, from large electric motors and line transformers to tiny replacement parts—prices, shipping weights, discount structures, production schedules, and the number of units presently in stock in each of twenty-six field warehouses and nineteen factory warehouses across the U.S. The equipment handles an average of 1,800 orders a day, and on busy days the total may go up to 2,400.

From the moment a salesman in, say, the Seattle office gets an order for an integral horsepower motor and hands it to a clerk, the whole order process is almost completely mechanical. The clerk looks up the number for the motor in a code book thick as a small telephone directory, supplies the customer's code number and the necessary details about the order, and teletypes it to Pittsburgh. From there on the computer takes over. Aside from some handling of data-processing cards, no human hands touch the order until the motor is shipped.

When the order comes in from Seattle, the monster first searches its memory to find the warehouse nearest the customer that has the item in stock. It then adjusts the inventory record. If the stock has now fallen to a predetermined danger point, the electric-motor factory in Buffalo gets the word to put the model back into production. Next the computer reaches into the memory bank for the customer's normal trade discount, figures out the state sales tax, shipping charges, and so forth, and types out an invoice. Finally the computer transmits the order to the proper warehouse, where it emerges a few seconds later from the teletype machine complete with bill of lading, addressed labels for the carton, and instructions telling the order picker what bin to go to.

All this takes no more than fifteen minutes on the average. By startling contrast, before Westinghouse installed the system in 1959, it used to take an average of *five days* to fill a similar order, five days that were often filled with worry and confusion. First the salesman had to waste precious time checking around to see where the item was in stock. (Now all he has to do is put a query on the teletype and the computer will have word back to him within ten minutes.) If the order was mailed to the warehouse or factory, that took a couple of days, and two or three days more were spent by the clerks figuring out the prices and processing the paper work. In the course of this, likely as not, the impatient salesman got on the phone or the teletype to see if the order had been shipped, and all that accomplished was to help jam up Westinghouse's communication system.

"We were always dealing with history," says David C. Mc-Alister, who is manager of distribution, accounting, and procedures and the chief architect of the computerized ordering system. No one ever quite knew the state of inventories on a national basis because both sales and inventory figures were weeks behind time. The tendency therefore was to keep large "protective" inventories on hand in order to guard against the danger of running out of stock, which is an anathema to a sales manager. Because the whole system was so slow, sales managers also pressed the company to maintain a large network of warehouses so as to be near as many customers as possible. Even so, Westinghouse found itself out of stock on a quarter of the orders received.

The speedy little monster has drastically altered all this. Westinghouse can now ship its orders from any point no matter how far away—even from the factory itself—and still get the goods to the customer faster than it once did. In many instances it can assure overnight delivery. The company has been able to close five of its field warehouses—one of them has been converted into a home for the computer—and some of the remaining twenty-six are scheduled to go. It has also slashed over-all inventories, and has cut the stocks of one line of products from $5 million to $1,700,000. Yet Westinghouse now is out of stock on only one out of every twenty orders.

"The Salesmen Never Had It So Good"

The treasurer's office has been made happy by all kinds of savings. Cash flow has been speeded up by five days because the invoices are mailed out to the customers the day the orders are received. Since the monster does all the bookkeeping, costs have been cut sharply; one factory has reduced its operating costs by more than $200,000 a year. And there has been at least one unexpected financial boon. Westinghouse, like any large industrial company, has a mélange of normal trade discount structures for its thousands of products. ("You name it; we've got it," says McAlister.) It is also changing prices constantly. In pre-computer days, there was always a lag between the time a price change was announced and the time the news got to all the 100-odd Westinghouse sales branches. Now the computer gets the news immediately and applies the new price at once. As a result, Westinghouse realizes an average of about one-half of 1 per cent more on the price of each item.

The sales force has mixed feelings about the new system. McAlister contends that "the salesmen never had it so good." They can assure faster service, and as one sales manager puts it, "We are able to ship when we say we are going to ship." On the other hand, the monster has automated the whole process of selling to a degree that is unsettling to many an older salesman. It used to be that the customer had several days' leeway if he placed an order, then decided to cancel. Now, with lead time down to fifteen minutes, the order has probably been invoiced and shipped by the time he changes his mind. The salesman then has the unhappy choice of reconvincing the customer that he needs the product—which may be difficult—or of having the goods returned.

McAlister has recently bypassed some salesmen altogether by putting teletype machines right into the offices of a few of Westinghouse's larger industrial customers, enabling them to order directly through the Pittsburgh computer center. "I give 'em a catalogue and let 'em buy," says McAlister. "I tell the salesmen that in the future all they will have to do is to carry an oilcan and keep those sending machines well oiled."

For major appliances (washing machines, refrigerators, etc.) Westinghouse has a second ordering system, located at a central shipping point in Columbus, Ohio. The problems here are different, and there is a somewhat lesser degree of automation. One of the important logistical considerations is to save freight costs by assembling full rail carloads of various appliances for pooled shipments to several dealers. Human brainwork is still required for putting together the mix. But the system has achieved enormous gains, similar to those for the industrial goods. The computer has speeded up the time needed to process an order from seven days to three days, has cut over-all inventories by 25 per cent, and has leveled out seasonal peaks and valleys on the production lines.

Transformers in the Drugstore

Sometime late this fall Westinghouse will cap four years of work by opening a glittering new Tele-Computer Center a few miles from Pittsburgh, built around one wonderfully versatile computer that will handle the work now done by both the Columbus and the present Pittsburgh ordering systems. This newest monster, a Univac 490 Real-Time computer, will be the brain for Westinghouse's entire teletype communication system, linking some 265 offices, factories, warehouses, and sales branches throughout the U.S. and Canada. More than 15,000 messages of all kinds each day will flow directly into Univac, which will sort out the 2,000 to 3,000 specially coded orders for industrial goods and appliances and put them through an even more highly automated process than now exists. (It will eliminate the need for using data-processing cards for the industrial goods.) And as a sideshow, the Univac will also be turning out sales, financial, and engineering data for corporate and divisional staffs. "My worst nightmare," says McAlister, "is that someday the machine is going to goof and I'm going to deliver a carload of line transformers to a corner drugstore."

To the Moon—or A & P

Westinghouse was one of the first corporations to experiment with the application of the computer to the day-to-day problems of distribution, and in four years it has advanced so far with its system that it has become a mecca for U.S. and foreign businessmen who are fascinated by the new possibilities of the electronic era. But many other companies have installed similar systems— General Foods, Armstrong Cork, Clark Equipment, Scott Paper, Chemstrand, and Pittsburgh Plate Glass, just to name a few. Throughout a broad segment of industry, engineers like Westinghouse's McAlister are shaking up sales and order-filling procedures, inventory handling, and production scheduling.

The historical turning point was the introduction of the random-access memory bank, which made it possible for a computer to get at millions upon millions of facts almost instantaneously, and match them up practically instantaneously, without having to search endlessly through a whole tape. This development came just in the nick of time, for distribution was getting out of hand. To send an ICBM across the seas or to put a man on the moon surely requires a computer. But matters have reached a point where General Foods can hardly send a mixed carload of Jello-O and Gaines Dog Food across the Hudson River to the A & P without a computer, either.

Electronics is enabling industry to live with what may aptly be called "the short-order economy," in which the problems are less and less those of production and more and more those of distribution. During the last decade, as the era of war-incurred shortages passed into history, the strains in U.S. industry shifted from productive capacity to the business of getting and holding markets. Now the buyer calls the tune, and he has the producer hopping. The situation was summed up recently by a du Pont sales manager who said ruefully, "The customer wants delivery tomorrow, and in our business he gets it."

This kind of competition poses a new challenge to industry. Unless the efficiency of distribution can be vastly improved, the cost of giving customers the service they demand could become crippling. The strain is intensified by the fact that, in a time of abundance, nobody has to hold inventories. Retailers and whole-salers pass the buck back to the manufacturer, who is expected to deliver what is wanted, where it is wanted, and when it is wanted. The manufacturer in turn is faced with the enormous problem of holding *his* inventories to a minimum without risking being caught short. In essence, what the computer does is to make corporations more sensitive to the marketplace and to cut down greatly their "time of response," a concept that is gaining increasing currency in today's economic climate.

"A Hero on Thin Margins"

The tension set up by the short-order economy is caught by glimpses of the handling of glass bottles and foodstuffs, a particularly significant example of interrelated distribution problems. The great glass furnace, like an open-hearth steel furnace, must be run continuously. Glass production is planned three months to a year ahead; even the rate of output or the mix can't be changed on less than two weeks' advance notice. The new "double gob" glass machines, developed in the last fifteen years or so—they produce two gobs of molten glass at a time, each of which is molded into a bottle—have almost doubled output, so that one machine produces 8,000 five-ounce baby-food bottles an hour, night and day, day in and day out—1,344,000 a week. The consumer of these bottles is the food-processing plant, which has filling lines that operate at the rate of 700 bottles of strained spinach, pears, or carrots a minute—or 1,680,000 bottles weekly in a forty-hour week. Any stoppage on this floor is costly. Even if just one bottle is defective and breaks, it might take fifteen minutes to clean up the mess, which would work out to a loss in production of more than 10,000 bottles.

The Armstrong Cork Co. glass plant in Millville, New Jersey, one of the biggest in the country, keeps several food processors supplied with baby-food bottles. Roger Hetzel, vice president and general manager of packaging materials at Armstrong, describes what he is up against: "We must meet fast, tight delivery schedules. At some plants the client sets the load right on the line the minute our truck arrives. They have minimal reserves of bottles, just enough so they don't have to shut down if the truck breaks down. If we don't provide continuous service, we won't be the supplier for long." Nor will Armstrong keep the business if flaws in its product cause its bottles to break on the client's filling line. And the customers are demanding lighter and stronger bottles, which means increasingly expensive production equipment and equally costly electronic quality controls. "The modern mass marketer," concludes Hetzel, "is a hero on thin margins and fast turnover."

A Million Different Chevrolets

The new market pressures not only introduce costly complexity into distribution and inventory planning, but also reach back to the manufacturing process itself. By its very nature, competition in an economy of abundance threatens to cancel out some of the efficiencies created by mass production. The height of efficiency, it has often been pointed out, is reached when most cars sold are Model T's and all Model T's are black. But customers today can demand all kinds of refinements and variations. The result is a proliferation of shapes, colors, sizes, and styles.

The Chevrolet Division of General Motors provides a vivid example of how far this sort of thing can go. It now produces thirty-four basic passenger cars, ranging from the compact Corvair to the two-seat sports Corvette, from station wagons to convertibles. Most of these cars are available in a four-door or a two-door model, and they come with or without radio and various other accessories. On top of this, the customer can choose among several types of transmissions, carburetors, power brakes, and power steering, and even among different hubcaps. And finally, Chevrolet offers a choice of fourteen solid colors, as well as two-toned combinations. Only a computer could keep track of all the possible variations; they come to more than a million.

The greater the variety of products manufactured on any given production line, the greater the tendency toward short runs, and the higher the setup costs. Furthermore, there is an increase in what methods-study people call "conveyer wastage." If a production line is working on a variety of models, the line has to slow down to the speed imposed by the slowest job. And for so many different products bigger raw-material inventories must be maintained. All this adds to production costs that are in reality hidden marketing costs.

The Dealer Just Takes the Order

These costs have also been pushed up by another, older tendency in U.S. industry. The manufacturer has been taking over from the merchant more of the job of selling goods to the ultimate consumer. This has raised proportionately the manufacturers' outlays for advertising as well as their expenditures for promotion at the point of sale and for the training of salespeople. Moreover, the producers have had to assume greater responsibility for the handling of their goods. Long ago they took over packaging—formerly a function of retailing and wholesaling—and they have become increasingly responsible for "breaking bulk"—i.e., sorting out goods at central points for transshipment in smaller lots. Now, particularly in the appliance business, manufacturers must often even deliver goods right to the ultimate customer's doorstep. And increasingly, manufacturers have had to supply credit to retailers to finance both inventories and consumer installment buying.

The great difficulty is that so many of these distribution costs, like those incurred on the production line by the proliferation of goods, are hidden. They are truly "the dark continent" of business, as Peter Drucker points out in the article on page 294. Some of these distribution activities, such as advertising and personal selling, are readily identifiable. But many other costs of distribution—marketing administration and research, warehousing, shipping, delivery, billing, credit, collection, etc.—tend to be scattered about in most corporations. Many of these costs are swallowed up in general and administrative overhead, and no two companies agree on how to report such costs, if indeed they break them out at all.

An obvious way to attack the distribution-cost problem is by controlling inventory. By itself, inventory represents a considerable investment in distribution. It must be warehoused. It often deteriorates or becomes obsolete. It is subject to "shrinkage," through theft and other losses. Businessmen figure that, as a rule of thumb, the cost of financing and holding inventory over a year comes to about 20 per cent of the value of the goods. The cost of tying up this capital was viewed more complacently in the earlier postwar years when inventory accumulation was justified, on more or less speculative grounds, by inflation. But with the subsiding of the inflationary spiral, and with the increasing risk of obsolescence because of the proliferation of new styles and new products, corporate financial officers have clamped down more severely and demanded that inventories be cut.

As Westinghouse has shown, the new electronic tools are admirably adapted to handling the inventory problem, and they extend management's control over its business forward, along the distribution pipeline, and backward, to the production line. The disjointed parts of distribution are drawn into one integrated system. What is perhaps even more significant, this tends to centralize corporate organization. An illuminative example is provided by General Foods, which began by dealing with the problem of giving the grocery trade faster, more reliable, and cheaper delivery, and is now changing drastically the way it conducts its entire operation.

How To Get Closer to Customers

General Foods was one of the first major corporations to recognize the existence of "the distribution problem," which in General Foods' case was the outcome of sheer growth, diversification, and decentralization. General Foods had originally been a highly centralized company, with a central sales staff. But by 1953 the divisions were fully autonomous, with complete control over production, sales, and distribution—and the company was beginning to have troubles. "We had as many distribution schemes as divisions," says one executive. The company's distribution and selling costs were rising sharply, and the customers were complaining about the service.

General Foods made the bulk of its shipments directly from plant to customers (mainly supermarkets and chain stores), frequently over long distances. The service was erratic and undependable and also penalized the smaller customers, who could not afford to save freight costs by buying a single product—for example, Baker's cocoa—in full carload lots. Unlike Westinghouse with its industrial goods, General Foods had to get physically closer to its customers to assure faster, surer service. And in view of the diversity of its products, it had to find some way to ship mixtures of goods at the cheaper carload rates.

In 1956 the company set up a task force to study the problem. Out of this came a sweeping proposal to build a network of central distribution centers handling most of the company's products. The centers were to be located so that no customer would be farther than three days' shipment by rail or overnight by truck. This posed quite a problem, since General Foods has many thousands of customers scattered all over the country. One subsidiary problem was how to optimize freight costs by placing the centers so that there would be a minimum of back-hauling from the plants. After what is now regarded as a classic case history in the use of operations research, General Foods decided to build twenty centers; the first one got under way in 1957. Since then it has completed sixteen centers.

The centers are run by a new division of General Foods called Distribution-Sales Services. The division is responsible for almost the entire distribution function, from the "dry end" of the machines in the factory to the customer's unloading dock. It handles all the technical details involved in ordering, invoicing, shipping, and bookkeeping. It also provides office space for the district salespeople of the various operating divisions, who have been grouped together in the centers. D.-S.S. charges each division according to the warehousing, shipping, and other services it performs for them.

It is no secret around General Foods that there was resistance within the company to this centralizing move. "Some of the divisions had to be legislated into joining," says one executive dryly. However, D.-S.S. now handles the bulk of the company's sales, which totaled $1,280,327,000 in the fiscal year ending March 31, 1962. It does not handle the Birds Eye frozen-food division, which because of the special nature of its product is establishing a separate central depot system, and it does not yet handle the bulk of Maxwell House coffee, though it probably will someday. The total cost of running the centers is about $15 million, and all together, with freight costs included, the company's total distribution bill for its finished goods is some $60 million a year. The new system has already brought about savings in freight and handling costs.

The main purpose of the centers was to get customers on a regular, automated system of ordering, so that in effect there would be a steady, constant flow of goods to them. So successfully have the centers adapted to the short-order economy that about half of the bulk shipped is ordered on such a routine basis, and the salesmen don't see the order until later. The customer, instead of ordering full carloads of one product from the plant, and having to figure his needs some weeks ahead, can order mixed carloads of a number of products just a few days ahead of time. The net effect is to increase the frequency of delivery and to cut the inventories the supermarket or store has to hold. General Foods figures that over-all its customers have cut their inventories of the company's products by 25 per cent, in some cases by as much as 50 per cent.

Less Jell-O on the Shelf

In the course of designing its system, General Foods realized that the inventory problem it was taking on itself might well turn out to be astronomical. The company was already aware of a related problem, which had been pointed out by its distribution task force: In the past there had been great unevenness and seasonal surges on the production line. This unevenness was partly the result of the long time it took for production to respond to sales. With more warehouses, and bigger inventories, the instability in the whole system was likely to become worse. So General Foods undertook another study, which resulted in the formation of a computer systems group at corporate headquarters in White Plains, New York.

For the past year this group has operated a system called COPT—Cost Optimization—which develops inventory, production, and shipping schedules through the use of computers. The system, applied first to the Jell-O division, is now being extended to others. The warehouses flash sales and inventory figures to the computer in White Plains on Fridays. Another computer digests them over the weekend. On Monday the plants receive production schedules and shipment estimates for as much as eight weeks ahead as well as raw-material requirements. The warehouses used to carry enough stocks of Jell-O products to cover an estimated nine weeks ahead; now they are down to six weeks and still going down. Over all, Jell-O inventories have been cut 30 per cent.

While overhauling its physical distribution, General Foods discovered that some significant changes had taken place in the nature of the salesman's job. These are not unique to General Foods or to the food industry. They have been characteristic of every industry caught up in the short-order economy. The first change has been cited by Herbert M. Cleaves, General Foods' executive vice president of marketing: "The day is gone when all you want to do is put the stuff in the customer's warehouse and depend on him to get rid of it. Our salesman is customer-oriented. He has to think about how best and most profitably to get the product through to the hands of the consumer."

The second major change is the growing importance of the *big* customer. In General Foods' case, the statistics are dramatic. Back in the 1930's, before the supermarket revolution had made its great impact, some 110,000 retail stores accounted for 70 per cent of its business. Today, 30,000 customers account for the same volume. "These customers have become very powerful. If one makes a decision not to carry our brand this could be a sizable chunk of our business," Cleaves notes. "So we have to take a real and continuing interest in his business."

The third big change has come about as a result of the computer revolution. The new central physical-distribution organizations, with their automated ordering, have freed the salesman from considerable drudgery and the burden of making out orders and reports. Hence, greater efficiency in the use of sales manpower becomes possible.

Fewer Salesmen, Lower Costs

General Foods responded to these changed conditions by reorganizing its sales organizations from top to bottom. They are still organized divisionally, but their character has been changed. The territories have been entirely redrawn along the lines of the distribution centers with the emphasis on major markets rather than sheer geographical territory. Field administration has been separated from actual selling. A system of account managers has been set up to handle the big supermarket-chain accounts. And, perhaps most significant of all, the actual number of salesmen employed by General Foods has been *cut by 8 per cent,* from over 1,600 to some 1,500. "On the average," says James D. North, vice president of marketing services, "we have higher-grade personnel. Actually, we come out with about the same costs, but we'll keep increasing the salesmen's quotas so we'll have an increased sales volume against the same cost."

Where the pressures of the short-order economy will finally carry General Foods and other corporations is still unclear. But one broad trend certainly appears to be in the making. As Cleaves puts it: "We went through what many companies go through, the decentralization to individual units. Then eventually and gradually we came to realize that in some areas we had lost some of our corporate strength from placing operating autonomy in smaller segments. The General Foods organization is still decentralized. The profit responsibility is still with the general manager of the division. But there is a greater awareness on his part that there is a corporate interest which may transcend his own division's interest."

Distribution may still be something of a jungle, but now that some corporations have cleared away a few trees, they can at least begin to see the forest.

The burdens and costs of marketing are constantly being shoved back onto the producer. Wholesalers and retailers want to hold as little inventory as possible, and many of them would prefer not to pay for goods until they have actually sold them. Under present conditions, as selling becomes more and more a matter of providing services that enable the customer to conduct his business more profitably, trade credit becomes an essential sales device. And if manufacturers do not grant it, customers frequently take it.

The Great Credit Pump*

by Carl Rieser

One of the most significant and least discussed statistics in the U.S. economy is the total of outstanding trade credit, the short-term credit that business extends to business. Estimates put it at nearly $10 billion more than the entire federal budget for 1963, some $20 billion more than the total value of all U.S. corporate bonds outstanding at the end of 1961, and about two and a half times the gross national product of Canada. It is in the neighborhood of $100 billion. But even more dramatic than its sheer size is its growth rate. In the decade between 1951 and 1961, while the U.S. gross national product, measured in current dollars, grew 58 percent and nationwide sales grew 37 percent, trade credit expanded by just about 100 percent.

A no less striking fact is that U.S. manufacturers are the main source of this credit. They account for about half of the total. The

* Vol. 68, February 1963, pp. 122–124, 148–157.

remainder comes from wholesalers, service industries, and the entire complex of other non-farm businesses put together. But the figure does not adequately state the entire investment in credit by U.S. producers of goods. For, in addition to short-term trade credit, they also extend to their customers untold billions of dollars in long-term credit through a number of different devices, such as the "captive" finance company. All together, the amount of credit supplied by manufacturers is far greater than that provided by the banking system, which at last count had some $42 billion in commercial and industrial loans outstanding. Since the banks are the base of the whole credit system, the manufacturers can be viewed as a great pump, vastly increasing the volume and velocity of the credit on which U.S. business operates.

The question arises: How did U.S. industrial corporations, whose main function is to produce goods, get into this formidable side business of financing trade? This raises other intriguing questions. Who, for example, pays for this credit? Or to put the question in the form that is of surpassing interest to business, who *should* pay for it? And in view of the extraordinary growth of trade credit, there is a still more important question from the over-all economic standpoint: Is it dangerous?

A Competitive Weapon

In answering these questions it is necessary first to examine the characteristics of trade credit and the reasons for its phenomenal growth. (This article will discuss long-term credit later.) Trade credit is strictly short-term credit extended by a seller of goods or services to a commercial customer—e.g., by a manufacturer to another manufacturer or to a wholesaler or retailer, or by a wholesaler to a retailer. It is entered on the current-assets side of the seller's books as a receivable. (It sometimes appears technically as a "note," a term commonly used in the jewelry trade among others.) The great bulk of trade receivables arises from sales of goods on open-account credit, where the buyer is expected to pay according to accepted trade terms. A typical statement of such terms is "two-ten-net-thirty"; translated, this means that the buyer has thirty days to pay, but if he pays in ten days, he gets a cash discount of 2 percent. There are other kinds of receivables, of course. Goods are often sold, for instance, on dating plans, whereby the customer accepts seasonal merchandise ahead of time and gets an extended time in which to pay. And there is consignment selling, in which the seller does not expect payment for the goods until the customer actually sells them.

In part, the tremendous proliferation of these devices in recent years can be explained by the current vogue for doing things on the cuff, whether it is buying a home, eating out, or taking a jaunt by air. So much attention has been fixed on the phenomenal growth of consumer borrowing that hardly anyone noticed that trade credit was growing even faster, and today has roughly twice the volume of consumer credit. This suggests that there are some powerful economic factors, independent of mere fashion, at work. What has happened is that trade credit has become an increasingly essential weapon in the sales arsenal.

Customers demand a longer time to pay for their purchases and the sellers have had to go along with this in order to get the business. In fact, they vie with one another in offering easier and easier terms, because in a number of businesses such competition has become at least as meaningful as price and quality competition, sometimes more meaningful. In hardly any business or trade have the traditional, decades-old credit terms been officially changed. But in instance after instance the seller quietly grants the buyer a longer time to pay, or the buyer quietly avails himself of more time. "We don't grant the credit," says the executive of a steel supply company ruefully. "The customers take it."

The Undercapitalized Middleman

The conditions that enable the customers to "take it" were created by the emergence of the "short-order economy," described in the preceding article. The burdens and costs of distributing goods are constantly being shoved back onto the producer. Wholesalers and retailers want to hold as little inventory as possible, and many of them would prefer not to pay for goods until they have actually sold them. They get their way because, in this economy of abundance, a producer frequently can hope to gain an edge only by catering more generously than his competitor to the needs of potential buyers. As was pointed out in an earlier article (see page 243) selling is more and more a matter of providing services that enable the customer to do *his* business more profitably.

By and large, both the middleman and the retailer in U.S. distribution are undercapitalized. They lack the assets and the credit ratings on which to borrow money cheaply. (Trade debt actually accounts for roughly *half* the borrowings of wholesalers and retailers.) Manufacturing corporations—especially the larger ones that are responsible for the bulk of U.S. industrial output—have huge assets and excellent credit ratings. They borrow at prime rates, and with a relatively plentiful cash flow, have ready access to cheap money. Consequently, the pressure is on them to take more and more of the job of financing the flow of goods through the distribution pipeline.

The whole subject of trade credit has been largely ignored until very recently by economists, and the over-all effects of this massive movement of money are little understood. However, one thing seems quite certain: The broad economic effect of trade credit tends to be strongly countercyclical. Consumer credit, on the other hand, generally rides with the cycle; when consumers feel an economic pinch they tend to stop buying on credit and start paying their debts. Bankers also become cautious in recession, and they tend to pull back in periods when money is tight. But trade credit tends to expand under both circumstances, as the customers clamor for more and easier credit and the suppliers, pushed by intensified competition, give in to the pressure.

This is not just a supposition. It has been documented in an exhaustive study on trade credit made by Dr. Martin H. Seiden, director of the Bureau of Economic Analysis, a New York consulting firm. Dr. Seiden notes that in the recession of 1954, when total sales volume fell $15.2 billion and bank credit fell $300 million, trade credit helped to offset the contraction by increasing $4.1 billion. On the other hand, when the monetary authorities sought to tighten credit in the 1955 boom, trade credit increased by $10.7 billion, while bank credit was expanding by only $6.3 billion.

The Lenient Sales Departments

But it is one thing to say that trade credit has proved a nice cushion against the relatively mild recessions of the past decade and quite another thing to predict that it can keep on growing

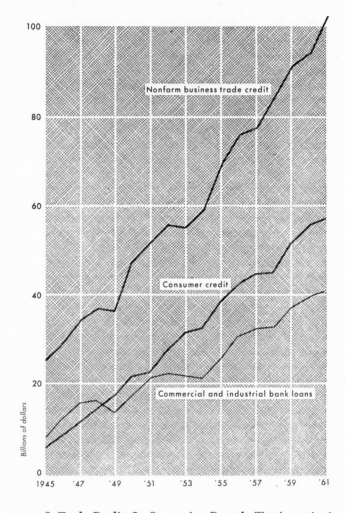

FIGURE 9. Trade Credit: Its Staggering Growth. The dramatic rise of the short-term trade credit that business extends to business is illustrated in the chart above, which is based on Federal Reserve flow-of-funds figures. In the past decade the volume of trade credit has increased far faster than that of the other two forms of credit. The principal reason, as the accompanying article explains, is that the granting of easier credit terms has become an important com-

at its present rate without posing an ominous threat to the economy. The question is: How sound is this credit structure?

A fair answer must take into account that in any company there is a conflict of interests, between the sales department, which above all wants to make a sale, and the finance or credit department, which takes a more orthodox view toward granting credit— how much and to whom. Inevitably, companies end up by taking a more lenient view toward a credit risk than would, say, a banker. In most trade credit there is no down payment, no lien on the goods, no collateral. The National Bureau of Economic Research reported last year that the dollar volume of trade-credit losses currently exceeds more than a billion a year. This probably exceeds the dollar losses in all other forms of credit combined.

Most companies, however, report that they are not concerned by their loss rates and it is unlikely that the overhanging threat of that $100 billion in trade credit would become a real menace unless the economy took a sharp turn downward. In that case, of course, it could have a spreading effect as devastating as the collapse of credit had in the 1929 depression.

The disturbing element in the situation is that in the recent past credit has been growing faster than sales. This trend shows no signs of abating, but there is no reason to assume that it will continue indefinitely. Conditions might change. For example, expansion of informal trade credit has undoubtedly been encouraged by the fact that the nation's total money supply in relation to the G.N.P. has gone back to the level of the Twenties, now that the excess liquidity generated during World War II has been worked off. As economic activity "grew up" to money supply, access to credit through existing financial institutions became

---

petitive weapon for manufacturers. Trade credit, which appears as receivables on the asset side of the seller's books, is, of course, balanced by trade debt, which appears as payables on the debit side of the buyer's books. Most corporations are simultaneously both lenders and debtors. Manufacturers extend about 50 percent of total trade credit, and about three-fifths of this goes to other manufacturers (for example, from a producer of electrical components to an appliance maker); the remainder is provided to retailers, wholesalers, and others.

more difficult and encouraged the resort to substitute devices. But the rein on the money supply can get looser as fears of inflation fade and the balance of payments is brought under control. Also, the competitive conditions resulting from today's buyer's market could well change. If manufacturers begin to find that their capacity is stretched, they might be less willing to give such generous payment terms.

In some areas of business, creditors have already begun to sense the need for caution. In retailing, the great discount revolution described earlier (see page 189), has produced a number of new operators who are skating on very thin ice. Typically, many discounters use trade credit to finance growth; they buy goods on credit, turn the goods over, put the money into new goods and stores, and count on a further fast turnover to pay off their suppliers. Turnover is the key to discount operation, and it gives the discounters a considerable power over suppliers, who are so eager to get the discounters' volume business that they are willing to extend credit well beyond the limits of prudence indicated by a retailer's assets and working capital. According to Dun & Bradstreet, which regularly surveys some 200 discounters, the median figure for discount stores showed current assets at one and a half times debt in 1961. (Department stores, by contrast, had current assets of roughly three and a half times debt.) There has been a disturbing number of bankruptcies among discounters, and some suppliers are trying to tighten up credit terms.

Another trouble spot is the highly competitive construction industry, notably in home building. There is, at last, a trend toward concentration in what has always been a fragmented industry dominated by many small operators. "Many of the tract builders have become economic giants who buy in big gobs and have bargaining power," says one supplier to the building trades. "They can get quantity prices and move large volumes at low margins." But smaller subcontractors in particular are being squeezed, because they make cutthroat bids to land contracts. The credit problem posed by these undercapitalized businesses, working on ever slimmer margins, is worsened by the manner in which builders and contractors are paid—in stages leading up to a completion payment that gives them their profit. A hard-pressed contractor will obviously make his suppliers wait for their money until *he* gets paid. Almost every supplier to the building trades reports that his receivables are disturbingly extended, and getting worse.

How To Cut Prices Quietly

The average age of receivables for all U.S. manufacturers rose from about thirty-five days in 1956 to nearly forty-five in 1962, according to the National Association of Credit Management. The pressure to extend trade credit, however, is by no means uniform throughout the economy. For manufacturers of mass-produced, high-consumption, high-turnover items such as food and toiletries, credit is not a big factor in selling. Velocity is the important thing, and the producers have concentrated on streamlining their distribution systems, speeding up shipment, reducing inventory, and moving the goods through to the consumer. The retailer orders, sells, pays for the goods on the usual terms, and orders more goods. Receivables held by Colgate-Palmolive, for example, simply tend to rise in proportion to sales.

But the story is quite different in a whole cross section of other U.S. businesses, from electronics to machinery, from textiles to chemicals. A big aluminum company reports that, in 1962, 29 percent of its trade accounts were overdue as against only 15 percent in 1955. The average age of receivables held by a major electrical manufacturer, to take another example, has jumped from forty days to more than fifty in the past five years.

The cost of carrying this liberalized credit obviously concerns these manufacturers. In general, they consider it an inevitable cost of getting more business. In a sense, the terms and conditions of sale are part of the price of the goods. Many businessmen are frank to admit that the easy extension of credit is equivalent to juggling prices. "The basic problem," says the chief financial officer of an electronics company, "is that most of the industry has excess capacity. So what can it do to sell more goods? It can use credit so that it amounts to a price concession."

There is a tactical advantage in so using credit. An outright price cut immediately alerts the competition, but credit can be extended quietly here and there without anyone's noticing, at least for a while. Some companies are worried about where this eventually leads to. "What does this giveaway generate?" asks an executive of a major steel company. "It doesn't generate more business because eventually everybody else will do it." And he adds, "Too much credit is about the worst thing that can happen."

"You Can't Do This to Joe Doakes"

Many corporations accept the role of financier reluctantly. The extension of credit is, after all, an investment of money—frequently of considerable sums that could otherwise be used elsewhere in the business, perhaps in new production facilities. This investment is increasing just when industry is trying its best to cut down other distribution costs, notably the cost of holding inventory. The distinction between inventory and receivables is becoming fuzzy. It makes little difference to a manufacturer whether he holds his products in his own warehouse until his distributor has orders for them, or pushes them along to the distributor, who won't pay him until he has sold the goods. Either way, the manufacturer gets hit with the cost.

The problem many manufacturers are facing is how to use credit as the vital sales tool that it is without paying too high a price for their sales. It is a highly complex problem, one that can no longer be solved simply at the level of the credit manager and his gimlet eye for credit risks.

An obvious way to solve it would be to charge the customer for the use of the money, with the double purpose of getting some return on the investment and at the same time forcing the laggard customers to pay up sooner. Some firms do charge interest on open-account credit when the customer extends his payment beyond the usual trade terms. Many companies have thought about doing that, but have shied away because, in the words of one corporate executive, "It would cost more to administer than it would be worth. Anyway, you're not going to make it stick. The customer says, 'Your lousy equipment isn't working,' or 'You didn't ship this piece,' or so forth. 'You can't do this to Joe Doakes,' says the sales department. 'He's a big customer.'" One of the country's major steel-supply companies once tried charging a fee on overdue accounts, but shortly abandoned the idea. The competition didn't go along, and besides, the company found that when a customer had to pay interest, he simply let his bill run, so that it was harder than ever to collect the overdue amount.

In some industries, however, it *is* often possible to put credit on a self-sustaining basis. A good example is in commercial electronics, particularly the manufacture and sale of tubes, semiconductors, and other components. This is a relatively new business, and by and large the distributors of these products are undercapitalized. Furthermore, it is a highly competitive business, due to the pressure from imports and the declining market for tubes. The result has been an enormous demand for easy credit, and the standard trade terms in the business (thirty days net) have become meaningless. Distributors now get as much as 120 or 180 days to pay—or longer. Manufacturers have recognized the problem for what it is, and in effect try to regularize the whole situation by extending formal inventory loans over longer periods. Under one such plan, for example, the manufacturer extends one- to three-year credit, at 6 percent per annum, to the distributors who will carry its line of components. The manufacturer recognizes this as virtually an advance of equity money to its customers. "They started out short of equity," says the financial vice president. "Now they're short of business."

Westinghouse uses a variant of this technique, not only for electronic components, but for a number of other products. "When the terms go from thirty to ninety days," points out an executive, "the manufacturer doesn't get any interest. It means a ballooning of working capital. The demand is for credit at no cost—to the customer. With capital equipment, normal trade practice is net thirty days. But this gets abused, and we keep hearing, 'I want two years to pay.' So what we want to say is, 'Our standard terms are thirty days, but we have a financing plan of up to five years.' We try to *sell* the customer on financing, since that gives him longer to pay."

How To Make a Profit on Credit

As the man at Westinghouse points out, "Financing of consumer goods has been going on for years. But in the last few years a lot of these techniques have been applied to industrial goods." The device Westinghouse ultimately adopted in 1954 in order to formalize its medium- and long-term credit arrangements was a captive finance company, the Westinghouse Credit Corp., which offers a wide range of leasing and financing arrangements to its customers. A number of other leading industrial corporations have done the same thing.

The captive finance company[1] gives a corporation many advantages, one of the most important being that it clears a mess of receivables off the parent company's books. It also segregates the corporation's credit-financing problem, and puts it under the management of financial experts who presumably are free of pressure from sales departments. It gives industrial companies a direct and easy contact with the money markets. And it makes it feasible for a corporation to amortize its credit costs, and even to make a profit on credit.

The device has some limitations, however. It is highly useful in such fields as transportation equipment, appliances, and capital goods—where purchases are commonly financed over rela-

---

[1] One of the phenomena of the financial world has been the remarkable rise of the so-called "captive" credit companies. Victor L. Andrews, of the Harvard Graduate School of Business Administration, recently made a study of the field and amassed some startling statistics. He identified, as of 1960, a total of 102 "nationally significant" credit subsidiaries. Of these, only fourteen had existed prior to 1946. Just between the years 1953 and 1957, no less than fifty-six such companies were set up, a trend that was tied in part with the tight-money policies of the federal government and the increasingly pressing need of corporations to find new ways to finance their customers. (New captive companies are still being founded, though the birthrate has declined somewhat.) The captive finance companies operate much like any independent finance company. They draw the bulk of their own financing from the money market. The great advantage that the parent company gets is enormous leverage—i.e., the dollars that it can borrow for each dollar of equity invested in the subsidiary. This advantage stems in large measure from the fact that the parent company's assets stand behind the subsidiary. Legally, in most cases, the parent company is not responsible for the debts of the subsidiary. But investors know that morally the parent company would be bound to take responsibility for making up any losses. Table 2 shows the power of some of the major captive companies, notably those of the big manufacturers, General Motors, General Electric, Whirlpool and Carrier, which lend both to commercial customers and to consumers; the one operated by Sears, Roebuck lends only to retail customers. These captive firms have a leverage ratio of better than eight to one. Ford is a special case; its credit company is new and the start-up costs have been high.

TABLE 2. OF THE TOP TWENTY-FIVE FINANCE COMPANIES
EIGHT ARE OWNED BY MANUFACTURERS

(Figures for fiscal year ending on or before June 30, 1962)

	Capital base* (000,000)	Borrow- ing ratio†	Stock- holders' equity (000,000)	Stock- holders' leverage‡	Gross volume§ (000,000)
G.M.A.C. (*General Motors*)	$867.6	3.5	$367.6	12.6	$10,047.4
C.I.T.	572.0	2.5	347.0	6.4	4,008.5
Commercial Credit	495.0	2.5	295.0	6.9	3,965.3
Associates Investment	294.2	2.8	169.4	7.3	1,761.6
Beneficial Finance	272.8	1.5	222.8	3.3	935.1
Household Finance	210.8	2.6	210.8	3.7	965.5
Pacific Finance	161.5	2.3	79.4	7.1	632.3
Seaboard Finance	124.4	1.7	70.6	5.2	308.6
G.E.C.C. (*General Electric*)	108.1	4.0	69.1	8.7	820.6
American Investment	107.3	1.6	58.7	5.1	443.5
Int'l. Harvester Credit	104.8	2.4	67.3	5.5	663.6
Ford Motor Credit	100.1	.51	100.1	1.8	394.4
James Talcott	99.2	2.6	49.9	8.1	1,453.9
Sears Roebuck Acceptance	92.6	6.1	67.6	9.9	976.8
Montgomery Ward Credit	79.9	1.9	54.9	4.3	364.6
General Acceptance	79.9	2.4	36.8	8.7	451.0
Walter E. Heller	76.4	2.7	44.2	6.9	1,272.3
Family Finance	70.3	1.9	47.4	4.6	303.9
State Loan & Finance	65.5	2.2	42.2	5.1	337.4
General Finance	63.9	2.4	34.7	6.8	373.3
Fruehauf Trailer Finance	54.5	2.3	27.7	6.5	79.7
J. I. Case Credit	53.4	1.9	31.4	5.1	167.8
Y.M.A.C. (General Motors)	51.4	3.4	21.4	11.5	344.2
Liberty Loan	51.1	1.9	31.4	4.9	208.0
Appliance Buyers Credit (Whirlpool, Carrier)	45.2	3.6	17.5	12.5	308.0

* *Stockholders' equity and noncurrent subordinated debt.*
† *Ratio of senior debt (current and long-term) to capital base.*
‡ *Ratio of total liabilities to stockholders' equity (deferred income excluded).*
§ *Total value of paper purchased.*

tively long periods. It is not so useful in such areas as food, though captives have been set up even there.

The captive does *not* spare the manufacturer the need to make an investment in credit; it is simply a different kind of investment, one that often brings a direct return. Not every corporation finds it a satisfactory way to commit its money. Recently Motorola got rid of its captive credit company, in which it had a $40-million investment. (It sold the subsidiary to an independent finance company, Associates Investment.) The captive was set up to finance the installment sale and leasing of Motorola's two-way radio systems. But the company found that it could use the investment more profitably elsewhere. E. P. Vanderwicken, vice president and treasurer, says: "We're going to be in new businesses we don't know about yet. The alternator is doing away with the generator in cars, and semiconductors are making the vacuum tube obsolete. Over the next ten years there will be many new businesses to go into, almost all better to be in than the finance business."

Everyone Wants a Piece

One factor that is making the finance business less attractive in some cases is the development of strong competition. Once U.S. manufacturers were lonely pioneers in merchandising credit; no one else wanted to touch it. International Harvester developed the farm-equipment market through credit. General Motors helped build the mass market for cars by setting up General Motors Acceptance Corp. (in 1919), to finance the purchase of cars both by dealers and consumers. Fruehauf created a market for trailers when the banks and other institutional lenders were leery of the infant trucking industry. The captive credit companies still perform useful functions that other finance institutions won't or can't perform. They provide a steady source of credit for customers when bank money dries up in tight-money periods or in recession. In the case of agricultural-equipment makers, the captives supply copious drafts of credit in rural areas where the banks are too small to do the needed job. Also, banks, independent finance companies, and others do not like financing dealer and distributor inventories, which is less profitable than the financing of consumer paper.

But generally speaking, everyone is now eager to get into the fields pioneered by the manufacturers. Many banks, independent finance companies, and old-line factoring concerns have diversified their financing activities, and are now competing with one another—and with the captives—for industrial or consumer time-installment business. Big finance companies have entered the leasing business, where they compete with Westinghouse Credit Corp. The banks, once so conservative, have become perhaps the most aggressive of all. As their source of funds has shifted more and more from demand to time deposits, raising the cost of their money, they have sought more profitable business. In the past five years their share of the new car-financing business has risen from about 40 percent to nearly 50 percent.

This new competition is having an interesting and significant impact on the nature and use of captive companies, and on their function in the marketing scheme of the parent companies. The auto industry offers a very dramatic illustration of what can happen.

Ford's "Last Resort"

For years, as one auto executive recently remarked, the auto industry "had it made" insofar as the smooth distribution of its product went. Broadly speaking, the sale of cars to the dealer was on a sight-draft basis. The factory made the cars; the dealer paid for them when he took delivery. The carmakers themselves were in the enviable position of carrying virtually no finished inventory at all. Indeed, in earlier years the dealer had to pay for the cars as they came off the production line, though this was modified after the mid-1930's when the carmakers began to give free transit time while the car was en route to the dealer.

G.M.A.C. long gave General Motors dealers an advantage over the dealers of the other carmakers, who did not have their own captive companies. G.M.A.C. today finances, at wholesale, some 74 percent of the cars handled by its dealers, and about 22 percent of the cars sold by them on time payments to consumers. Its dollar share of total U.S. new-car installment paper is about 17 percent, nearly equal to that of all independent finance companies combined (they have about 20 percent). This situation galls the independents, who would like to have Congress pass an antitrust law severing G.M.A.C. from G.M.

A few years ago Ford, which had chafed under G.M.'s competitive advantage, decided to do something about it. (Ford had started a captive in 1928 but soon sold it to C.I.T. Corp., which handled most of the Ford business thereafter.) Several developments in the car business seemed to make some move imperative, not the least being the enormous proliferation of new car models and types, which threatened to balloon dealers' inventories. (Many large dealerships require an average inventory of around $200,000; some require $500,000 or more.) This began to give G.M.'s one-half of 1 percent margin on wholesale paper a very real significance. First Ford tried to get the independent finance companies to bring their rates down to meet G.M.A.C.'s. But, says Theodore O. Yntema, the chairman of Ford's finance committee, the company had no luck. "The largest independent finance company [C.I.T.] told us bluntly it would not meet G.M.A.C. rates." So, in a move that Yntema has described as a "last resort," Ford three and a half years ago re-entered the finance business by setting up Ford Motor Credit Corp.

Ford's bid has been costly and it offers a nice illustration of what is required when credit is used as a sales tool. The company had to build a nationwide credit organization of some 100-odd branch offices, and the start-up costs have been high. Ford has plunked $25 million in capital stock into the subsidiary, plus $75 million in paid-in surplus. As of 1961, on receivables of $160 million, Ford realized a miniscule net income—$64,159—and it will be some time before it reaches a desired yield of, say, 10 percent on its investment.

But the rewards have been great, too. F.M.C.C. has already achieved a very signal victory. It has been responsible for driving down finance-company rates on auto financing to a level comparable to G.M.A.C.'s, which is what Ford had in mind in the first place. What Ford didn't particularly have in mind but has resulted is a benefit also to Chrysler and other dealers.

A $250-Million Bump

Meanwhile the carmakers, like other manufacturers, came under pressure from their customers (the dealers), who insisted on passing back some of the burden of carrying inventory. A little more than a year ago, with the introduction of the 1962 models, G.M. dramatically reversed the industry's hoary no-inventory policy. It initiated a free-wholesaling plan that in effect puts the autos into the dealer's showroom on consignment up to fifteen days. The other carmakers, of course, were compelled to introduce similar plans.

The effect was arresting. The move automatically transferred dealers' debts on G.M.A.C.'s books, where they yielded interest, to the parent company's books, where they didn't. This increased G.M.'s receivables by a whacking $250 million, pushing its total receivables of all kinds to slightly under a billion dollars. Ford's receivables were bumped more than $200 million.

Detroit's experience shows how, even in a mighty industry enjoying one of its most prosperous periods, the manufacturer has to keep the massive and costly pump of trade credit at work.

Leasing frees capital or makes it unnecessary for companies short on cash to borrow for equipment. Lease payments, where there are no purchase options, are tax-deductible business expenses. On government cost-plus contracts lease charges count as costs whereas interest paid on a loan to buy the same equipment does not. Thus, more and more companies are leasing, not owning, production machinery. Here is an examination of the leasing business and some speculations about future developments.

Machines without Owners*

by Staff
of
FORTUNE

Without a factory to its name, and with only a utilitarian second-floor office at the foot of Nob Hill in San Francisco and twenty-one small branch offices around the U.S. and Canada, United States Leasing Corp. nevertheless owns enough lathes, drill presses, and other industrial equipment to fill a couple of hundred plants. No one in the company has ever seen or used any of this equipment and no one ever will; and this is just the way the company's executives like it. Their business is to find out what their various clients want in the way of equipment; buy it with money borrowed from banks, insurance companies, and pension funds; and then collect lease payments over the years. In 1961, U.S. Leasing bought over $22 million worth of oil-drilling machinery, electronic testing gear, and other equipment, collected leasing fees of $5,300,000, and had a net profit of $594,000.

* Vol. 66, August 1962, pp. 112–114.

This is a small business, but U.S. Leasing is a window on a much bigger world—the world of industrial leasing. In one sense, of course, the practice is nothing new. Producers of railroad rolling stock have for many years leased freight cars to shippers and carriers. United Shoe Machinery, International Business Machines, American Machine & Foundry, still do a lot of renting of their products rather than selling them, and this business runs into billions annually. Autos and trucks have been leased on an ever larger scale since the late 1940's. But over the last decade there has been a phenomenal growth in so-called general-equipment or finance leasing. Corporations have discovered that it pays them to rent rather than to buy equipment of all kinds, and to use middlemen, like U.S. Leasing, to finance the transaction.

On some estimates as much as $700 million worth of general-equipment leases are now written annually in this country. While this is only a fraction of the total of $34.5 billion spent on plant and equipment in 1961, there is considerable evidence that leasing is growing in size and certainly in scope. Today, just about anything can be leased by anybody with good credit. A midwestern printer, for example, recently rented a $380,000 Miehle four-color offset press; Utah Construction Co. took on a fifteen-year lease on a $4-million hydraulic dredge; a carpet company leased $1,600,000 worth of weaving machines.

Leasing comes high. Surcharges run to 4 to 6 per cent per year of the original cost of the equipment. Thus a company that could buy a machine tool for $50,000 may finish up a five-year lease paying out $60,000 to $65,000, and still not own it. But there are also solid reasons for the growth of equipment leasing and for the growth and proliferation of leasing companies. Small manufacturers just getting started, and medium-sized growing ones, often don't have the cash to buy all their equipment. Leasing offers them the financing to get what they need without a down payment. Moreover, lease payments are a tax-deductible business expense (so long as there is no option to purchase). And if a corporation signs a five-year lease on a piece of equipment whose normal life is ten years, it gets in effect the benefits of accelerated depreciation.

Government procurement policy has also favored the growth of leasing. On cost-plus contracts, lease charges are counted as part of the costs whereas interest payments on money borrowed to buy the same equipment aren't. Hence leasing has been avidly adopted by a host of rapidly growing firms. The former Ramo-Wooldridge Corp., for example, when still a small company in 1954, found it could not possibly swing its business if it had to buy all the equipment needed, and it turned to leasing. Indeed, at the time of its merger with Thompson Products in 1958, it was leasing 70 per cent of all its equipment.

The Pioneers

It was in fact Ramo-Wooldridge's turn to leasing that gave a powerful boost to pioneers in the leasing business, and helped get the U.S. Leasing Corp. on its feet. This company was founded in 1952 almost by accident by D. P. Boothe Jr., then head of a small California food company. The Boothe company was turning out ration packages for the Army and needed a lot of packing and processing equipment. Rather than tie up his limited capital, Boothe tried to rent. "This was a hell of a job," he recalls. "Nobody quite knew how to handle the necessary arrangements. In fact, nobody really knew what the necessary arrangements were." But Boothe persevered and eventually got his equipment. In the process, he got the idea that other firms might be having the same difficulties.

They were. And presently Boothe got a contract from another California food packager for the lease of $500,000 worth of machines. On the strength of this order, Boothe and three partners set up U.S. Leasing, with a capital of $20,000, and persuaded the Bank of America to extend a $500,000 line of credit to purchase the equipment. Two years later U.S. Leasing discovered that Ramo-Wooldridge needed the same kind of service, and with Ramo-Wooldridge hooked up, U.S. Leasing later went on to sign contracts with Ampex, Raytheon, and dozens of other electronics firms, many of them located on the peninsula south of San Francisco. By 1954, U.S. Leasing was writing some $3 million of contracts per year.

This in fact proved almost too much business for U.S. Leasing to handle with its slender capital structure. The expenses of writing lease after lease were actually greater than income from leases previously made. Boothe tried to persuade his partners to make a public offering of stock. They refused and he sold out to go off and found a separate company of his own—Boothe Leasing Corp. Eventually U.S. Leasing did go public and its business grew. In 1960 management responsibility passed to Richard J. Elkus, the company's present president, a man of strong ideas and large experience in both industry and banking. Elkus cut back personnel, set up a bank-like credit department, and established $12 million worth of open-line credit with banks and insurance companies around the country. And he reorganized the company into departments: a lease engineering department to tailor-make leases for major customers; separate departments to handle leases over $100,000, and under; and a sales-aid division to work with manufacturers. "People in the leasing field," Elkus says, "have always looked at the business from the point of view of the customer who wants to acquire the equipment, and I thought we should also look at it from the equipment seller's point of view and perhaps try to turn his salesmen into leasing advocates."

And Now There Are Hundreds

The success of U.S. Leasing in constantly attracting more business sparked many another similar venture. Today there are hundreds of independent leasing companies all over the country, from U.S. Leasing down to small brokers handling an occasional lease now and then. National Equipment Rental, for instance, wrote over $15 million in general-equipment leases last year. Nationwide Leasing Co. of Chicago writes about $1 million in leases a month and has set up manufacturer sales-aid plans with Sperry-Rand, A. B. Dick, and others.

Until very recently, D. P. Boothe himself, the original pioneer, was a doughty independent. When he first set up Boothe Leasing in San Francisco, he had in capital $400,000 from the sale of stock to friends. As he needed more money, he sold more stock to the public and issued subordinated notes. At the end of 1961, Boothe had capital funds of $8 million and his business was second only to U.S. Leasing in the general-equipment field, with 4,800 outstanding lease schedules with 2,700 customers for equipment worth about $66 million. But Boothe was constantly disturbed by the fact that his company never really had enough money and that his borrowing costs were well above prime rates. "I realized very quickly," he says, "that a leasing company is fundamentally buying and selling money." Last March he found a solution to his problems. He sold Boothe Leasing to Greyhound Corp. for $15 million in convertible preferred stock, a deal made only after Boothe agreed to stay on as head of the new Greyhound subsidiary. "This was an ideal marriage," he says. "Greyhound throws off an awful lot of cash each year—between $15 million and $20 million. A leasing company is always in need of cash, and its field has great opportunities to employ that cash for a good return."

Boothe's merger with Greyhound points up the fact that all kinds of companies are today edging into the leasing business. Walter E. Heller & Co., for instance, bought almost 40 per cent of Nationwide Leasing as a diversification move. Other finance companies, such as C.I.T., Commercial Credit, and James Talcott, have established leasing subsidiaries. The Hertz Corp., long famous for its leasing of cars, is now in the general-equipment rental business. Another new arrival is Electric Autolite. Last year it completed the purchase of Equilease Corp. Machine-tool makers like Jones & Lamson have long leased their own products. Recently J. & L. expanded its operations and now leases competitors' products.

This expansion has given a measure of stability and scope to the leasing business that it lacked only a few years ago. And leasing companies, large and small, are filling an important gap in the money market. Banks have long been the source of short-term money for business (i.e., less than five years). Insurance companies have provided long-term funds (i.e., over ten years). But five-to-ten-year money has been harder to come by. Now leasing companies are filling this need by borrowing at long term and leasing their equipment on a five-to-ten-year basis. Further, they are also becoming more sophisticated in the kinds of leasing deals they can arrange. Tishman discovered in real estate that a good way to obtain cash is to sell and then lease back property; in this way he could have both cash and the use of the real estate over a long term. The sale-and-leaseback arrangement is now becoming increasingly popular in the general-equipment field.

There are some limiting factors to any expansion of the leasing business. Changes in accounting practices may make leasing less popular. Today when a company leases machinery it may or may not drop a note to this effect on its balance sheet, but it does not include the leases in its normal liabilities. Thus a corporation can manage, through leasing, to take on additional debt without distorting its debt ratios. This practice may soon come to an end. Most accountants are advocating full disclosures of all leases. Once creditors and stockholders have complete information at hand on the amount a company is leasing, the hidden advantage will disappear.

There is also some worry as to just how leasing will stand up in a major economic downturn. The leasing companies have survived recessions until now, but the business was still young, small, growing, and resilient. In the future, there could be trouble; companies that lease a lot of equipment might well find themselves unable to meet rental payments. Since no leasing company would have any enthusiasm for repossessing the equipment, it would have to extend and reduce the terms of the lease.

Even so, leasing is likely to grow relative to the economy. Robert Sheridan, president of Nationwide Leasing, predicts that leasing will rise from 2 per cent now to at least 10 per cent of capital expenditures by 1970. "Leasing," Boothe says modestly, "did not come to save the world. It is not some kind of exotic money falling from the sky or saving people from death and taxes. Leasing is another financial tool. It costs more than conventional financing but it can do a lot more in some situations."

Availability of products and competitive position in markets
depend largely upon events outside the company. Thus, distribution policies and distribution systems must take into account
the entire flow of products regardless of lines of ownership and
legal responsibility. Exploration and development of this "dark
continent" may require new concepts which could restructure
traditional management practices and channels of authority.

The Economy's Dark Continent*

Almost fifty cents of each dollar the
American consumer spends for goods
goes for activities that occur after the
goods are made, that is, after they have   by Peter F. Drucker
come in finished form off "the dry end of
the machine," to use the papermaker's
graphic term. This is distribution, one of
the most sadly neglected, most promising areas of American
business.

The activities that are encompassed by the broad term distribution include sorting and cutting, invoicing, billing, and other
paper work; labeling, packaging, storing, moving, shipping—plus
wholesaling, retailing, financing, and insuring. Physically, distribution contributes little; it can only mar, soil, tear, scratch, or
otherwise damage or downgrade the product. Economically, however, distribution is the process in which physical properties of
matter are converted into economic value; it brings the customer
to the product. But how much of the distributive cost is really
"value added," how much is merely "waste added"?

* Vol. 65, April 1962, pp. 103, 265–270.

We know little more about distribution today than Napoleon's contemporaries knew about the interior of Africa. We know it is there, and we know it is big; and that's about all. There are plenty of experts on individual phases: on transportation and warehousing, on retailing and consumer buying habits, on labeling and packaging, on factoring and insurance. But when a major government department recently looked for two or three men to advise it on distribution, none of the many people consulted in industry, government, and the universities could name even one qualified candidate.

To reach a real understanding of the role and structure of distribution in the American economy we need new concepts of economic theory and economic analysis. Most of our present concepts focus on production or on the stream of money and credit, rather than on the flow of physical goods and its economic characteristics. We also need new data; our figures today, such as those of the Census of Business, obscure distribution rather than report on it. (And only the high-speed computer can analyze anything as complex as the distributive system.)

G.M.'s Grand Design

Business need not wait until this work is done. An industry or a company can make its own distribution manageable. This was proved more than a generation ago by the automobile industry and especially by General Motors. Henry Ford, in building River Rouge, had had the premature but great vision of the manufacturing plant as the central switchboard in a flow of physical matter from mine to customer (and from there to scrap heap and back into the furnace as raw material.) With this as its starting point, General Motors, in the middle and late Twenties, built its business around the economic characteristics of the distributive process—beginning with the customers' buying habits, proceeding thence to the structure and characteristics of dealer finance, dealer inventories, and dealer compensation, going back further to the design, location, size, product mix, and scheduling of assembly plants, and finally all the way back to corporate organization. For well over three decades General Motors' distribution system has made the automobile the highly engineered mass-consumption product with the lowest total distribution costs.

By now this system may be obsolescent in important parts. How much economic sense, for instance, does the "franchised dealer" still make in a world of supermarkets and discount houses? How meaningful is his fixed commission? But G.M.'s achievement still stands as a useful example of how distribution can be brought under control. The example has been only too rarely followed. Only lately have things begun to stir—mildly. The American Management Association, for instance, has run a number of conferences on physical distribution. A few large consumer-goods companies have made distribution a specific corporate responsibility; H. J. Heinz of the "57 varieties" has a vice president-distribution. The results are encouraging. It does help, for example, to have someone around who points out that a proposed new packaging design will double freight costs, instead of having this come to light only after millions of the new packages have been made—as happened a few years ago at one of the big soap companies.

Why Distribution Lags

But even at their most successful, the new approaches attempt only to do a little more systematically and a little more cheaply the old jobs of transportation, inventory keeping, and warehousing. And they are still isolated attempts rather than a broad trend. A recent study by Professor Michael Schiff of New York University (published by the Financial Executives Research Foundation under the title *The Financial Management of the Marketing Function*) found that the importance and cost of distribution are recognized in fewer than half of the twenty-eight large companies analyzed.

Getting at the distribution problem requires cutting through a hard-rock overburden of legal, managerial, and organizational concepts. Few companies think of their distributors when they speak of "our business." Their horizon is set by the legal boundaries of their corporation. Few companies, for instance, know how large their distributors' inventories are and what is in them; this ignorance is a major cause of the persistent inventory booms and inventory busts that beset our economy. Distribution is no respecter of legal corporate boundaries. In industry after industry the price the consumer pays for the merchandise delivered and installed can be double the manufacturer's factory price or more. This means that perhaps half of the dollar the consumer pays for "our products" goes to distributors who are not legally part of "our business." The competitive position of industry and company, the reputation and availability of its products, and the use the customer makes of them, all depend more on events outside the legal business boundaries than on what the manufacturer does within his legal four walls. Perhaps the single most important lesson the generation-old G.M. approach still has to teach us is that distribution policy and distribution system must take into account the entire flow of the product regardless of lines of ownership and legal responsibility.

For example, the manufacturers who make the bulk of the products sold by Sears, Roebuck are legally and financially independent, as a rule. Yet every Sears buyer is expected to know as much about the making of the product—the manufacturer, his plant, his process, his materials, his people, and his costs—as he knows about selling it in the Sears stores. He often gets into product design. He is, in other words, responsible for the entire process even though he legally controls only a small part.

As restrictive as the legal boundaries are organizational and managerial boundaries within the manufacturing business itself. These tend as a rule to keep distributive costs out of sight and distribution activities unmanaged. Even in the few companies that have such a title, the "manager of distribution" usually takes over only when the product is ready to be loaded and shipped away. The major distribution costs within the manufacturing business tend, however, to lie before this stage—and so do the major opportunities for significant savings.

The Mob in the Shipping Room

In a well-managed manufacturing plant the machine areas are —and should be—quiet places. There aren't too many people in sight. They don't rush around. They do not seem to exert themselves unduly but move with measured calm. There is a good reason why the "drama of industry" so rarely comes through in paintings or photographs: in a well-managed plant there is no "drama."

But even in the best-managed plant things change drastically as soon as one goes through the door labeled "Finishing Room" or "Shipping Department." There is suddenly a mob of people. Everybody seems to rush and no one seems to know why and where. If the machine areas are soporific, the areas where products are sorted, cut to size, packaged, labeled, stored or shipped, are pandemonium.

The board of directors tends to hit the ceiling whenever the monthly scrap figure in the plant goes up by one percentage point. But few boards, to my knowledge, have ever been told how much spoilage there is in the distributive activities under the plant roof, and they have not been very interested in finding out. Yet this area is where the costs are in a modern plant—for this is where the people are. An aluminum rolling mill, for instance, may employ four workers in distributive plant jobs to every one actually employed at "making." To be sure, this distribution work is unskilled work, done usually with the simplest tools. But no matter how unskilled the job, there are no more "unskilled wages." Yet the costs of these distributive activities are rarely known and almost never shown. They disappear in general catch-alls: "allocations," "indirect labor," "administrative expense" or "burden." The industrial engineers sweat to pare one mill off the costs of making. But they rarely pay any attention to the dollars that might be saved in finishing, cutting, packaging, and shipping. I know of one company where a small team of industrial engineers put in ten days of routine work on the areas between the machines and the loading dock. As a result of the study, the company was able to reduce its fleet of forklift trucks from over 200 to fifty, to cut its manpower needs by half, and to speed up shipping time of the finished products from seven to four and a half days.

Typically, no one is individually responsible for these distributive activities in the plant. Organizationally these activities normally come under manufacturing management. They are lucky, however, if they are treated even as stepchildren. For people with a technical orientation—the production man, the chemical engineer, the plant manager—these activities are low-grade nuisances. And because, to a technically oriented man, most of the distributive work is donkey work, he tends to put a donkey in charge—more often than not a man of proved incompetence for "more demanding" work as a manufacturing supervisor.

"Solutions" That Don't Solve

As we apply management science and data processing to segments of the distribution process it becomes even more important to make sure that distribution is seen and managed as something that crosses legal and organizational boundaries. I have a suspicion—strengthened by a good deal of the work I have seen—that high-powered operations-research "solutions" for inventories, warehousing, transportation, order handling, and so on often increase the costs of distribution. For many managers tend to try and fit operations-research into the existing legal and organizational boundaries as if these were physical facts. In straightening out one kink in the stream they may only create expensive, new turbulences some place upriver or downriver, in what may be somebody else's job, if not "another business," but is still part of the same distribution process and part of the cost structure of the same product.

I have seen one example of this in a steamship line, where an operations-research team overhauled the entire loading and scheduling process. The team produced what the operating vice president wanted: a schedule that gave the fullest possible utilization of ships, that is, of expensive capital equipment. But no one told the team that there are different rates for different kinds of freight, and that therefore freight-mix has even more to do with final results than turnaround time. And the new scheduling system put such a substantial premium on getting a rather unfavorable freight-mix that total earnings plummeted even though the rate of capital utilization went up by half.

To get control of distribution, therefore, requires seeing—and managing—it as a distinct dimension of business and as a property of product and process rather than as a collection of technical jobs. Whenever this has been done (with or without a separate "manager of distribution") substantial benefits and savings have resulted.

The Discount House and Its Lessons

But effective and economical distribution also requires, in many cases, that an entire business be run differently. This is evident in three big areas in the American economy where we know distribution to be ineffectual and costly: retail selling, the new multibillion-dollar scientific-equipment market, and the buying of industrial supplies.

The discount house, it is commonly said, can sell at a lower price because it concentrates on the brands with fast turnover. Plausible—but simply not true. Many brands that turn over slowly in the ordinary retail store turn over rapidly in the discount house. In different discount houses the same brands often perform quite differently. And even the retail store's best seller turns over much faster as a rule in the discount house (or at Sears, Roebuck). The truth is that concentration on staple items is what gives the discount house both low costs of distribution and fast turnover. (See page 202.)

Ninety per cent or so of all business in a given line—for a manufacturer as well as for a retailer—is contributed by a very small percentage of items, 5 to 8 per cent as a rule. The remaining 90-odd per cent of all items, however, account for 90-odd per cent of the costs. For while revenue is roughly proportionate to volume, costs tend to be proportionate to the number of items or transactions. A slow seller requires just as much shelf space as a fast seller and ties down just as much capital. One requires as much paper work as the other—and paper work is so expensive that a major wholesaler has concluded that orders with a net profit of less than $10 do not even cover their ordinary paper-work expenses. In transportation, as every one knows, the smaller the unit the higher the cost—and the same goes for crating, for collection, for inventory control, for insurance, and so on. Even spoilage and losses in transit, according to the meager figures available, seem to be higher proportionately, the smaller the unit of transaction or shipment.

Markets without Middlemen

For the last two years I have watched the building of a fair-sized medical center. The buying of a good many million dollars worth of hospital and classroom equipment—from beds to benches—was a reasonably well-organized job. Ample technical help was available both to design facilities and to choose equipment; there were a good many distributors, well equipped with products and competent to give technical advice; and information enabling the center to weigh the consequences of decisions—say between initial costs and cost of upkeep—was reasonably easy to obtain.

But when it came to buying the scientific equipment for laboratories and testing facilities—in biology, chemistry, bacteriology, pathology, electronics, and so on—chaos took over. No one apparently had the faintest idea what would be needed, how much, and where. No one seemed to know what was available on the market and from whom. The laboratories took at most one-tenth of the total equipment budget. But in time, they took more than all of the other equipment together. And worse, a score of men who should have been getting on with their scientific work spent months as amateur lab designers and purchasing agents. Even so, no one is very happy with the results: there is too much stuff that will be needed only rarely, and not enough of the bread-and-butter items; the wrong equipment is centralized, creating bottle-necks; and far too many pieces are not where they are needed the most.

Scientific equipment has become a multibillion-dollar market, with thousands of producers and with a multitude of customers: government agencies and industry, hospitals and schools of all kinds. But it is still organized as if it were a small "specialty" business in which one or two manufacturers supply a few odd customers. No wonder that the cost of equipment is going up twice as fast as the number of qualified research people—to the point where equipment costs may soon force us to cut back research. No wonder that, even on some apparatus in standard use, distribution costs take 80 cents of the customer's dollar.

This is a peculiar market: each individual buyer buys once in a lifetime—but then he buys a great deal at once (though there is, of course, also a constant replacement and expansion demand). Yet there are enough buyers to provide a constant order flow. Such a market, more perhaps than any other, needs a middleman —and it has none. A middleman knows both the market in an area and the available supply. Typically, the middleman of such a market is an adviser to the buyer—either the architect type who receives his pay as a fee from the buyer, or the advertising-agency type who receives his commission from the supplier. But out-and-out wholesale distributors also can supply such a market—

as they do in many other hospital and school supplies. And there may be room for a cooperative buying organization of major users, such as the design and purchasing cooperatives some of the major universities are talking about. But without effective middlemen this rapidly expanding market cannot be supplied properly, let alone cheaply.

The scientific-equipment situation gives a conclusive answer to the old charge that the middleman is a "parasite." So, by the way, does the paperback book market, our fastest-growing market in the last few years. Cheap, paper-bound books have been around a very long time—at least since the days of the Haldeman-Julius "Little Blue Books" more than forty years ago; the "serious" reading public was there all along too—though in smaller numbers. What created the industry was the discovery and development of new distribution channels, such as the campus bookstore, and the bookrack in drugstore and supermarket.

The Semi-Literate Buyer

A good deal of work has been done these last ten or fifteen years on the marketing of industrial goods. Yet marketing men all say that selling and distribution in this field still leave much to be desired. Above all, they would increasingly agree that the key to efficient and effective industrial marketing is not the supplier but the buyer. And the buyer of industrial products and supplies is in many cases semi-literate, or even illiterate, in a business sense.

One example is paper. For many a business, paper is a major supply: the carrier of its communications, of its "image," its relations within and without; the carrier very often also of its product, its product appearance, and its product message. It is also a substantial cost item. But few companies buy paper as a major supply—if indeed they even know that they buy paper at all. Thus, in some very big banks the paper bill may be the second-biggest expense item after wages. Yet not only is there no accounting for the costs of paper, there is usually no one who knows anything about paper or about the graphic arts, no one who supervises the bank's paper buying, no one who knows what papers are available and what they can and should do in terms of end results, such as graphic representation, easy control, or accessible information. Typically, forty or fifty people in as many different departments buy paper as an "incidental" office supply—and through whatever printer, merchant, or stationer they happen to have come across (check paper is an exception—it is bought as a highly engineered product for a specific end use). As a result the bank is likely to end up with far more varieties of paper than it needs, and yet with little paper that is really right for the job. This is costly for the bank—if only because it pays retail prices for wholesale quantities. It is costly above all for the manufacturer, who has to maintain a meaningless product variety with its high expenses, both in making and in distribution. What the bank needs is a paper buyer who knows the needs of the bank and the end results it aims at, as well as the paper industry's technical and economic structure. The "old battle-ax" in accounting who, only too often, places the paper order for her department knows none of these; as a paper buyer she is illiterate.

Another example is the ordering of generating equipment for electric-power companies. Technically these buyers are extremely highly qualified. But economically they know little—especially about the economics of their supplier, the equipment producer. As a result many buyers tend to insist on their own special designs —rather than order by performance specifications, most of which can be satisfied by standard designs. If the apparatus producers could build standarized models to performance specifications and on a planned even-flow basis, their costs would tumble. It is probably not entirely accidental that one major utility system which manufacturers say really understands the economics of equipment production, American Gas & Electric, also has turned in a truly superior performance in respect to growth, technical performance, and profits.

An Urgent Job

The industrial purchaser has to know his own business, of course—and the progress made here in the last few years is all to the good. He has to know what the product or supply he buys is supposed to contribute to his company's end results, has to buy it as cost per unit of his own output rather than just by the price tag. But he also needs to know just as much about the structure of the supplier industry and its economics.

This sketch of the distribution challenge oversimplifies and overgeneralizes, of course. There are countless exceptions to its sweeping statements. But my purpose is to point to distribution as an area where intelligence and hard work can produce substantial results for American business. Above all, there is need for a new orientation—one that gives distribution the importance in business design, business planning, and business policy its costs warrant.

At a time when American business faces great competitive pressures from abroad—especially from a unified Europe whose industries can hold their own in technology, manufacturing knowledge, equipment, and salesmanship—raising the effectiveness and cutting the costs of the American distributive system may be a more important and a more urgent job than most managements yet realize.

The soap industry is an oligopoly where three great companies —Colgate-Palmolive, Lever Brothers, and Procter & Gamble— clamor for consumer preference and compete with one another for profit. Until recently the marketing strategy and tactics of the soap makers were well-kept secrets. But a recent court action opened records that revealed many details about some classic marketing campaigns, including Procter & Gamble's fabulous success with Tide and Lever Brothers' ill-starred introduction of Surf, and the effects of these campaigns on market share and company profits.

The Soap Wars: A Strategic Analysis*

Few secrets in American business are more closely guarded than the strategy and tactics of selling soap. It is no secret, of course, that advertising is the ammunition on which the big U.S. soap companies mainly rely in their perpetual wars with one another. Colgate-Palmolive, Lever Brothers, and Procter & Gamble, the three companies that make close to 85 percent of all the soap and synthetic-detergent products consumed in the U.S.—they also make some non-soap products, like shortening and toothpaste—spend approximately $250 million a year to advertise their wares. They spend an additional $150 million or so on sales promotion—e.g., on prize contests, price-off coupons, distributing free samples. But the broad strategies that underlie the firing of all this ammunition are ordinarily invisible to the neutral observer. Such reports as

by Spencer Klaw

* Vol. 68, June 1963, pp. 122–125, 182–198.

find their way into the pages of the trade press are inaccurate at worst and sketchy at best. One learns that detergent X, which Cleans Everything Washable, has been routed by detergent Y, a similar product that Cleans Like a White Tornado. The maneuvers that led to victory, the enemy weaknesses that were exploited, the cost of the victory, and its effect on the balance of power among the big soap companies—all these remain obscure.

Last January, however, the secrecy surrounding some of the great battles of recent years was at least partially dispelled. The occasion was the trial, in New York, of an antitrust case arising out of a 1957 deal in which Lever Brothers obtained from Monsanto Chemical the right to market a product called "All"—a laundry detergent, of the variety known as a low-sudser, that Monsanto had developed and had been selling in competition with the big soap companies. The government's contention was that the deal tended to lessen competition in the detergent business, and therefore violated Section 7 of the Clayton Act. At the trial Lever made two main arguments in opposing the government's demand that it divest itself of All. One was that All's sales had been falling off in 1957, and that Lever had actually served the cause of competition by taking the product over and marketing it more effectively than Monsanto could. The second argument was that Lever, having recently suffered a series of defeats at the hands of Procter & Gamble, needed a best-selling detergent like All if it was to remain a serious competitor in the laundry-products business.

These arguments evidently impressed the court, and several weeks ago the government's suit against Lever and Monsanto was dismissed. But the record of the trial will stand as a document of extraordinary interest. For days Lever executives testified in rich detail about the strategy of the soap-and-detergent business, and about the humiliations inflicted upon them by Procter & Gamble. Moreover, at Lever's request—though over the strong protests of Procter & Gamble's chairman, former Defense Secretary Neil H. McElroy—the court forced P. & G. to reveal certain facts about *its* operations as well. These included figures showing how much P. & G. had spent to advertise and promote certain brands, and how much money it had made in certain years from the sale of its laundry soaps and detergents—information that the big soap companies often deny even to their own advertising agencies.

The trial dealt with only one class of soap products: so-called heavy-duty soaps and detergents that are used mainly for washing clothes. The big soap companies also sell toilet soap, shampoos, all-purpose liquid cleaners, light-duty liquid detergents for washing dishes and delicate fabrics, and other kinds of cleaning products. But the heavy-duty products are the heart of the soap business: of the five billion pounds of soap and detergents that Americans will consume this year, well over three billion pounds, costing about $900 million at retail, will be consumed in washing machines, and it is for the privilege of supplying the American housewife with laundry products that the big companies wage their most costly and bitter wars. Last winter's trial not only shed light on the way these wars are fought; it also made clear some of the reasons why they have so consistently been won in recent years by Procter & Gamble.

Miraculous Tide vs. No-Rinse Surf

The balance of power among the big soap companies has, in fact, shifted radically in favor of P. & G. since World War II. The shift began with that company's introduction, in 1946, of a product called Tide, which was billed as a "revolutionary wash-day miracle." Tide was not a soap, but a synthetic detergent—i.e., it was made by chemical synthesis, not by the simple processing of animal fats. While there had been detergent powders on the market for years, Tide was the first one strong enough for washing clothes as well as dishes. It did such a good job, in fact, that before the end of 1949 one out of every four women was doing her laundry with Tide.

Confronted with this flight from old-fashioned soap powders, both Colgate and Lever Brothers hastily introduced heavy-duty detergents of their own. Colgate's was called Fab, and in time it sold moderately well. But Lever's entry, Surf, did such a mediocre washing job that it was withdrawn from the market. In 1949 a new, reformulated Surf was introduced, which was said to be so efficient that it obviated the need for rinsing clothes after they had been washed. This impressed housewives to such an extent that very soon Procter & Gamble advertisements were proclaiming that Tide, too, "washes clothes so miracle clean NO RINSING NEEDED." The claim was also appropriated by Colgate, and since Tide and Fab were available in almost every grocery store in the U.S., while Surf had up to then been introduced in only a few markets, almost all the benefits of the no-rinse story, as it was known in the trade, accrued to P. & G. and Colgate. Whether any benefit at all accrued to housewives is another question; the FTC insisted that rinsing *did* make clothes cleaner, even if they had been washed with a detergent, and eventually all three companies agreed not to make any further claims to the contrary.

By the end of 1953, according to evidence given at last winter's trial, about all that Lever had to show for six years of effort on behalf of Surf was a $24-million loss. The company was still bent on having a best-seller in the laundry-detergent field. But the feeling was strong, a Lever executive testified, that "we couldn't make that soufflé [i.e., Surf] come up for a second time," and so a decision was made to start over again and try promoting a new detergent called Rinso Blue instead. Lever's hopes for Rinso Blue were based in part on the results of blind tests, a procedure in which consumers are asked to try two different products, each in an unmarked box, and to say which one they prefer. While Surf appears not to have shown up too well in such tests, a Lever witness testified that housewives seemed to like Rinso Blue just as well as Tide, and even better than a second Procter & Gamble detergent called Cheer.

When one of the big soap companies launches a new product, it must, as a rule, commit itself to a huge outlay for advertising and promotion; otherwise, grocery stores are loath to stock the product. The amount of such investment spending, as it is called, is determined partly by the level of sales the new product is expected to reach after it has been on the market for a few months: the bigger the expected sales volume, of course, the bigger the investment that can be risked. Encouraged by Rinso Blue's showing in blind tests, Lever was confident that its sales would eventually hit at least $70 million a year, at which level the gross profits would amount to between $20 million and $25 million. On this assumption, the company felt justified in investing a very large sum—nearly $22 million—to get Rinso Blue into national distribution as quickly as possible.

When Rinso Blue reached the market, Procter & Gamble reacted with unexpected vigor. In the two areas where the new detergent was first placed on sale—the West Coast and the middle Atlantic states—P. & G. increased by hundreds of thousands of dollars its local advertising budget for Tide and Cheer. At the same time, it took other and more direct steps to neutralize any effect of Lever's introductory sales campaign. While Lever handed out millions of free sample packages of Rinso Blue, P. & G. handed out coupons good for the purchase, at reduced prices, of Tide and other P. & G. products. In Baltimore and Philadelphia, a Lever executive testified, P. & G. adopted the "highly unusual practice for them of delivering coupons on a door-to-door basis . . . they came in so hard and heavy that as our sampling crews were going up one side of the block, the Procter men were coming down the other side handing out the Tide coupons." P. & G. also used straight price-off deals to accomplish the classic defensive maneuver known as "loading the customer." Vast quantities of merchandise were put on sale at big price discounts, so that a woman who had tried her free sample of Rinso Blue, and had gone to the supermarket intending to buy a box, would be tempted to load up on Tide or Cheer instead.

Partly as a result of these countermeasures, by the end of 1955 Lever had lost more than $7 million on Rinso Blue, in addition to the $24 million it had already lost on Surf; and in those areas where the new detergent had been introduced, its sales had leveled out, not at 10 percent of the market for detergents, as Lever had hoped, but at a little over 4 percent. The J. Walter Thompson agency, to which the Rinso Blue advertising account had just been shifted, studied the situation and reported gloomily that it was unlikely to improve. Tide and Cheer were so profitable, the agency pointed out, and P. & G. could therefore afford to spend so much money in their defense, that Lever would be able to achieve its sales goal for Rinso Blue only at a ruinous cost. Thompson underlined its conviction that Lever's situation was all but hopeless by gallantly proposing a 60 percent cut in the Rinso Blue advertising budget. The proposal was accepted, and Lever's executives did some painful thinking. "This led to the conclusion," the company's chairman, William H. Burkhart, testified last winter, "that we were facing apparently a hopeless task to get a real entry, a winner, into this field [and] we came to the conclusion that we would give up any further attempt to force our way into a winning position in the heavy-duty field."

The full dimensions of P. & G.'s triumph and Lever's defeat emerged clearly at the trial. Before the war, the two companies had been fairly evenly matched in the laundry-soap business. But between 1940 and 1956, P. & G.'s estimated share of the market rose from 34 percent to nearly 57 percent, while Lever's share fell from 30 percent to 17 percent. (Colgate's share was unchanged at approximately 11 percent.) This shift naturally had a profound effect on the earnings of the big soap companies. From 1951 through 1956, according to figures reluctantly provided by P. & G., the sale of Tide and its other laundry soaps and detergents yielded profits totaling about a quarter of a billion dollars before taxes. In the same period, Lever and Colgate were both *losing* money in the laundry-products field. P. & G.'s net earnings nearly tripled in the postwar decade, rising to $59 million in 1956 on sales of just over $1 billion. Meanwhile, Colgate's earnings on its domestic business declined from $16 million in 1946 to $5 million ten years later. Lever's record was even worse: in the early 1950's the company barely broke even, and the $3 million that it earned in 1956, on sales of $282 million, was only about a third of what Lever had earned in a good prewar year.

That Old Blue Magic

While the Rinso Blue fiasco had impressed on Lever Brothers the folly of making frontal assaults on entrenched positions, the company's management did not intend simply to abandon the field to P. & G. When Lever was given the opportunity to acquire All, and thereby to occupy an entrenched position of its own, it gladly seized the chance. Before turning, however, to the new series of battles into which Lever Brothers was plunged, it may be useful to consider in a general way the evolution of marketing strategy in the soap industry since World War II.

Probably no event in this period has more greatly influenced the strategy of the big companies than the successful launching by Procter & Gamble of its second heavy-duty detergent, Cheer. By 1950, four years after the introduction of Tide, Procter & Gamble had at least two good reasons for wanting to market another laundry detergent. One was that it might appeal to housewives who just didn't like Tide. The other was that it would get P. & G. a larger share of the limited shelf space in the grocery stores. Often the big soap companies contrive to get additional "facings" for a brand by bringing it out in a variety of different-sized packages. But Tide was already being sold in three sizes—

regular, medium, and giant—and there was obviously not much more that could be done along this line.

Although Cheer was not a bad product—in cool water, for instance, it was considered by P. & G. to perform better in some ways than Tide—the company could not at first get women interested in buying it. Then it tried a scheme for giving Cheer a new and distinctive personality. Like other detergents on the market, Cheer contained an optical bleach—a dye, that is, that made clothes look very white in sunlight by causing them to reflect some of the sun's ultraviolet rays in the form of blue light. The scheme was to add blue coloring matter to Cheer, which had been sold up to then as a white powder, and make a great point of the "blue whiteness" it imparted to shirts and sheets. This worked so well that by 1953 the new Cheer ("It's New! It's Blue! . . . *only* Cheer has the Blue-Magic Whitener!") was outselling every other brand of laundry soap or detergent except Tide.

If It Isn't "New," It's "Improved"

The success of Tide had shown the enormous benefits to be reaped from a basic improvement in a soap product. The lesson soap men drew from Cheer was that even what they call a "me-too product"—i.e., one essentially similar to others on the market—can be marketed successfully if it at least *looks* new and different. This discovery has led the big soap companies to put much less emphasis than they did before the war on devising new claims for old products—inventing B.O., for example, and announcing that Lifebuoy would cure it, or suggesting that the way to avoid "undie odor" was to use Lux Flakes. The emphasis today is on making constant changes, often of a fairly superficial kind, in the products themselves.

Soap products are constantly being brought out in new colors and new forms, or at least in new containers. Light-duty liquid detergents have successively been marketed in bottles, in cans, and in plastic containers, and they are now sold in three different colors. P. & G., for example, offers the housewife her choice of Creamy Pink Thrill, Ivory Liquid ("the gentle white detergent"), and New Sparkling Clear Joy. Elsewhere in the soap-products section, the shopper is confronted with a rich variety of laundry powders and laundry liquids; of all-purpose cleaners with am-

monia, and all-purpose cleaners without ammonia; of toilet soaps
that contain bacteriostatic additives, and toilet soaps that contain
cold cream; of low-sudsers that are "condensed," and low-sudsers
that are "fluffy"; of detergents that come in small, soluble packets,
and detergents that come in the form of large tablets. Most items
are labeled "New!" or "Improved!" As a Colgate executive observed recently, "If the package doesn't say 'New' these days, it
better say 'Seven Cents off.'"

The fact that soap companies are putting more stress on product changes does not mean that they are putting any less stress
these days on advertising. On the contrary, the rise of the self-
service store has caused soap manufacturers to cut back on promotional efforts aimed at storekeepers, and to concentrate even
more single-mindedly than in the past on selling the consumer
directly. As a group, the big soap companies today spend more
money on advertising, in proportion to their total sales, than they
did twenty years ago; P. & G. salesmen are informed when they
sign on with the company that "nearly one billion Procter &
Gamble messages are delivered to the housewives of America
each week."

It is hard to find new things to say about a soap product (apart
from the fact that it is "new"), and as a result the advertising
claims that are made on behalf of competing brands in any given
category of products—e.g., laundry powders—tend to sound a lot
alike. In 1953 the Chicago *Tribune* commissioned a study, by a
firm called Social Research, Inc., of women's feelings about laundry soaps and detergents, and their feelings about the way these
products were advertised. The resulting report listed a number
of advertising slogans that were current at the time, and observed, "For a woman to learn to distinguish between product
claims like these requires her to become a scholar in the subtle
evaluation of textual difference . . . to decide whether a wash is
whiter when it is 'whiter *without* a bleach' or when it is 'whiter
than bleach.'" Most women, the report added, simply stop paying
attention to the claims.

Puralin Plus and New Germaseptic Dreft

Since 1953, there have been some changes in soap advertising.
Humor is in vogue, and soap commercials abound with humorous
lady plumbers and humorous washing-machine repairmen; P. & G.

even has a commercial featuring an Oriental houseboy, who says, "Lady know Joy not hurt pretty little hands . . . Joy mild as lotus blossom." But the specific advertising claims sound pretty much the same, and there is evidence that many women find them just as hard to sort out—and to take seriously—as ever. Oxydol "bleaches as it washes," New Super Suds offers "a *brighter* wash, a *whiter* wash than ever before," Dreft is "New Germaseptic Dreft," Cascade has Chloro-Sheen, Lifebuoy has Puralin Plus, Spic-and-Span contains Germ-Fite, Salvo is "the *fortified* detergent," Tide is "New Improved Tide," and offers "the cleanest, freshest-smelling wash in Tide history," while Fab has "five extra launderatives" and produces "a wash that's not just detergent clean—but clean right through."

But whatever they think about such advertising claims, housewives seem to have a special confidence in detergents that *are* advertised. One evidence of this is the relatively poor sales record of private-label soaps and detergents. Private-label laundry detergents, which have been found by independent testing organizations to perform, in general, about as well as brands like Fab or Cheer or Tide or Rinso Blue, are now available in most supermarkets. But nine out of ten women prefer to buy a nationally advertised brand, even though it may cost them as much as 40 to 45 percent more.

The big soap companies themselves, it is true, frequently offer their own products at bargain prices. In a particular store, on a particular day, half a dozen different brands of soap products may be on sale in boxes prominently marked "Five Cents Off Regular Price!" Cents-off deals of this kind are initiated by the manufacturer, who offers retailers for a limited time a chance to buy a particular brand at a big price reduction if the retailer will agree to pass the saving on in full to his customers. But the fact that a soap company can resort to this maneuver again and again is in itself proof of the power of advertising, since it is on advertising that the manufacturer mainly relies to persuade housewives that the product they were offered at 27 cents a box last week is still a pretty good value now that it is back at its regular price of 32 cents.

If a new product is to be profitably marketed by one of the big soap companies, it must normally meet certain basic requirements. It must fill a real need—or one that can be demonstrated by advertising to be a real need—and it must work reasonably well. All together, the Big Three are now spending around $30 million a year on efforts to develop such products. In addition, a product must strike consumers as giving good value—although this does not necessarily mean that it must be sold at the same price as similar products already on the market. In 1959, for example, P. & G. introduced its liquid cleaner Mr. Clean in a twenty-eight-ounce bottle, and charged as much for it as the makers of Lestoil, a similar and very popular product, got for a thirty-two-ounce bottle. However, since Mr. Clean had some inherent advantages (unlike Lestoil, it was non-inflammable), and since the Mr. Clean bottle was not only more conveniently shaped than the Lestoil bottle but was cleverly designed so that it looked just as big or even bigger, consumers overlooked the discrepancy, and within two years Mr. Clean was outselling Lestoil two to one.

Muddying the Test Waters

But even if a product performs well and seems to offer a good value, it is impossible to tell a priori what the actual demand for it will be. Overestimating its potential sales can cost many millions of dollars, as Lever's experience with Rinso Blue demonstrated, and soap companies ordinarily test the market very carefully before launching a new brand. Colgate, for example, will spend over $16 million this year on market tests.

Putting a product on sale in a test market has one obvious risk, however. While the test may furnish a good line on the potential sales of the product, and on the amount of advertising and promotion that will be required to sustain that volume, it is very hard to keep this information secret. If Lever Brothers puts a new product on sale in, say, Grand Rapids, P. & G. and Colgate will be among the first to buy it. Often they will not only analyze the product in their laboratories, but try it out on consumer panels in blind tests. Furthermore, by keeping a close watch on what Lever is doing to advertise and promote the new product, and by auditing its sales in a few Grand Rapids grocery stores, Lever's rivals can learn almost as much as Lever does about the product's potentialities.

Actually, market tests in the soap business often more nearly resemble a poker game than a scientific experiment. When player A puts a new product on sale in a certain market, player B, who has a similar product already in national distribution, may raise the stakes—that is, he may triple his advertising of that product in the area where player A is making his test. This confronts player A with a difficult question: Does player B intend to triple his *national* advertising budget if player A puts his new product on sale nationally? Or is player B bluffing? He may only be engaged in what is commonly known as "muddying the test waters."

A classic demonstration of water-muddying was staged some years ago by the Toni Corp., then the leading producer of home-permanent preparations. When Colgate began a market test of a product called Lustre Creme Home Permanent, Toni launched a counteroffensive referred to, in intra-company memoranda, as Operation Snafu. Toni already had three home permanents on the market, Toni, Prom, and Bobbi; in addition to stepping up greatly its local advertising of all three of these brands, the company introduced a fourth brand, called Epic, in the cities Colgate had chosen for its test. The object was to scare Colgate off entirely or, failing that, to make Colgate underestimate the potential sales of its new product, and therefore to launch it with a relatively small advertising and promotion budget—which would, of course, make life easier for Toni. Whether or not Operation Snafu was the deciding factor, Colgate did in fact drop its plans to market Lustre Creme Permanent nationally.

Why Nobody Wanted All

When Lever Brothers acquired All in 1957, no market test was needed to find out if there was a big demand for it. All had been on the market for more than ten years, and recently it had been selling a lot better than either Rinso Blue or Surf. It was, in fact, outselling every other brand of packaged soap or detergent apart from Tide and Cheer and Colgate's Fab.

All's popularity was doubtless an irritation to the big soap companies. Although they expect stiff competition when marketing toiletry items like shampoos and home permanents, they have, for some forty years, almost completely dominated the market for basic soap products. The only important exception to this rule, apart from Monsanto's success with All, has been Armour's success in marketing Dial soap. For years, the Big Three did not consider the market for a high-priced deodorant soap like Dial big enough to be interesting. Then, when they realized their mistake, Armour was so solidly entrenched in the soap business that not even an all-out offensive by P. & G., which in 1958 introduced a deodorant soap of its own, called Zest, was able to dislodge Dial more than temporarily from its position as the best-selling toilet soap on the market.

But if Armour has shown that the big soap companies can be beaten in their own territory, the story of Monsanto's venture shows how great are the dangers that threaten an invader. The history of All goes back to the early 1940's, soon after the development by Westinghouse of a device it called the Laundromat. The Laundromat was an automatic washing machine of the kind known as a front-loader, in which the clothes are washed by being tossed around in a revolving drum. In a washer of this type, the cleaning action is impeded by too many suds, and Westinghouse asked Monsanto if it could develop a synthetic detergent that would wash well without making a lot of foam. In 1945, Monsanto came up with a low-sudsing product, called Sterox, that did the trick, and began looking around for a company that would be interested in putting it on the market.

But very few automatic washers were in use as yet, and none of the companies first approached by Monsanto—they included all three of the big soap manufacturers—was interested in a product for which the demand would presumably be so limited. The deal that Monsanto finally made was with a new company called Detergents, Inc. It had been formed, with the encouragement of Westinghouse, for the specific purpose of buying Sterox in bulk from Monsanto and selling it to consumers under the trade name of All.

In 1946, when All first went on sale, many of the new automatic washers then coming onto the market were of the top-loading variety, in which the clothes were swished around by a mechanical agitator, or paddle. In most such machines there was no harm in having lots of suds; ordinary soap powders, or high-sudsing synthetic detergents like Tide, worked well in them, just as they did in old-fashioned non-automatic washing machines. Detergents, Inc., however, promoted All as the ideal product to use in *any* automatic washer, not just in front-loaders, and as the number of automatics in use rose into the millions, sales of All grew rapidly. They grew so rapidly, in fact, that Detergents, Inc., soon had more business on its hands than it could cope with. The company had been formed with very little capital, and by 1951 it was strapped for working funds and heavily in debt to Monsanto. Monsanto decided it had better buy out the company's stockholders and market All itself.

For two years everything went beautifully. Then, in 1954, P. & G. introduced a low-sudsing detergent of its own, called Dash, and Colgate soon followed with a product called Ad. While Colgate's efforts on behalf of Ad were modest, Dash was launched with heavy expenditures for advertising and promotion. Some of the money spent by P. & G. went into tie-in deals with washing-machine manufacturers. Detergents, Inc., had hit on the notion of promoting All by persuading manufacturers of automatic washers to put a sample box of All in every machine they sold. P. & G. now offered the manufacturers large amounts of free advertising on its television programs if they would agree to stop packing All in their machines and pack P. & G. products instead. Specifically, P. & G. proposed to manufacturers of top-loading machines that they pack Tide, and to manufacturers of front-loaders that they pack Dash. By 1957, every manufacturer had deserted All and gone to Tide or Dash.

The Horrifying Ad Budget

At first, Monsanto tried slugging it out with P. & G. In 1955 the company spent what Monsanto's chairman, Dr. Charles Allen Thomas, described at the trial as the "rather horrifying" sum of $12 million to advertise and promote All. But even so, sales fell off, and Monsanto's Consumer Products Division, which had been organized to market All, reported a $3-million loss for the year.

It was obvious that part of the difficulty arose from the fact that All was the only consumer product Monsanto had. There was talk of adding a conventional, high-sudsing detergent to the company's line. Nothing came of this, however, partly because the big soap companies were good customers of Monsanto—in 1956, they bought some $27 million worth of its phosphates and other chemicals—and the company's management was reluctant to antagonize them. Monsanto also considered buying the Clorox Corp., the largest U.S. producer of household bleach, but nothing came of this either. Monsanto's estimate was that it would take at least

$22 million to buy Clorox, and Thomas testified that "being of technical background we thought it rather ridiculous to pay this much money for water to which some chlorine and caustic soda had been added."

Meanwhile, P. & G.'s campaign was continuing to cut into the sales of All, and Monsanto soon concluded that the best thing to do was to sell off the All business before it was too late—that is, to turn the All trademark over to some company that could market the product successfully, and that would therefore be in the market for lots of Sterox. Talks were held with several companies, and for a time a deal with Armour seemed likely. But after several months negotiations broke down—mainly, it appears, over the question of how much Armour should pay for the Sterox.

Then, early in 1957, Monsanto approached Lever Brothers. Two years before, Lever had put a low-sudsing detergent of its own into test markets. But the product had been withdrawn in the face of complaints that it solidified when it was left standing too long, and Lever was delighted at the prospect of acquiring All. It was agreed that for five years Lever would buy the finished product (that is, Sterox) from Monsanto, and that during the same period it would buy an additional $80 million worth of Monsanto chemicals. Monsanto, congratulating itself on having withdrawn from the field in fairly good order and with no serious losses, handed the All trademark over to Lever.

"Makes White Clothes Greener!"

At the trial Lever witnesses gave a number of explanations for Monsanto's unimpressive showing against P. & G. They pointed out that Monsanto had been selling All through food brokers, and allocating 12 to 13 percent of the net sales receipts to direct selling expenses. By contrast, a Lever executive testified, his company (or P. & G.), having a big sales force of its own, was in a position to do a much better selling job for only about 3 percent of sales. Lever also argued that the ability to get volume discounts in buying network television time gave P. & G. a significant advantage that was not available to Monsanto. (For very big buyers, like P. & G. and Lever, these discounts amount to as much as 25 or 30 percent off the card rate.) Thomas Carroll, Lever's vice president of marketing, testified that Monsanto, partly because of inexperience, had in any case made a mistake by concentrating too much of its advertising in newspapers, where, he said, "the delivery of messages to homes is very expensive" compared to television.

Another cause of Monsanto's difficulties, Lever witnesses said, was that All had had some serious deficiencies as a product in the days when Monsanto was marketing it. According to tests made by Lever in 1957, a good many women didn't think it smelled as nice as Dash. More important, All had a tendency to cake, it sometimes left sandlike grains in the bottom of a washing machine, and in cities where the air was badly polluted it was apt to turn white shirts and sheets an apple-green color. "Dash was a superior product," Carroll testified. "It was being introduced with vast quantities of television advertising . . . . Their selling was good. They introduced it with sampling. They would go from door to door, and knock on the door, and ask a woman if she owned an automatic washing machine. And if she did they gave her a sample of Dash. . . ." Carroll added, "They followed it up with couponing, price packs, and other very strong promotions. They had a sales force that numbered nearly a thousand men . . . and, in short, they were coming in and it was pretty clear that All was going to suffer the ravages of this warfare."

When Lever took over All, the tide of battle began to turn. The market for low-sudsing detergents was expanding rapidly, and between 1956 and 1959 Lever was able to increase All's sales from $30 million to $44 million. This was brought about, moreover, with an annual outlay for advertising and promotion amounting to only about half of what Monsanto had spent on All in 1955. As a result, profits on All rose to more than $8,500,000 (before taxes) in 1959.

This was the first decent piece of business Lever had done for many years in the laundry-products field. Since 1956, it is true, the company had been making around $4 million a year before taxes on the sale of its four conventional high-sudsing detergents. (Besides Rinso Blue and Surf, they included two other low-volume brands called Breeze and Silver Dust Blue.) But these profits had been made possible only by reducing advertising and promotional expenses so drastically that sales had begun to decline, and Lever's management was unhappily aware that the four brands were gradually being milked dry.

In 1960, Lever introduced "New *Active* All," which smelled nicer than the old All and didn't have the same tendency to cake or to turn shirts green. Up to this time, sales of Dash had been increasing even faster than sales of All. But in 1961, even though P. & G. appeared to be spending more money (figured on a dollars-per-case basis) to advertise and promote Dash than Lever was spending on All, the trend was reversed. For the first time since the introduction of Dash, its share of the market fell, while All's share rose. Lever's joy at this development was mingled with apprehension, however. A Lever executive recalled at the trial that "we, for once in our life, had a reversal of the classic position . . . and we were observing Procter & Gamble spending on a much higher per-case basis, and it was our conjecture as to just how long they would be willing to play this game. . . ."

As it turned out, P. & G. had already thought up a new game. Lever and P. & G. had both been testing the market for a low-sudsing detergent to be sold in tablet form, and in 1961 both companies began to put their products into national distribution. P. & G., however, appeared to be investing a lot more money in the introduction of its product, Salvo, than Lever felt it could afford to invest in Vim, its own low-sudsing tablet. It was obvious that Procter's strategy was to shift the battle of the low-sudsers to new ground, where Lever would not have the advantage of an entrenched position; by the end of last year, it was also obvious that the strategy was working. While Lever's Vim had captured only 8.5 percent of the total market for low-sudsing detergents, Procter's Salvo had captured 20 percent. Although Dash still lagged behind All, sales of Dash *plus* Salvo were running well ahead of sales of All plus Vim. P. & G. had thus succeeded, at last, in becoming the leader in the low-sudsing field.

While these facts were being recited to the court by a Lever witness, the trial judge, Archie O. Dawson, broke in impatiently at one point to ask what they all added up to. He added, "I can see that the witness is annoyed with Procter, there is a competitive feeling there, and all that, and this is the poor little boy with the rich relative or rich uncle who's got lots of money to spend, but what has that to do with this case?" In reply, Lever's principal trial attorney, William L. McGovern, said that he assumed the government would contend that Lever, in acquiring All, had acquired the power to lessen competition. He went on to say, "The purpose of this testimony, Your Honor, is to show that not only did we not lessen any competition, but with all of our own talents and skills and funds we have been scarcely able to keep our head above the water."

The Fruits of Victory

It can be argued that P. & G. is not quite so irresistible a force as Lever Brothers made it out to be at the trial. Lever's toilet soaps—Lux, Lifebuoy, Dove, and Praise—have, for instance, been giving P. & G.'s Ivory, Camay, and Zest a very good run for their money. And Colgate's Liquid Ajax has recently replaced P. & G.'s Mr. Clean as the best-selling brand in the $100-million-a-year market for liquid cleaners.

But while P. & G. may lose now and then, its batting average is still very high. More than half of all the cleaning products sold in the U.S. are manufactured by P. & G., and last year, as the following table shows, it made more than three times as much money as its two big competitors made between them; if foreign earnings are excluded, it made seven times as much, as shown in Table 3.

TABLE 3. SALES AND NET INCOME OF PROCTER & GAMBLE, LEVER BROTHERS, AND COLGATE

	Net sales (*000 omitted*)	Net income (*000 omitted*)
PROCTER & GAMBLE		
Domestic and foreign	$1,619,000	$109,300
Domestic only	N.A.	89,100
LEVER BROTHERS	413,000	10,200
COLGATE		
Domestic and foreign	673,800	22,900
Domestic only	327,000	2,400

These figures, coupled with some of the evidence given at last winter's trial, raise an interesting question: Why doesn't P. & G. go after an even bigger share of the soap-and-detergent business by cutting substantially the price of Tide and of its other heavy-

duty detergents? Within the industry, P. & G.'s restraint is sometimes attributed to fear of the Department of Justice's antitrust
division. But P. & G. may well figure that it can make more money
by keeping the price of its laundry detergents at a high enough
level to assure a copious flow of profits, and by investing a portion
of those profits in fields outside the soap-and-detergent business.

Another Secret Weapon: Toothpaste

In any case, P. & G. in the past ten years has added to its
product line such non-soap items as scouring powder, bleaches,
facial and toilet tissue, peanut butter, and cake mixes. It has also
added toothpaste, and sales of its two brands, Crest and Gleem,
now account for almost half of all U.S. toothpaste sales. Crest and
Gleem have benefited P. & G. in two ways. Besides contributing
handsomely to company profits, their success has cut into the
profits that Lever and Colgate had been making in the toothpaste
business, and has thereby deprived them of money they might
have been able to use against P. & G. in the soap-and-detergent
business.

As the evidence at last winter's trial demonstrated, to play the
kind of game the big soap companies play takes a lot of money,
and the fact that P. & G. has so much more money than its competitors has certainly been one important reason for its long
winning streak. Ever since its early triumphs in the synthetic-
detergent field, P. & G. has been able to invest the kind of money
in the launching of a new product—Salvo, for example—that its
rivals find it difficult to match.

But it is not just P. & G.'s ability to outspend its rivals that
makes it so formidable a competitor. The fact is that it is also
an extremely well-managed company. At various times since
World War II both Lever and Colgate have had difficulty in
finding capable top executives. By contrast, P. & G.'s managers
have been successful in recruiting and training successors as
tough and able as they are themselves, with the same natural
flair for poker, and the same willingness to play as a member of a
big team. As P. & G.'s president, Howard Morgens, has said,
"Everything we do is created, adjusted, and tested by the team."
This way of doing business is not everybody's dish of tea, but
there is no doubt about the fact that it sells a lot of soap.